PITCH UP
EAT LOCAL

Published by AA Publishing, a trading name of
AA Media Limited, Fanum House, Basing View,
Basingstoke, Hampshire, RG21 4EA, UK.

Registered number 06112600

First published May 2015

A CIP catalogue record for this book is available
from the British Library.

ISBN: 978-0-7495-7708-7

A05245

Art Director: James Tims
Editor: Donna Wood
Design and layout: Tracey Freestone and Nick Johnston
Reprographics: Jackie Street-Elkayam
Production: Nathan Clark

Illustrations © Matthew Midgley

Printed and bound in Dubai by Oriental Press.

www.theAA.com

PITCH UP eat local

Where to camp, what to eat and how to cook it

Written by
ALI RAY

Contents

Foreword

When the Camping and Caravanning Club launched its Eat Local initiative in 2004 you would have needed a very large crystal ball to predict this book – but here we are, more than a decade later, with the finished product. Welcome to *Pitch Up, Eat Local*.

You may, like me, already be an advocate of 'eating local'; that's to say buying from and supporting local food suppliers and producers, whenever possible, and in turn supporting their local economies.

It's as important now as ever that we help sustain these communities. What Eat Local stands for is to show commitment to local areas, drawing on the expertise and knowledge of the people within them, while we as tourists enjoy visiting and learning about new places.

It's a noble campaign and I don't think there's a better person to be behind this book than Ali Ray, the Club's Eat Local expert. On her camping travels in the aptly named Custard the Campervan, she's visited all manner of folk who are keeping the home fires burning so far as great locally produced food is concerned.

It has been hugely enjoyable for me to work with Ali at Eat Local demonstrations held by the Club – we're kindred spirits when it comes to how we think about food and drink. We both agree that food is an experience that should be savoured. I distinctly remember cooking up some wonderful pork chops in a cider and cream sauce with her at one event, and anyone who knows me will tell you that there's nothing I enjoy more after a good walk than a refreshing pint of cider – from local apples of course.

Ali's enthusiasm for food is infectious and that will come across as you enjoy her food stories, read her suggestions for where to pitch-up, and recreate her many tasty camping recipes – Ali's passion for great ingredients is clear for all to see.

This book will help prepare you for your next adventure; what you might find when you arrive and where you can gather all the ingredients for a remarkable and memorable camping experience.

Enjoy, and remember to Eat Local!

Julia Bradbury
President
The Camping and Caravanning Club

Introduction

Here in Britain we are blessed with a fantastic food culture. Up and down the country, astoundingly good food is being created by dedicated farmers, small-scale growers, passionate chefs and creative artisans. If you care to look, you will find them – as well as their supportive network of farmers' markets, farm shops and independent shopkeepers.

They are the antidote to the industrialised and anonymous food chains in which we buy all our food under one roof and have no relationship at all with the people or places that produce it. It's a system that corrodes our basic connections to the landscape, the seasons and the natural world.

As campers who love the great outdoors, it is within our interests to make that connection again. Put simply, where we choose to buy our food has a direct effect on the countryside around us. Local farmers are the caretakers of the landscape and the open spaces we love to camp in. Good farmers maintain our hedgerows and take part in schemes to encourage wildlife and insects. They give back to the environment as much as they take, rotating crops in a way that puts the good stuff back into the land and future-proofs their part of the world.

There is no denying that the simple sight of a hedgerow heavy with autumnal berries or an apple orchard in full spring blossom is a real spirit-lifter. We can choose to buy apples grown by local farmers rather than the ones in plastic bags from New Zealand; that way we are giving our farmers a reason to keep those orchards, and enhancing our sense of wellbeing.

It's not just about looking after the countryside. Food, how we grow it, how we cook it and how we eat it, is at the heart of so much that we do and love in this country. It is food that makes the places we travel to distinctive, diverse and interesting. To understand the food of a place is to understand what makes a place tick.

So many of our customs and festivals that bring our communities together are based around food, from agricultural shows to wassailing ceremonies in the cider orchards of Somerset or 'blessing the nets' celebrations in Cornish fishing villages.

Look around the towns and villages of this country and you'll find links to food history everywhere; the distinctive long, low forced rhubarb sheds of Yorkshire tell a cultural tale of a determination to grow fresh fruit in a cold northern climate, the smoking sheds on the northeast coast are the legacies of communities that survived by preserving fish to send to the cities, the long-gone Lancashire farmhouse cheesemakers have left signs

> ## To understand the food of a place is to understand what makes a place tick.

of their craft in the form of huge cheese stones strewn in the fields. Market places, laverbread huts, drover's roads, hedgerows and fields of grazing cattle ... it all comes back to food.

This book is a celebration of all of this. It's about inspiring campers to leave the tins and packets of food at home, bypass the big brand shops and seek out the bounty of delicious, locally and sustainably produced food around the places they are staying. It's about doing our bit to protect the things we love, but it's also about having a good time and cooking and eating great food.

I taught myself to cook during the year that I travelled around Australia living in a knackered old yellow Mazda campervan that I called Custard – which is probably why I still tend to cook better meals when I am outside. I discovered there is definitely a peace to be had from cooking outdoors.

Being the sentimental fool that I am, I couldn't be parted with my van after the year was up – so I rammed it full of all the cooking gear I'd bought – along with a handsome man of suitable husband material – and brought Custard home to the UK.

Since then, still with my trusty, rusty yellow campervan, I've been seeking out and sampling Britain's edible treasures – even managing to turn it into a job, becoming a food and travel writer and writing a column called 'Eat Local' for *Camping & Caravanning* magazine.

I've had the privilege to meet the most inspiring, passionate and dedicated farmers, growers, cooks, bakers and wine makers. I've bustled in markets, tasted on tours and been taught how to fish for my supper. I've also found so many great places to camp along the way, and used fresh and interesting local ingredients to create easy meals 'of that place' while I'm there.

The following chapters are the results of my gastronomic camping adventures in Custard. This culinary camping tour of the country shares the feasts I have cooked, reviews the beautiful places I have camped and tells the tales of the people who produced my ingredients.

Now it's your turn.

This book will give you all the information you need to just Pitch Up and Eat Local. It provides inspiration to explore the regions by telling the food stories behind the places you visit. From the whisky regions of Scotland to the fish sheds of the Suffolk coast, the Morecambe Bay shrimps and clotted cream in Cornwall, there's a fascinating tale to be told, and wonderful food to taste.

For every food area featured, I've suggested some great campsites to pitch up at. There's something for everyone, from the super-organised, well manicured sites with hot showers right through to the bumpy field with a single water tap and the best view this side of heaven. Each campsite featured is close to great locally grown or produced foods.

The book has full details, first-hand descriptions and general listings of farmers' markets, farm shops, pick-your-own farms, vineyards and breweries. There are also recommendations for eating out in quirky cafes and pubs that are committed to using locally sourced produce.

Finally, there is a recipe to go with every food story and region, and a few more beside. They are all things I cook when I camp. I am not a chef, I am a happy camper, wife and mum who uses good ingredients with as little fuss as possible to make meals that taste wonderful. They are inspiring, simple and really easy to cook on a gas hob, barbecue or over a fire. Most importantly, all the ingredients needed can be bought in the farm shops and markets listed.

Happy camping!

Five Reasons
to Eat Local

Eating Local ... supports local and rural communities

We all know that good pubs make good holidays. We need to keep them open.
By eating locally and choosing food produced in the places we travel to, we are putting
our money back into local pockets. That goes back into local communities and the rural
economy. It keeps the good food pubs, cafes and restaurants open.

Eating Local ... nurtures and protects our countryside

Who wouldn't want to put money straight into the pockets of the farmers who look after the
landscapes that we love? Obviously just being 'local' isn't enough. We can avoid intensive
farming practices by buying directly from farm shops or farmers' markets where we can meet
the person involved in growing the food – and ask them questions. Farmers who are proud of
their high standards of animal welfare and care for the environment will let you know about it!

Eating Local ... keeps local traditions and skills alive

Choosing local dishes and specialities keeps regional distinctiveness alive and supports
traditional and local skills. Morecambe Bay potted shrimps, Welsh laverbread and Somerset
scrumpy cider were originally made by folk who simply used ingredients available from
the landscape and water around them. The results tasted so good that these drinks and dishes
have now become the edible blueprint of a place. Let's keep them going.

Eating Local ... tastes better

Buying from a farmers' market means your food is likely to be in season and fresher than
if it has been freighted across the world. Food made in small batches, like a just-baked loaf
from an artisan baker or plums plucked ripe from the orchard, is likely to have more flavour,
care and (yes, I'll say it) 'love' in it than an item mass-produced in far-off factories. The food
miles and packaging are happily low, too.

Eating Local ... is good for the soul

Camping holidays are about making memories – and food can be a huge part of that.
Why on earth would you choose to trudge around the same big chainstores buying the
same things on holiday as you do every other week of your life at home? Instead, you can
explore the farmers' markets, breathe in the smell of freshly baked bread in the high street
bakers, loiter to hear local gossip in the farm shop, head to the beach and eat freshly caught fish
with crispy chips while watching the fishing boats come in, and have a good reason to sample
the local ales. This is what holidays are about. Not shopping in the supermarket.

For the Love of Camping

Camping keeps the craziness of life in check. Whether you pitch up in a tent, campervan or caravan or enjoy a spot of glamping, camping is great for the soul. Stripping life back to the bare essentials of finding and cooking food, lighting up the barbecue, making fires, and washing your dishes in a field is a brilliant way to switch off from the stress of our busy lives. Camping gives us back time – time to think, time to watch our children play and time to notice small details that pass us by during our normal busy routines.

The British are certainly feeling the love again when it comes to camping. The Camping and Caravanning Club has about 500,000 members in this country, making it the world's largest and oldest club for all types of camping.

Despite its size, this member-run club still sticks to its values set out in 1901 by six cycling friends who camped together in an orchard near Wantage: to enable, encourage and promote the enjoyment of camping in the great outdoors. By 1905 the Club had opened its first site at Weybridge in Surrey and boasted several hundred members. Captain Robert Falcon Scott, better known as Scott of the Antarctic, became President of the Club in 1909, a position later held by Lord Baden-Powell, the founder of the Scouts.

Today, the Club has 109 sites across the country, most of which are open to members and non-members alike. It also has a network of more than 1,600 'Certificated Sites' for members. These are small, five-pitch sites on farms, in woods, or tucked away in corners of large estates, some of which cost less than £10 per night to stay. And through a joint venture with the Forestry Commission, it manages a further 16 Camping in the Forest touring sites.

If you enjoy big social events, being a member of the Club gives you access to thousands of Club rallies that take place throughout the year. Members also get the opportunity to stay on Temporary Holiday Sites which open for a limited period of time in popular holiday destinations and countryside retreats. It's a really good-value way to camp. The Club even offers an impressive range of escorted tours and other camping holidays across the world.

Every recommendation, campsite, cafe, farm shop, market and pub in this book has been chosen by me, but I'm grateful to have been ably supported by two of our country's oldest, and most trusted, camping and travelling organisations. Firstly, the Camping and Caravanning Club, for whom I've written many of my food stories in the past and who have sent me on countless adventures. And secondly the AA, who are publishing this book. They are no stranger to camping either. Although this vast membership club, set up in 1905 by a small group of motoring enthusiasts, is first and foremost a motoring organisation, it now inspects and grades more than 900 campsites.

Both organisations have search facilities for campsites on their websites that you can explore – once you have exhausted all the sites in this book.

www.campingandcaravanningclub.co.uk
www.theaa.com/self-catering-and-campsites

A Word on Campsites

No two campers are alike. One camper will spend the night in a luxurious motorhome with double beds, satellite telly, microwave and en suite toilet while another sleeps in a bag under a thin layer of canvas with little more than a head torch and single gas burner. The rest of us are somewhere in between with our rusty campervans (me), cavernous family tents, and glamping tipis. And while each style of camper may never appreciate the other's approach, we all share a common goal – to travel around this beautiful country, breathe in the fresh air and to live a little bit closer to nature.

Luckily, there is a campsite to suit every breed of camper, and I have reflected that in the book by recommending three levels of campsites for each location:

1. Where possible I've included an all-singing, all-dancing site complete with home comforts of electric hook-ups, hot showers, laundry facilities and on-site shop.

2. The mid-range site will be a fabulous place to stay but will have fewer facilities. Maybe a shower block but no electric hook-ups.

3. And then there are the 'rustic charm' sites. These are for the folk who don't choose campsites on the standard, or even the existence, of a shower, but look for a place that's away from the crowds and is the closest thing to beautiful wild camping on offer. I've pointed out if the only facility is a water tap or if you have to bring your own chemi-loo.

What all the sites have in common is a magical quality. Maybe it's in a beautiful setting, has a fabulous view, is in a great location or has wonderfully friendly owners. And of course they are all close enough to a source of really good local food.

Read the entries and it will be easy to spot which type of site is which. I have included website addresses for all the campsites so you can look up all the extra details you need to know.

Some of the sites featured are **Camping and Caravanning Club Sites**. The majority of them are open to all and have high standards of cleanliness, facilities and friendly site managers on-hand to help you with any part of your camping holiday. They are great if you are looking for an easy camping experience – somewhere to wash and dry your clothes and easily clean the mud from your children.

I have also included some **Camping in the Forest Sites** that can be found in places such as the New Forest or the Forest of Dean, giving you access to some of this country's most special woodland locations and the excitement that camping in the woods brings.

The **independently run sites** range from great traditional holiday parks to stylish labours of love, perhaps with a few tipis and shepherd huts. The best are run by people wanting to share the beauty of their land and provide a wonderful holiday experience.

Finally I've picked a selection of **Certificated Sites**, part of the Camping and Caravanning Club's network of more than 1,600 small sites, which take up to five caravans or motorhomes plus tents, space permitting. These exclusive locations are member-only sites and ideally you'll have joined before you arrive. However, if you aren't a member you can join on arrival. Don't let this put you off, as the minimal effort it takes to join rewards you with access to some of the most fantastic, uncrowded camping experiences, not to mention all the other benefits of being a member of the Club.

Certificated Sites listed in this book are marked (CS) after the name.

Campsite Cooking

Cooking on a campsite is surely the best form of meal-making. None of the usual kitchen rules apply: schedules, timings, whizzing gizmos are left behind at home. In fact, outdoor cooking is a pretty relaxed affair. Being alfresco lets you watch the world go by; you can listen to birdsong and the kids yelling while enjoying a glass of something cold. A bit of freeform creativity and ingenuity may be called for on occasion – but that's all part of the fun.

I've made every effort to offer recipes throughout this book that can be cooked on a selection of heat sources: gas stoves, barbecues (both gas and charcoal) as well as campfires.

Cooking on Gas Stoves

Think of campsite cooking and most people immediately think of barbecues. But, from my observations, many campers actually tend to favour the gas stove. From the single pocket-sized glorified Bunsen burner with one small collapsible pan, to the dual ring stove with added grill, gas is probably going to feature somewhere in your cooking kit.

If you have a double gas burner I'd recommend getting a suitable cast-iron griddle or hot plate that will sit on top of it; this will give you ultimate versatility in your cooking. Alternatively you can use a heavy-bottomed griddle pan.

I've tried and tested many gas barbecues as part of my job, but the ones I return to again and again are the Cadac Safari Chef, which has a gazillion different cooking surfaces – paella pan, wok, pizza stone, griddle and gas ring – to use over a single central gas source. My other staple is the trusty old Outwell dual burner that I can sit on a table top and get the kettle on in a flash.

Obviously, if you are in a caravan, campervan or a motorhome then you will probably have a gas stove as part of your kitchen.

Barbecues

Sizzle, spit and smoke – a barbecue should feature at least once in any camping weekend. Here are some thoughts and tips:

Cooking on barbecues can be done in two ways
- **Direct heat method** The food is put directly over the main heat source. This method is perfect for grilling items that will cook quickly like steaks, burgers and pieces of fish.
- **Indirect heat method** is best used for larger pieces or joints of meat, where you would otherwise use an oven at home. It involves moving the glowing charcoals to either side of the barbecue and leaving a cooler area in the middle. Once the barbecue lid is down, the heat circulates and cooks the food evenly. Gas barbecues sometimes have heat deflection attachments or you can turn the burners off on one side to achieve the same effect.

Charcoal Barbecues

These are seen as the genuine article by many. After all, real fire is involved! The upside is that you get great barbecue flavours in your food, and you can take the grill off after cooking and chuck on some more charcoal or wood and feel like you are sitting around a camp fire. For me, the only disadvantage is the time it takes to heat up to the right temperature when you have hungry children.

Tips on lighting a charcoal barbecue

- Open the vents on the side of your barbecue. Add a single layer of coals/briquettes on the grate, then pile them into a pyramid with about 3-4 firelighters. Try to use the waxy firelighters made specifically for barbecues. The ones for domestic fires or liquid lighters are more likely to taint the taste of the food. Light with a long match!
- If your barbecue is big enough, pile some coals higher on one side. That way, if you need a high heat to sear your meat first, you use this area, where the heat will be more intense, before moving it to a cooler area.
- Natural charcoal tends to start more quickly than briquettes and burns with about twice the level of heat. It smells cleaner, too.
- Generally it will take about 30 minutes or so for your barbecue to get to cooking heat. It is ready when the coals are covered in a layer of white ash, and you can't hold your hand 15cm above for more than three seconds.

Gas Barbecues

You don't get the lovely smoky flavours with gas, but you do get more control over your cooking temperatures, and of course you are ready to cook immediately. Marinating your meat is even more important if cooking on gas in order to add those extra flavours.

If you haven't been able to get all of the residue off your barbecue from its last use, turn the gas on, let the bars get hot to burn off the residue, then give them a brisk brush with a wire brush.

It is also worth taking all the fat trays, grates and burners out now and again to give them a really good clean to get rid of the gunk. It helps to prevent the flare-ups and too much smoking – which can affect the flavour of your food.

Lightly brush the bars with some oil before cooking to prevent the meat sticking.

Disposable Barbecues

My advice is just don't – unless you like the taste of lighter fuel in your food. You can buy reusable 'bucket barbecues' using charcoal that cost next to nothing.

Campfires

It's a rare treat to find campsites that allow campfires, but I've hunted out some good ones for this book.

Sitting around a campfire has been a vital part of human ritual since one lucky soul discovered the spark. Even now it fulfils the basic need for warmth and cooking in many cultures. Our need might no longer exist, but the desire to sit around a fire is still as strong as ever. The crackle of burning logs and glowing embers draws people in like moths. A fire encourages good old-fashioned late-night storytelling and singsongs with guitars. And, there is satisfaction to be had from cooking a meal over a fire that is hard to beat. The best way of cooking on a campfire is to use old pans or aluminium trays set on a low metal trivet or triangle of bricks over the glowing embers around the edge. Potatoes and bananas wrapped in foil are also great nestled in the embers. If you are a regular campfire cook, I'd recommend investing in a steel tripod from which to hang your cooking pot.

Barbecuing Tips

• Be prepared

Barbecuing is so much easier if you do all your prep before you start cooking. I don't always listen to my own advice here, but a successful barbecue usually requires constant prodding and basting – which won't happen if you are still busy cutting veg.

• Let the meat get up to ambient temperature

If you put meat straight from the cool box on to the barbecue the outside is likely to burn before the inside begins to cook. The closer you can get the middle temperature to the outside temperature the less likely you are to suffer from barbecuer's-curse – black on the outside and raw in the middle.

• Keep watching

The best piece of advice is to stay with your barbecue and watch what you are cooking. I have learnt to my peril that getting distracted chatting to friends and family has too often ended up in over-cooked food.

• Don't turn the food too often

Just turn once if you can get away with it. It will be easier to turn and gets those lovely grill marks across it if you leave it alone for longer. Use tongs, not a fork, so that the meat doesn't pierce and start to lose its juices.

• The perfect steak

If grilling meat, sear it briefly over the hottest part of the coals, then move it further away from the coals to cook it more evenly and slowly. Putting a lid on will help it cook through.

• Cooking a large joint

Wrap it in foil before you cook it as this will keep it juicy. You will need a lidded barbecue for this, which will cook the meat like an oven. When the meat is almost cooked, take it out of the foil and finish it off directly over the heat on the barbecue to colour up and soak up the smoky flavours.

• Talking of smoky flavours …

if you don't have a smoking box but still want an extra smoky flavour, throw some twigs of rosemary or thyme or untreated woodchips on to some of the cooler coals. The smoke will slowly infuse the flavours into the meat.

• Rest Up

ALWAYS rest your meat once it has cooked. A piece of meat hot off the barbecue will be tough, but letting it rest for 5-10 minutes (covered in foil so it doesn't go cold) will allow the meat to relax, soften and re-absorb all the lovely juices.

Food Safety and Hygiene

It goes without saying but always use separate utensils, plates and chopping boards for raw and cooked food.

Never pour any leftover marinade from the raw meat on to the cooked meat at the end.

The only way to make sure those sausages and chicken pieces are cooked through is to cut one in half to check. If there are any pink juices when pressed, it's not cooked and not safe to eat! Put it back on the grill.

General Campsite Cooking Safety

NEVER EVER use a barbecue or any other cooking appliance in your tent or awning – it can cause carbon dioxide poisoning, which can be fatal.

Check the coals are fully extinguished or the gas is turned off properly before leaving your barbecue unattended. It's worth having a fire extinguisher or bucket to hand. Keep children and pets well away.

Tricks of the Trade

Here are a few campsite cooking techniques I have developed over the years that make life a little easier.

• Marinating

Marinating is the perfect way to add flavour and also makes the meat tender. Marinate for as long as you can for best results.

Don't add salt to your marinade! It will draw all the moisture out of your meat and it will end up dry.

Also, if your marinade contains sugar, don't put the meat over a high temperature otherwise the sugar will burn too quickly.

Most meats benefit from marinating. The easiest way to do it is in a large, resealable freezer bag. Put the empty, open bag into a bowl so that you can fold back the opening of the bag around the rim of the bowl. This holds the bag steady and open for you while you put your marinade ingredients in, then your meat. Seal the bag, squish it all around to coat the meat, then pop it into the cool box. It saves on space in your fridge and there is no washing-up or mess.

• Foil Parcels

This is a nifty way to make a meal. I've cooked lots

> ## " The crackle of burning logs and glowing embers draws people in like moths. "

of things in a foil parcel, such as Rhubarb Crumble (page 293) and Hot Cheese and Cider Dip (page 266), and also made small parcels of potato dauphinoise. Layer thinly sliced potatoes, add some butter, a little cream, grated cheese and salt and pepper and lay the parcel on the medium hot grill for 20 minutes.

The trick for foil-parcel food is to make sure you have at least a double layer of foil. Even better, place three large rectangles of foil on top of each other, put your food (be it fish or vegetables) in and fold it over like a padded envelope.

• Smoking

I've included a simple recipe for smoking mackerel in this book (page 63).

Smoking food on the barbecue is fun, tasty and really easy. You can buy a 'smoking box' from camp shops or online, or you can easily make your own.

Use a small aluminium tray, the kind you get takeaway food in. In a separate bowl soak a couple of handfuls of natural (untreated) wood chips in water for 30 minutes to stop the chips burning too quickly. You can buy smoking chips in garden centres and hardware stores.

Drain the soaked chips then put them into the aluminium tray, cover the top with tin foil and make lots of holes across the top to allow the smoke to come out. Put the 'box' in between the elements of your gas barbecue or nestled down in the charcoal.

Heat your barbecue up with the lid on until you notice the wonderful smoky smells coming out. Quickly open the lid and put your meat or fish on the grill and put the lid down. Cook it as normal, allowing it to 'soak up the smoke'.

A Word on Ingredients

It's simply not realistic to suggest that all of your cooking ingredients need to be sourced from the field next door. Eating local certainly isn't about setting rules on where you must buy all your food. It is about enjoying the process of buying some of your ingredients from interesting places and people who are passionate about their products, farm shops and markets.

You will find details of all the farmers' markets local to the campsites in this book, as well as certain country markets. To be called a farmers' market, stalls have to be certified under the rules and regulations set out by FARMA (the National Farmers and Retail Association, www.farma.org.uk). All the produce on sale at a farmers' market should have been grown, reared, caught, brewed, pickled, baked, smoked or processed by the stallholder. There are also about 300 weekly Country Markets (www.country-markets. co.uk) held in village halls and town squares across England and Wales. They tend to run for an hour or two and sell homebaked goods, preserves and garden-grown vegetables and fruit. I've included many in the book. Check markets are running before you travel.

Making an effort to locally source key ingredients like meat, vegetables, quirky local cheese or freshly caught fish can make a huge difference to your meal. It will taste better simply for not having been freighted halfway across the world. It will also taste better because you will cook it differently. When you meet the person who produced that food, or know a bit about its provenance and the way it was produced, you are bound to care more about it and get more pleasure from eating it than if it came wrapped in clingfilm and polystyrene from the supermarket.

The Camping Store Cupboard

Every camper should have one – a pre-packed bag or box of store cupboard basics to take with you on every trip. Get this bit right and you'll find campsite cooking a delight and a doddle.

Having the all the basics to hand, such as rice, pasta, herbs and oil, leaves you the flexibility a buy a couple of steaks or fresh fish from the local market knowing you've got everything you need to transform it into a great meal back at the site.

No-one wants to buy a whole pot of honey each time they need one teaspoon of it for a recipe, so stock up on basics and keep them all in a neat lightweight box and it will save you money and make you smug. Trust me!

Here is a list of what I have in my transportable store cupboard – it's the kind of thing you can add to whenever you come across handy travel-size or mini versions of things.

Store Cupboard Kit

Salt	Mayonnaise
Pepper	Rice
Mustard	Pasta
Worcestershire sauce	Couscous
Sweet chilli sauce	Plain flour
Sugar	Harissa paste
Plastic bottle of	Tinned chickpeas
lemon juice	Tinned kidney beans
Olive or rapeseed oil	Tinned cannellini
Balsamic vinegar	beans
Runny honey	Tinned tomatoes
Garlic	White wine vinegar
Soy sauce	(great for making
Stock cubes	salad dressings)
Dried herbs: mixed	Soft tortilla wraps
herbs, oregano, mint	
Spices: smoked	**Bought on arrival,**
paprika, chilli powder,	**or brought in your**
cumin, coriander,	**coolbox from home:**
cinnamon	Butter
Curry powder	Milk
Ketchup	Eggs

Cooking Gear Checklist

I keep two large plastic storage boxes ready packed with all my camping cooking gear. Here's what's in them:

Good quality re-sealable freezer bags of varying sizes

Aluminium foil

Chopping boards – each year I buy a set of three cheap coloured boards: green for veg, red for raw meat and blue for fish. Easy, hygienic and disposable at the end of the holiday

Grater

Three sharp knives – one for cutting raw meat, one for veg and a thin-bladed one for fish

Pans – two saucepans with lids. One quite large

Frying pans – one small, one large

Skewers

Camping kettle

Nest of plastic bowls – big enough to mix all-in-one recipes like burgers

Serving plates, bowls and cutlery

Wooden spoons

Gas lighter and matches

Plastic measuring jug/cup

Washing-up bowl, liquid and loads of tea towels

Aluminium trays – great for cooking over the fire without wrecking your posh trays from home

Barbecue tongs

Spatula

Bottle opener

Tin opener

Kitchen roll

Water carrier

Cool box with freezer blocks

Bin bags

Tupperware pots with lids

Cooking appliances – campfire grill, gas stove, ideally with two burners, and a bottle of gas

SOUTH WEST ENGLAND

Pasties, cider, Cheddar and clotted cream are the specialities of this region, where food, farming and tourism combine to great effect. The stunning coastline, fields of Friesians in bucolic Devonshire farmlands, cider orchards in Somerset and busy farmers' markets are what we all want to see when we head south for our holidays. So enjoy the farmhouse cheeses and make the most of freshly caught seafood while supping the golden cider. You'll be protecting all that we love about the area.

CRABBING BUCKET

01 ABSOLUTELY CRABULOUS

Forget surfing and sailing. Take a stroll around the pretty South Devon harbour towns of Dartmouth and Salcombe and you'll be convinced that 'crabbing', with line and bucket, is the region's most popular pastime.

On sunny days, sitting space on quaysides and harbour walls is at a premium as families, teenagers, couples, young and old happily wait patiently for a catch.

This South Devon coastline positively bristles with crabs. Most of those in tourists' buckets are shore crabs – small and green in colour. But these waters are best known, certainly among the culinary world, for the edible Brown Crab. The heaviest of the crab species in British waters, it is described by the Marine Conservation Society as looking 'a bit like a pie with legs on, with its distinctive reddish brown shell and pastry crust rim'.

Rich in vitamins and minerals and low in fat, about two-thirds of the meat from a crab is the sweet-tasting white meat and a third is the flavour-packed brown meat – absolutely stunning mixed with a little mayonnaise and lemon juice.

Local crab fisherman Nick Hutchings has been fishing these waters nearly every day of his working life. He, his wife Anita and family sell fish throughout the local area via post offices and village stores. But, if you want someone else to cook it for you, they'll do that too. They run **Britannia @ The Beach**, a brilliant no-nonsense cafe with a menu of home-made crab cakes, hand-dived scallops and fish pies, as well as home-made pizzas and chips for the less adventurous. This much-loved landmark – known to the locals as 'The Shack' – is positioned directly on the shingle beach. It used to be the family's bait store but now doubles up as the village store and a traditional fishmongers, too. Grab yourself a crab sandwich and a cool drink, look at the sea and feel the warm glow of discovering simple holiday pleasures.

Britannia @ The Beach

The Shack, Beesands Beach, Devon TQ7 2EH • 01548 581168
www.britanniaatthebeach.co.uk

Pitch Up

Slapton Sands Camping and Caravanning Club Site

Middle Grounds, Slapton, Kingsbridge,
Devon TQ7 2QW • 01548 580538
www.campingandcaravanningclub.co.uk

With the beach literally across the road, many
of the pitches have perfect sea views and you can fall
asleep to the sounds of the waves. The site is right
next to Slapton Ley, a freshwater lagoon that is
part of a National Nature Reserve teeming with birds
and wildlife.

Campers benefit from regular visits from the local
bakery van and a fish-and-chip truck. However, for
a real gourmet gem head to **The Tower Inn**, tucked
away among the thatched cottages of picturesque
Slapton village. If it is a warm summer's evening, eat
in the shadows of the atmospheric ruin of a 14th-
century tower in the pub garden.

Silver Gates (CS)

Churchstow, Kingsbridge, Devon TQ7 3QH
01548 857997 • www.southdevoncamping.com

Being a large flat field, there might not be as many
bells and whistles as on other sites, but what there is
is of a very high standard. Caravans are welcome and,
unusually for this area, the approach roads aren't too
windy and narrow. You'll feel at one with the wildlife
here; the hedgerows flicker with butterflies, inquisitive
rabbits sit nearby while you marvel at the vast
countryside views rolling down towards the sea. Oh,
and did I say that there's a good pub walkable from
the site? The 13th-century **Church House** is all dark
beams and bare stone and serves up honest home-
made food. Gorgeous.

Karrageen

Hope Cove, Bolberry, Malborough, Kingsbridge,
Devon TQ7 3EN • 01548 561230
www.karrageen.co.uk

The narrow approach to Karrageen campsite is
pretty tricky, so only the most confident of
caravanners will make it this far. But, hidden away
in the secret little world of Hope Cove, this campsite
offers unbeatable sea views, peace, tranquillity and
great facilities including its own spring water supply.
What's not to love?

Eat Local

From vibrant food markets to cosmopolitan eateries
and cool beachside shacks, the South Hams area has
an embarrassment of gourmet riches.

Stokeley Farm Shop

Stokeley Barton, Stokenham, Kingsbridge,
Devon TQ7 2SE • 01548 581605
www.stokeleyfarmshop.co.uk

They claim to offer the largest range of local produce
in the South Hams, and I believe them. There's a
food market, deli and restaurant here. As well as
produce from their own farm, the folk at Stokeley are
passionate supporters of local producers. You can
get all your holiday supplies here and it's only five
minutes from Slapton Sands campsite.

Ashby's Easy Stores

East Charleton, Kingsbridge, Devon TQ7 2AP
www.ashbysonline.co.uk

I have to mention Ashby's. It's a petrol station
like no other and the locals love it. It has an
astounding stock of local produce, meats, dairy and
vegetables but also sells surfboards, paddleboards
and camping equipment.

Moby Nicks

24 Fairfax Place, Dartmouth, Devon TQ6 9AB
01803 839070 • www.mobynicks.com
Nick and Beverley Henry have been selling Devon-caught fish to wholesalers for over 25 years. Luckily for us, they have decided to open a shop in the middle of Dartmouth for the general public. Fresh crab is on offer, as well as cooking advice, should you need it. Closed Mondays.

Catch of the Day

54 Fore Street, Kingsbridge, Devon TQ7 1NY
01548 852006
Straight off the boats in Plymouth, this town-centre shop has a good range of wet fish, mussels, scallops and crab as well as home-made sauces to complement your fish when you've cooked it on your barbecue.

Farmers' Markets

Totnes Good Food Market

High Street, Totnes, Devon • www.totnesgoodfood.co.uk • 3rd Sunday of the month
I love this market – there is always a party atmosphere. From home-made fish cakes, charcuterie meats, hedgerow cordials and a huge choice of hot dishes to lunch on, a morning spent here will feature in your great holiday memories.

Kingsbridge Farmers' Market

Town Square, 1st and 3rd Saturday of the month

Dartmouth Farmers' Market

Market Square, 2nd Saturday of the month

Eating Out
Sharpham Vineyard Café

Sharpham Estate, near Totnes, Devon TQ9 7UT
www.sharpham.com
This is my 'must-visit' restaurant. Hidden in a deep valley, the rustic outdoor dining area has exclusive vine-framed views of the River Dart. The setting is divine, the kitchen is a tarted-up static caravan and the food is fantastic. Kingsbridge crab, local charcuterie or a board of local smoked fish are served with wine and cheese made on-site. It's laid-back, stylish and unforgettable. The staff even bring round blankets if the breeze gets up.

Britannia @ The Beach

The Shack, Beesands Beach, Devon TQ7 2EH
01548 581168 • www.britanniaatthebeach.co.uk
Rustic on the outside, delicious on the inside. Owner Nick Hutching fishes for crabs and scallops daily and brings them straight back to his cafe, which is also the local post office ... and the village store. Welcome to Devon village life.

The Crabshell

Embankment Road, Kingsbridge, Devon TQ7 1JZ
01548 852345 • www.thecrabshellinn.com
A favourite pub of mine, set on the edge of Kingsbridge's estuary. The outdoor tables on the quay catch the sun all day, and after your meal you can try your hand at crabbing, with buckets and crab lines provided at the bar. The menu is suitably crustacean-themed – the crab bisque is fantastic.

South Devon's unique voluntary management scheme, the 'inshore potting agreement', prevents fisherman from fishing the crabbing area and vice-versa. This protects the crab neighbourhoods, making South Devon one of the best places for pot-caught crab in the UK. It's nuts then that over 60 per cent of these crabs are exported to France, Spain, Hong Kong and China. Why don't we eat more? It's time we got a taste for one of our best natural resources.

CRAB LINGUINE

I will confess to buying my fresh crab meat already cooked and picked. I have neither the skill nor the patience to pick it from the shell. But even ready-prepared it is still a reasonably priced, sustainably-sound option at the fishmongers.

Serves 4

300g linguine pasta

salt and pepper

For the sauce

300g fresh cooked white crabmeat

a good glug (approx. 2 tbsp) of olive oil

1 garlic clove, finely chopped

¼ fresh red chilli, very finely chopped

4 spring onions, very finely sliced

grated zest and juice of ½ lemon

a splash (about 50ml) of dry white wine

a handful of parsley leaves, chopped

- Cook your linguine pasta according to instructions — probably around 8 minutes in salted boiling water.

- Heat the oil in a deep frying pan or saucepan. Add the garlic, chilli, spring onions, lemon juice and lemon zest. Fry for a couple of minutes then add the crabmeat. Heat through for about a minute.

- Pour the wine into the pan and heat until most of it has evaporated.

- Add a spoonful of the pasta water to the crab sauce pan, then drain the pasta into your sink. Put the drained pasta and most of the parsley into the pan with the sauce, and mix so that everything is well coated.

- Season to taste with salt and pepper and serve, with the remaining parsley sprinkled on top.

02

AN UNCTUOUS DOLLOP

"Is clotted cream originally a Cornish product or a Devonshire one?" I asked innocently of Nicholas Rodda, managing director of Rodda's, the largest clotted cream producer in the UK. "There's no definitive evidence," is the firm reply, but I'm left in no doubt as to which county he believes owns the crown.

Nick and his brother Adam are the fifth-generation of Roddas to immerse themselves in this regional product. Based near Redruth, Nick's great great grandmother started making clotted cream in her farmhouse kitchen in 1890. As Nick says, "It was a hit with the locals before she started 'exporting' it to England."

In 1998, Nick's grandad, Alfred Rodda, achieved the much-coveted Protected Designation of Origin (PDO) status for his family's beloved product. This stipulates that only Cornish clotted cream made using stringent traditional methods in Cornwall from Cornish cows' milk of no less than 55 per cent fat can be called 'Cornish Clotted Cream'.

Using a method that has remained largely unchanged for over 400 years, clotted cream is produced by 'scalding' milk in an enamel pan in a *bain marie* (container of hot water) for a few hours. This thickens it, and it forms a crust or 'clot' over the top. It was probably made for practical reasons originally, in the days before the fridge. The crust on the top sealed the cream, keeping it fresh for up to two weeks (it is fabled that the crust can withstand a pound weight without breaking).

Of course, on the scale that Rodda's now make the cream, the process is far more mechanical but the basic techniques are the same. The milk is sourced from 151 dairies within a 30-mile radius of the creamery. It takes six pints of milk to make half a pound of clotted cream.

No holiday in Cornwall is complete without a cream tea. Which brings me to the other debate: jam first … or cream? It's not just provenance that gets the locals a little heated. Apparently in Devon it's cream first then jam – Cornwall is the other way around.

Rodda's Clotted Cream

Scorrier, Redruth, Cornwall TR16 5BU • 01209 823300
www.roddas.co.uk

Pitch Up

Elm Farm (CS)

Tram Road, Nancekuke, near Redruth, Cornwall
TR16 5UF • 01209 891498 • www.elmfarm.biz

Surrounded by lush green pastures, this is a chilled-out, naturally beautiful and friendly place. Two top sandy surf beaches, Porthtowan and Portreath, are a walk or cycle ride away.

Hugged by trees and shrubs, the pitches are level and sheltered. Tents, campervans, caravans and motorhomes are welcome, but if you fancy a spot of glamping then there is Gertrude the Horsebox – a beautifully converted ned-shed right next to the stream. To top off that perfect campsite experience there are braziers and wood for evening campfires.

They like to keep things green here at Elm Farm so there are composting toilets. If you prefer a flushing loo then head up to the farmhouse.

The beach-hut style licensed cafe is small but big in style, offering local beers, ice-creams, and simple lunches. If you are going to cook for yourself, then **Etherington's Farm Shop** is just two miles up the road, and Rodda's creamery is a short cycle ride away.

Beirut Roots

Clotted cream's origins are firmly in Devon and Cornwall … and Lebanon. This rather unexpected connection comes from the Phoenicians' trade links with Cornwall around 500BC when they came here as part of the tin trade and shared their cream-clotting techniques along with their trading.

Tehidy Holiday Park

Harris Mill, Illogan, Redruth, Cornwall TR16 4JQ
01209 216489 • www.tehidy.co.uk

Don't let the term 'holiday park' put you off. This gem of a place is family run, quiet and characterful. Static caravans, pitches, camping pods and wigwams nestle among the trees, flower borders and wildlife and there's a comforting old-fashioned air about the place. There's a play area and games room for the children but the site is also well positioned for some of the best beaches in the country.

Veryan Camping and Caravanning Club Site

Tretheake, Veryan, Truro, Cornwall TR2 5PP
01872 501658 • www.campingandcaravanningclub.
co.uk

This well-equipped site with hard standings for caravans, pitches for tents, electric hook-ups and sparkling facilities is hidden away on the Roseland Peninsula. It's close to the pretty villages, stunning beaches and coastal paths that make holidaying in this unspoilt part of the country such a delight. There's a small lake worthy of a pre-bedtime stroll.

Eat Local

Etherington's Farm Shop

Wheal Rose, Scorrier, Redruth, Cornwall TR16 5DF
01209 890555 • www.etherington-meats.co.uk

Naturally you can get all you need for your barbecue here: top-quality chicken, pork and lamb including Cornish-bred beef fed only on the grass you see around you. 'Keeping it Cornish' is the mantra, so you'll also find locally made beer, cheese, vegetables and the most delightful Cornish Pasties – handmade on-site by Ian Trevethick, who makes them to his mother's recipes.

Callestick Ice Cream

Callestick Farm, Truro, Cornwall TR4 9LL
www.callestickfarm.co.uk

Head 15 minutes up the road from Elm Farm to
enjoy another product of this luscious grassland.
The family at Callestick have been making ice-cream
for 25 years at their conservation farm. It's completely
natural with no added nasties – just fresh flavours
like strawberries, clotted cream and honeycomb.
The water for the sorbets comes from the farm's own
spring. It's as close to guilt-free ice-cream as you'll get.
There's a cafe, small farm shop and a chance to see
ice-cream being made.

Berrymans Bakery

Pednandrea, Redruth, Cornwall TR15 2EE
01209 215534

A real 'proper job' of a bakery as they say in these
parts. Baking is in Robert Berryman's blood: he grew
up in the flat above the bakery, spent his childhood
lulled to sleep by the muffled sound of the machinery
and woke to the smell of fresh bread. Sourdough,
ryebreads and wholegrains share the shelves with
award-winning pasties and traditionally made
Cornish saffron cake.

The Cream of Society
Rodda's Clotted Cream has further
pedigree. This dairy in Cornwall is the
provenance of the oozy dollop on the
Wimbledon strawberries, it was served
at Prince Charles' wedding (first time
around) and on Concorde on its final
flight from London.

Farmers' Market
Truro Farmers' Market

Lemon Quay, Truro, Cornwall • Saturday and
Wednesday • www.trurofarmersmarket.co.uk
Regular stalls of fresh bread, organic veg, venison,
local pork and honey as well as seasonal stalls.

SIRLOIN STEAK
WITH BRANDY, MUSTARD
AND CLOTTED CREAM SAUCE

Don't be constrained by scones and jam. Clotted cream is a versatile ingredient for cooking savoury dishes – and a great way of making rich, quick and easy sauces.

This recipe is a favourite of Nicholas Rodda, so thanks are due to him for giving it to me. With ingredients all sourced from Etherington's Farm Shop, you'll be able to stand by your pitch as you cook and enjoy the landscape, pastures and sea breezes that contributed to the great taste of this dish.

Serves 2

- Get your frying pan as hot as you dare, then add oil and butter to sizzle.

- Add the steaks and sear quickly on both sides until brown.

- Next, add the shallot and cook the steak to your liking. Cooking times obviously depend on the thickness of a steak but as a guide: for 2.5cm thick, allow 1½-2 minutes on each side for rare, 3 minutes for medium and 4 minutes for well done.

- Remove the steaks and put to one side to rest.

- Meanwhile, reduce the heat under the frying pan, pour in the brandy and light it with a match, then cook until the flames die out. (If it doesn't singe your eyebrows it will impress the neighbours.) Burning it takes some of the alcohol out, but leaves the flavour. If using wine, just let it bubble briefly.

- Spoon in the Cornish clotted cream and mustard, and stir well. Finally, season the sauce with salt and pepper and leave to simmer for 1-2 minutes.

- Serve your steak with some boiled new potatoes and salad. Pour the sauce over the steak.

2 steaks (I used sirloin)

½ tsp olive oil

1 tsp butter

1 large shallot, finely chopped

3 tbsp brandy (or red wine if you don't have brandy to hand)

100g Rodda's Cornish Clotted Cream

2 tsp wholegrain mustard

salt and pepper

03 CHEDDAR, SOMERSET
GORGING ON CHEDDAR

Despite their best efforts, the packed coaches and gaudy gift shops populating the small town of Cheddar fail to detract from the impressive majesty of the wild gorges in Britain's largest canyon. Within moments of leaving Cheddar high street, you'll find yourself in staggeringly beautiful and refreshingly wild limestone escarpments and plateaus offering 360-degree vistas.

The attraction of the town and the fame of the cheese go hand-in-hand. An awe-inspiring landscape like this will have drawn visitors for centuries, visitors who no doubt ate the local cheeses and took some away with them, as I suspect you will too.

No-one knows for sure how long cheesemaking has been associated with Cheddar, but the info in the Cheddar Gorge Cheese Company's visitor centre (the only company to still make cheese in Cheddar) tells us the earliest references to Cheddar cheese are in 1170. Pre-refrigeration, turning excess milk into cheese was the done thing and the cool temperature of the caves was perfect for storing the truckles.

But it was the technique for making this cheese that made it distinct, to the point that 'Cheddaring' is now a noun. Someone somewhere worked out that if you pressed all the excess moisture from the curd then the cheese would last longer, and by cutting this curd up and stacking the bits together then pressing again to drain out all of the whey then you ended up with a pretty great cheese. I doubt that the farmer or farmer's wife who discovered this could ever have imagined that their invention would dominate the cheese world.

Visitors can watch cheesemakers using traditional skills to handmake the cheese. The cheeses are wrapped in cheesecloth and left to mature for up to 18 months. Over time the cheese grows a rind and changes texture, developing the flavours along the way. To finish things off, it's matured in the caves, as it used to be. Cheese matured in vacuumed plastic doesn't come close.

The Cheddar Gorge Cheese Company
The Cliffs, Cheddar, Somerset BS27 3QA • 01934 742810
www.cheddargorgecheeseco.co.uk

According to The Cheddar Gorge Cheese Company a truly authentic Cheddar cheese should be made from unpasteurised milk taken from cows grazing in the pastures surrounding the town of Cheddar. The calcareous (meaning chalky and limey) grasslands that the cows graze around the Mendips influence the flavours of the milk, which in turn affect the flavour of the cheese.

Pitch Up

Cheddar Camping and Caravanning Club Site

Mendip Heights, Townsend, Priddy Wells, Somerset BA5 3BP • 01749 870241
www.campingandcaravanningclub.co.uk

This is the perfect place to get among the locals. It's situated in Priddy, the highest village in the Mendips, known for its annual folk festival in July and sheep fair in August. A few yards from the site is the **Priddy Good Farm Shop**, renowned for fantastic home-made pies and the rustic little cafe selling scones, teas and breakfasts. The location may be suitably rural and wild, set high up there on the Mendips, but the facilities at this lovely campsite are slick, clean and impressive. The site is slightly sloping, but if you drink enough cider you are unlikely to notice.

Wookey Farm (CS)

Monks Ford, Wookey, Wells, Somerset BA5 1DT
01749 671859 • www.wookeyfarm.com

This campsite-on-a-goat-farm is brilliant for kids (no pun intended). Families can learn all about the day-to-day running of a goat farm, as well as seeing the sheep, donkey and rare-breed pigs, and help collect the eggs from the free-range hens. The on-site farm shop is housed in a nifty conversion of a horse trailer and sells goat's milk and cheese and free-range meat. The diced goat's meat makes fantastic curries and the pork sausages are massive. Facilities are basic but good, and there's water and a composting loo. There aren't showers, but you could take a refreshing dip in the River Axe via the rope swing.

The Old Oaks Touring Park

Wick Farm, Wick, Glastonbury, Somerset BA6 8JS
01458 831437 • www.theoldoaks.co.uk

Being a parent of two young children this 'adults only' site wouldn't usually be on my radar, but it deserves a mention for its consistent awards and excellent reputation in the camping world. So, if you are child-free and in the area, this will offer you a high-class, spacious, quiet option.

Eat Local

Priddy Good Farm Shop

Townsend Farm, Priddy, Somerset BA5 3BP
01749 870171

Just a few yards from Cheddar Camping and Caravanning site, this is a proper 'locals' farm shop. Dodge the tractors as you wander through the farmyard to the shop with its great variety of home-raised beef and lamb. The home-made pies are tasty, well-filled and rather addictive. There's a small selection of fresh produce and an on-site cafe that serves a proper farmhouse fry-up every morning.

Nyland Hill Farm Shop

Decoy Pool Farm, Nylands, Cheddar, Somerset BS27 3UD • 01934 744802
www.nylandhillfarm.co.uk

I tripped over ducks and chickens in the farmyard on the way in to the cosy shop invitingly full of fresh produce and fabulous beef from the farm but also cakes, pickles, cheese, jams and bread all made by the farmer Nick Hill's friends and neighbours. A side room is full of fruit and vegetables from local suppliers – some of it organic. There is an impressive selection of home-made ready meals, many of which could be heated in a saucepan over your gas stove.

Batch Farm Cheesemakers

East Pennard, Shepton Mallet, Somerset
BA4 6TH • 01749 860319

Batch Farm is set on picturesque Pennard Ridge, with views of Glastonbury Tor and the Mendips. The Gould family have farmed here for 70 years and have been making cheese for the last 40 of those. Milk from their 260 Friesian cows travels about 0.75 miles to the dairy each day to be made into a rich, tangy farmhouse cheddar. The cows drink the whey that is left over and the process begins again. There is a small shop selling the cheese next to the farmhouse. Ring the bell and someone will come over from the dairy.

Farmers' Markets

There is a good selection of farmers' markets in the county. It's worth checking **www.somersetfarmersmarkets.co.uk**

Wells Farmers' Market

Every Wednesday

Wow. This is such a good market. It bustles and buzzes in the beautiful old market place in the shadow of Wells Cathedral. You can buy some great traditional farmhouse cheddar from Greens of Glastonbury or Batch Farm Cheesemakers, and there's Charlton Orchards Apple Store in season, where the two very knowledgeable ladies will slice rare and unusual varieties for you to try before you buy. Also on offer is fresh fish, organic meats and hot lunches to take away.

Axbridge Farmers' Market

1st Saturday of the month

WEST COUNTRY SALAD

Serves 4

This is a simple West Country lunch, a good hot alternative to a ploughman's as a showcase for great cheese. It is only worth making if you use a decent local Cheddar – a really mature one, with the kind of flavours that give the inside of your cheeks that mild burning feeling when you eat a chunk of it. And let's face it, you won't be short of choice.

- Slice the cooled new potatoes lengthways, about 5mm thick. Season them with salt and pepper and mix with a little olive oil.

- Put the potato slices along with the mushrooms in a frying pan with half the butter and 2 tbsp oil, and sauté until they begin to brown. Add the garlic for the last couple of minutes. Transfer to a large serving bowl, using a slotted spoon or spatula, and set aside, covered in foil, to keep warm.

- Now add the asparagus, if you have it, to the frying pan with the remaining butter and another 2 tbsp oil and lots of black pepper. Cook for around 5 minutes, then set aside under the foil with the potatoes.

- Bring a pan of water to the boil, and poach the eggs for 2—3 minutes until soft-boiled.

- As that is happening, mix the potatoes, mushrooms, asparagus, parsley and cheese gently in the bowl, along with the lemon juice. Divide between 4 plates.

- Place a poached egg on each plate and drizzle with olive oil. Serve and enjoy!

200g new potatoes, cooked and cooled

salt and pepper

olive oil

200g fresh field mushrooms, thickly sliced

50g butter

4 garlic cloves, finely chopped

200g asparagus stalks, trimmed (if you can get it)

4 small eggs

2 tbsp roughly chopped flat-leaf parsley

200g West Country Mature Cheddar, shaved with a potato peeler

juice of 1 lemon

The Dorset Charcuterie Company
www.thepork-of-interest.co.uk

Dorset Frying Chorizo
A sumptuous mix of British
Pork Shoulder, Smoked
Paprika, Garlic, Cumin,
Fennel, Coriander & Port!

Best Before Frozen

0200676 005239

Use By
01-10-2012

Batch no
£/kg   kg   £
9.99   0.526   5.25

Bere Farm, Lytchett Minster BH16 6ER

04

THE PURBECK CURE

Saucisson, prosciutto, salami, chorizo, piled into crunchy baguettes or adorning antipasti platters … however it comes, we Brits consume it with a passion. Charcuterie, the process of curing, smoking, drying and spicing meat (usually pork), is a centuries-old practice intended to preserve the spare meat from a slaughtered animal so it could be consumed later in the year.

Charcuterie is a food product that we mostly associate with the continent, but in recent years British charcuterie companies have begun to take a slice of the market. One of these is the Dorset Charcuterie Company, run by friends Lee Moreton and Ben Sugden. Lee is a third-generation butcher, who shares a passion with Ben for working with small-scale local farmers.

So, with help from the Prince's Trust, the two set up their company in 2010, taking a unit on a farm in Lytchett Minster, part of the Purbeck region in Dorset. They take great pride in creating new and exciting products that have a real connection to their region.

"Absolutely all the meat we use in our products comes from Purbeck, a unique peninsula area of Dorset. We also use other foraged products from the landscape such as samphire and wild garlic," explained Lee. The meat is always free-range, wild or from traditional breeds and bought directly from small, very local farms. "We use a fantastic breed of pig called the Mangalitsa. It's a heritage breed, originally from Hungary, that has a wonderful layer of fat and marbling throughout its meat, which is great for charcuterie. We hang, butcher, season, cure, dry, smoke and mature all our own products from start to finish, coupling age-old traditional methods with state-of-the-art modern techniques."

I have had the pleasure of using Dorset Charcuterie in some of my campsite cooking. I've used their chorizo in paella and also their black pudding in breakfast röstis, both of which are wonderful, but the one that sticks in my mind is a sensational Dorset pancetta, rolled in hay ash. You may think it sounds weird, but it tastes extraordinarily good: salty, smoky, earthy and sweet all at the same time. I can't recommend it highly enough. You can buy the charcuterie directly from Bere Farm or The Salt Pig in Wareham (see page 45).

Dorset Charcuterie

Bere Farm, Wareham Road, Lytchett Minster, Dorset BH16 6ER
01202 625688 • www.dorsetcharcuterie.co.uk

Pitch Up

Corfe Castle Camping and Caravanning Club Site

Bucknowle, Wareham, Dorset, BH20 5PQ
01929 480280 • www.campingandcaravanningclub.
co.uk

Right in the heart of Enid Blyton country, Corfe Castle Club Site is a perfect place for idyllic childhood holidays with sandcastles, picnics and lashings of ginger beer. The iconic Corfe Castle ruins that can be seen for miles around are only a 15-minute stroll from the site. The village of Corfe, with its attractive grey houses and village square, has some good pubs and a National Trust cafe.

At the foot of the Purbeck hills, the site is in a beautiful setting. You can choose between grass or hard-standing pitches, some of which are sheltered by trees. The site shop sells its own honey and has daily newspapers, although you'll probably be too busy exploring to read them. Blue Flag beaches are a short drive away in Swanage.

Burnbake Campsite

Corfe Castle, Wareham, Dorset BH20 5JH
01929 480570 • www.burnbake.com

One of my all-time favourite sites. With a myriad of delightful nooks and crannies, created by trees, hedges and streams, to camp in, it oozes a laid-back, festival atmosphere. This is where families come to play together, and children have adventures in the woods and swing on the ropes across the stream. It's wild camping with the basic comforts and a bit more besides. There's a small site shop, picnic benches to hire and the cooked breakfast hut is a good recent addition, not least because it serves a much-needed coffee after a night of wine-fuelled singing around the campfire.

South Lytchett Manor Caravan Park

Dorchester Road, Lytchett Minster, Poole, Dorset BH16 6JB • 01202 622577 • www.southlytchettmanor.
co.uk

This site has won many awards, and receives high praise from the campers that return year after year. It's a well maintained and well managed site loved by families and dog owners in particular.

In a lovely village setting, the campsite is set in 20 acres of stunning parkland 9 miles from Bournemouth and 3 miles from Poole. There's a pub/restaurant 10 minutes' walk away or you can catch the regular bus service at the park gates to get into Poole. The amenities blocks are enjoyably posh, with fresh flowers, piped music and professional hair dryers. You can choose a deluxe pitch with a picnic bench, dustbin, electric hook-up, TV connection and WiFi.

Eat Local

Wilkswood Farm

Valley Road, Swanage, Dorset BH19 3DU
01929 427970 • www.wilkswoodfarm.co.uk

It may only be open from Thursday to Saturday each week but the quality of the Purbeck-raised meats are worth the wait. Wilkswood is a National Trust farm run by tenant farmer Paul Loudoun for over 25 years. The farm encompasses over 600 acres of land devoted to conservation and environmental protection of a wide range of habitats. The quality of the fauna and flora creates great grazing conditions for the meat from the farm – which contributes to the amazing taste. There is a butchery on the farm, so you can get any cut you need. They also sell wonderful barbecue-friendly selections with several varieties of sausages, smoked and unsmoked bacon, faggots, and lamb meatballs.

The Salt Pig

6 North Street, Wareham, Dorset BH20 4AF
01929 550673

A cafe, a deli and fresh meat and fish counter in one. This is an utter gem, packed with character and fabulous food that is unpretentious and utterly delicious, from full-on roasts to quiches and salads. The Dorset Charcuterie Company has good connections with The Salt Pig and provides the deli meats, plus it runs the local meat counter here, so it's well worth a visit.

Clavell's Cafe & Pantry Room

Kimmeridge, Dorset BH20 5PE • 01929 480701
www.clavellscafe.co.uk

In truth it's much more cafe than shop but I'd recommend making the most of both sides of the business. The cafe serves meat from the farm and fish from local boats in Kimmeridge Bay in honest, hearty dishes. The family farm 2,000 acres of Purbeck and are passionate about protecting the special character of the landscape in their methods. You can buy the farm's dairy products, lamb, beef and pork when you visit the cafe.

Chococo

Commercial Road, Swanage, Dorset BH19 1DF
www.chococo.co.uk

You can't come to the Purbeck region and not visit Chococo. It's an artisan chocolate shop that hand-makes fresh chocolates. What's local about that, you ask? It's what's on the inside. The chocolate is of the highest grade, ethically sourced from Venezuela or Grenada, but the fillings are the most exciting

combinations of Dorset's products. Try chocolates filled with milk vodka, the only one of its kind in the world, made in Dorset, or Dorset Blue Vinney cheese ... it sounds weird but it's one of the best taste sensations I've had in years. There's a little cafe too, serving the most heavenly real hot chocolate you can imagine and light lunches where there's even chocolate in the salad dressing.

Farmers' Markets
Wareham Farmers' Market
Wareham Town Hall, East Street, Wareham, Dorset BH20 4NS • 2nd and 4th Thursday of the month

Wimborne Farmers' Market
Riverside Park, Station Road, Wimborne, Dorset BH21 1QU • 3rd Saturday of the month
At the monthly market in this attractive 15th-century market town you'll find stalls selling lamb, beef, pork, poultry, game, shellfish, trout, vegetables, eggs, bread, cakes and bakes.

Purbeck Food Producers' Market
Commercial Road, Swanage, Dorset BH19 1DF www.purbeckproducts.co.uk • 2nd Saturday of the month
Purbeck Food is a co-operative of local farmers, cooks and craftspeople all hailing from the unique landscape of Purbeck. Between them, the group produce high-quality, environmentally friendly and locally made products such as meat, vegetables, bread, preserves, pies and cakes. They sell at a monthly market that takes place on Commerical Road in Swanage, mostly on the 2nd Saturday of the month, but check the website first, as dates do change.

> **Absolutely all the meat we use in our products comes from Purbeck, a unique peninsula area of Dorset.**
>
> Lee Moreton, Dorset Charcuterie

Eating Out
The Tickled Pig
26 West Borough, Wimborne, Dorset BH21 1NF 01202 886778 • www.thetickledpig.co.uk
This is a very special place to eat. It's a brilliant bolthole of a place in the centre of Wimborne that takes Dorset specialities and makes them shine even brighter in imaginative meals. Every single element of the menu has been grown or reared from local Dorset suppliers. The menu is designed around the seasons and all salads, herbs and vegetables are grown in their own kitchen garden. Slow-roasted shoulder of lamb with lavender and balsamic shallots, or pork belly with quince aïoli get my vote.

The Square and Compass
Worth Matravers, Dorset BH19 3LF • 01929 439229 www.squareandcompasspub.co.uk
The stuff of pub legends. Just off the coastal path and perched on the cliff, this wonderful relic of a pub serves pints of real ale from a hatch in the wall, and massive pasties to go with them. Everyone must visit at least once in their lives.

PAELLA

I make this dish when I'm camping with friends. It looks and tastes great, and can be scaled up or down to suit your numbers. It's the kind of dish that's got something for everyone: seafood, spicy sausage, chicken, peppers and vegetables.

The important thing is to use paella rice, a short stumpy rice that absorbs lots of liquid. The idea behind a good paella is for the rice to absorb the flavours of the stock and the other ingredients. It's all about the rice!

8 boneless chicken thighs

16 large raw prawns

2 large handfuls of mussels
(enough for about 2 or 3 each)

olive oil

150g cooking chorizo, sliced

1 large onion, chopped

2 garlic cloves, crushed
and finely chopped

1 red and 1 yellow pepper,
both seeded and chopped

500g paella rice

1.8 litres chicken stock
(stock cubes are fine)

a large pinch of saffron strands,
soaked in 2 tbsp boiling water

150ml white wine
(roughly a small glass of wine)

1 small bunch of fresh
parsley, roughly chopped

2 lemons, cut into wedges

- Leave the skin on the chicken, it adds to the flavour. Take the heads and shells off the prawns, but keep the tails on. Clean and scrub the mussels, throwing away any that do not close when tapped (they could be dead).

- Heat up a good glug of olive oil in the paella pan or large frying pan. Brown the chicken pieces on both sides, about 6 minutes each side. Take the chicken out of the pan and keep somewhere warm.

- Now put the chorizo into the pan and fry it until it begins to colour and all the lovely red oil and juices come out. Remove the chorizo from the pan, and pop it on a plate.

- Add the onion to the pan, and after a couple of minutes add the garlic and pepper and gently cook until both onion and peppers have softened.

- Now add the rice and mix it all around the pan so that it gets coated in the remaining oil. Immediately add the stock, plus the saffron in its water. Put the chicken and the chorizo back in, and let the whole thing simmer gently.

- While that happens, drink some of your glass of wine, then pour the last half into your pan.

- It's important to keep an eye on the stock levels. With such a wide open pan, the stock evaporates as well as being absorbed into the rice. Keep topping it up if it seems to be reducing very quickly. Remember, though, the idea is for the rice to be cooked, but relatively dry at the end, not too wet like risotto. It will need stirring only occasionally. It should take about 20 minutes to absorb most of the liquid.

- Just before it is ready, add the prawns to the pan. If you are using mussels, now is also the time to add them. Keep the pan simmering and turn the prawns over to cook through. The prawns very kindly tell you when they are cooked by turning pink, and the mussels will open. (Discard any that remain closed.)

- Check the rice is just tender to the bite. Add the chopped parsley, and squeeze in a wedge of lemon. Mix gently. Finish by popping lemon wedges around the edge of the pan if you want to it to look fancy.

- Call the troops to serve themselves from the pan.

SUNSHINE HASH

Serves 4 very generously

I discovered the joy of the 'hash breakfast' during my student years. A small cafe around the corner from my flat served generous and restorative plates of sautéed potato and onions, topped with sausages, egg, bacon and mushrooms every Sunday morning.

It's perfect campsite food, and the great thing about 'the hash' is the limitless variations on the theme: goat's cheese and roasted tomatoes, field mushrooms and Stilton, black pudding and a bit of chilli ... You can make them your own with whatever you have left over from last night's meal, or what you can get your hands on in the site shop. It will always taste like a meal for kings, and costs very little.

- You'll need a large, deep frying pan. Over a medium heat, cook your sausages in the frying pan for about 10-12 minutes. Then remove from the pan and put to one side. Wipe the pan with a piece of kitchen roll.

- Chop the potatoes into small cubes. Put 2 tablespoons olive oil into the frying pan over a low/medium heat. Cook the potatoes for about 15-20 minutes until they have turned golden in colour.

- Add in the pieces of bacon and cook for a further 5 minutes.

- Add in the chopped tomatoes and cook until they just start to soften, but don't let them go too mushy. Stir in the chopped spring onions and garlic if using. Then add the sausages (I like to slice them thickly before adding to the pan). Season well with salt and pepper.

- Push the hash to one side of the pan and add another tablespoon of oil. Crack two eggs in the space, and fry until they are cooked to your liking.

- Divide the hash between 4 plates, and pop an egg on top of 2 of them. Return the pan to the heat and fry the remaining eggs for the last 2 plates.

- Serve with ketchup and mugs of tea.

4 sausages (take the opportunity to buy an interesting flavour from the butcher, like caramelised onion, sweet chilli or apple)

800g new potatoes, scrubbed clean

olive oil

8 rashers streaky bacon, roughly snipped or chopped

4 large ripe tomatoes, chopped, or 12 cherry tomatoes, halved

4 spring onions, chopped

1 garlic clove, finely chopped (optional)

salt and pepper

4 large free-range eggs

05 A PASSION FOR VEGETABLES

Farmer Guy Watson started his family business delivering 30 veg boxes to friends and family in 1993. His company, Riverford Organic Farms near Buckfastleigh in Devon, now delivers over 47,000 boxes per week. That's a lot of vegetables. But although this is now a slickly run large-scale business, it hasn't compromised its ethical beliefs.

I visited with a bunch of mates and our children when we were camping nearby. In between summer showers we learned that the farm grows 100 different varieties of produce, from globe artichokes to runner beans, rhubarb to kohl rabi (a turnipy thing resembling a Teletubby). We learnt about the challenges of the unpredictable Devonshire climate, meaning that a crop might be ruined or delayed by the weather but the boxes still have to be filled. The contents vary weekly according to what's ready, and customers are emailed with recipe ideas to use the up-coming ingredients.

Being organic is central to the farm's existence. They work in a way that will sustain wildlife and nurture the soil. In order to meet demand across the UK, and not over-farm the land, Riverford has joined forces with 'sister farms' in other parts of the country to supply their local areas, thus keeping down food miles where possible.

The on-site restaurant, The Field Kitchen, is a light, airy building surrounded by fields of produce. A set menu is served to the communal tables and the atmosphere is relaxed and friendly. Dishes included a delectable braised carrot and beetroot dish with orange, a spinach gratin, perfectly crispy roast potatoes with red onion, thyme and rosemary, and a delicious roast duck on kohl rabi, celery and hazelnuts. The local landscape and season on a plate – delicious.

You can enjoy a visit to Riverford on many levels: for starters the food is fantastic. A guided tour provides a fascinating education on the practicalities and politics of producing food, or if you are aged four it's a great big muddy playground complete with tractor rides. Riverford proves that vegetables are not just 'extras', they are the stars of the show. In fact, after a visit here you'll never look at a vegetable in the same way again.

Riverford Farm Shops
Yealmpton, Plymouth, Devon PL8 2LT • 01752 880925

Pitch Up

Tavistock Camping and Caravanning Club Site

Higher Longford, Moorshop, Tavistock,
Devon PL19 9LQ • 01822 618672
www.campingandcaravanningclub.co.uk

A great site for soaking up the wild beauty of
Dartmoor. Traditionally laid out, the site provides all
the comforts you need for an easy camping holiday:
there are plentiful electric hook-ups and a selection
of hard-standing pitches. For local produce there's a
country market in Tavistock every Friday and farmers'
markets twice a month (see right).

River Dart Country Park

Ashburton, Devon TQ13 7NP • 01364 652511
www.riverdart.co.uk

This site scores highly for children wanting an action-
packed, lively camping trip. There are playgrounds,
zip wires, pirate ships, rivers and streams with rope
swings and little riverside beach areas. The facilities
are great and there's an on-site cafe and restaurant and
a well-stocked campsite shop.

Five Wyches (CS)

Bovey Tracey, Devon TQ13 9LE • 01626 832310
www.campingandcaravanningclub.co.uk

Very small, secluded site on Dartmoor taking just
five vans and a few tents. This is perfect if you
like back-to-basics rustic camping. Compost loos,
campfires, utter silence and big skies. The magic of
the moor is on the doorstep, yet Bovey Tracey and its
cool outdoor pool is a few minutes' drive away, as is
Ullacombe Farm Shop (see right).

Eat Local

Riverford has three great farm shops in the area selling
organic meats, sausages and bacon, vegetables and an
exciting array of pastas, sauces, breads and cakes.
The Yealmpton Shop has a selection of fish too.
Both Yealmpton and Staverton shops have cafes.
www.riverfordfarmshop.co.uk

Lunch

* Roast duck & Confit
leg on Kohl rabi, celery &
hazlenuts

* Roast potatoes with red
onion, thyme & rosemary

* Braised carrots & beetroot

Dartmoor is home to small traditional farms and other businesses, many of which sell their goods direct to you, the customer. As you are travelling around, keep a look out for farms selling their own produce direct, or alternatively visit the Dartmoor Farmers website: www.dartmoorfarmers.co.uk

Riverford Farm Shops

Yealmpton, Plymouth, Devon PL8 2LT
01752 880925

Staverton, Totnes, Devon TQ9 6AF • 01803 762851

38 High Street, Totnes, Devon TQ9 5RY
01803 863959

Ullacombe Farm Shop

Haytor Road, Bovey Tracey, Devon TQ13 9LL
01364 661341 • www.ullacombefarm.co.uk
Just down the road from Five Wyches campsite is this fabulous shop and cafe.

Dart Farm Shopping Village

Topsham, Exeter, Devon EX3 0QH • 01392 878200
www.dartsfarm.co.uk
It started as a farm shop hut 40 years ago, and now this 'village' offers home ware, gifts and even beauty treatments. The farm shop is still at the heart though, offering food that is locally grown, reared, baked or caught. There's an on-site master butcher, fishmonger, baker, deli, cider maker and restaurant.

Farmers' Markets

Tavistock Farmers' Market

Bedford Square, Tavistock, Devon
www.tavistockfarmersmarket.com • 2nd and 4th Saturday of the month. Extra markets take place in summer so check the website
Everything you will find on sale is produced within the local area.

Bovey Tracey Farmers' Market

Union Square, Bovey Tracey, Devon
www.boveytracey.gov.uk • Every 2nd Saturday

Okehampton Farmers' Market

St James' Chapel Square, Okehampton, Devon
www.okehamptonfarmersmarket.co.uk
1st and 3rd Saturday of the month
A small market selling organic veg, free-range eggs, cakes, cheeses and local meats.

COURGETTE AND HALLOUMI KEBABS
WITH GREEN TAHINI DRESSING

The chefs at Riverford have kindly given us this recipe for *Pitch Up, Eat Local*, which pairs courgettes – a perfect camping season veg – with halloumi on the barbecue. You will need some bamboo kebab sticks.

Serves 4

2 x 150g packs of halloumi, cut into large cubes

3 large courgettes, chopped into large, bite-sized pieces

2 green chillies, deseeded and finely chopped

olive oil

For the dressing

2 tbsp light tahini (sesame paste)

2 tbsp plain yoghurt

1 garlic clove, crushed

2 tbsp olive oil

juice of 1 lemon, more to taste

a handful each of finely chopped coriander and mint leaves

salt and pepper

- Soak the skewers in a bowl of cold water for 20 minutes.

- Make the dressing: stir the tahini with the yoghurt to make a smooth paste. Whisk in the garlic, olive oil and lemon juice with a few tbsp water, just enough to get the consistency of pouring cream. Stir in the chopped herbs. Season and add more lemon juice to taste.

- Thread the halloumi and courgette pieces on to the skewers. Mix the chillies with 4 tbsp of the oil. Brush a little over the kebabs.

- Heat a griddle, non-stick frying pan or barbecue.

- Fry the kebabs, brushing with more oil and chilli and turning carefully every few minutes, until the courgettes and halloumi are golden.

- Remove from the heat and drizzle over the dressing to serve. This is good alongside lemony couscous and some griddled peppers.

06 LYME REGIS, DORSET COAST

FISH 'N' TRIPS

My early morning arrival at The Cobb harbour in Lyme Regis coincides with calm sea and sunshine. My relief at the lack of the adjective 'choppy' is immense until I catch sight of the boat I must board for my fishing trip. No trawler this – it looks more like something my son might draw at school, complete with pirate flag.

Lyme Bay is the site of numerous shipwrecks. We drop anchor over *The Heroine*, which sank in 1852 while carrying emigrants to Australia. I'm told that a wreck on the seabed acts as a meeting point for sea life, almost like a ready-made town for fish – so it's a perfect place to head to if you want to catch them.

Our skipper tells us what we might catch at this time of year: black bream, red gurnard, pollack, whiting and mackerel. He says if I catch a conger eel then he won't be able to bring it on board as the boat is too small to cope with a thrashing eel. That's comforting.

The rods are handed out. Each has a thick line, weight and what looks like tinsel attached to it. They are short, unlike beach casting rods, as we won't need to cast out far. Instead we just drop the line to the bottom and slowly reel it up so the tinsel attracts the attention of the fish. It works. Five minutes later my rod strains and winding the reel gets difficult. I try to play it cool, reeling slowly until I spot the rather large-looking catch just below the surface. Our skipper helps me haul in three mackerel on my one line. I'm chuffed to bits.

The morning continues in the most relaxing fashion. With sunshine on my face and banter on the boat, there's a decent amount of fish being landed. With each fish caught, our skipper gives suggestions on how to cook it – even the much-maligned dog fish that most fishermen don't think highly of. It has been 'rebranded' as rock salmon in certain circles to make it sound more appealing. Our skipper says it tastes similar to monkfish if cooked correctly.

Within 15 minutes of my return to shore, I've fired up my little barbecue and my mackerel fillets are sizzling away. Taking the skipper's advice I wrap the filleted dog fish in foil, pour on a glug of wine, add fresh herbs and cook until the flesh turns white. I serve it as 'rock salmon' to my unsuspecting (and very impressed) friends.

Harry May's Sunbeam boat

www.mackerelfishinglymeregis.com or call 07974 753287

Pitch Up

Charmouth Camping and Caravanning Club Site

Monkton Wyld Farm, Scotts Lane, near Charmouth, Dorset DT6 6DB • 01297 32965
www.campingandcaravanningclub.co.uk
A truly great site spread across a few fields surrounded by established hedges and trees. There's a big shop and a playground for the children, but the best entertainment is a few miles away at the stunning Jurassic Coast. You are close to the market town of Axminster too, with the fabulous **River Cottage Canteen** and **Millers Farm Shop**.

Crabbs Bluntshay Farm (CS)

Whitchurch Canonicorum, Bridport, Dorset DT6 6RN • 01297 489064 • www.crabbsbluntshayfarm.co.uk
A superb site in the heart of the attractive Marshwood Vale valley. Sheltered by hedges, this 2.25-acre flat field is suitable for all kinds of camping. There is a facilities cabin with showers, toilets and a kitchen area, as well as eight electrical hook-ups. Crabbs Bluntshay is a small working farm, active in conservation schemes and farmed by the same family for nearly 100 years. Campers can buy home-made cider at the farm gate, along with chutneys, fruit, vegetables and honey.

Freshwater Beach Holiday Park

Burton Bradstock, near Bridport, Dorset DT6 4PT
01308 897317 • www.freshwaterbeach.co.uk
Along the lines of a traditional summer holiday camp with indoor and outdoor pools, a clubhouse, on-site restaurant and static caravans. The touring pitches are spread over the 13-acre site and offer hard standing, electric hook-ups or just a grassy field if you prefer. With its own private (pebbly) beach on this glorious heritage coastline, family fun is pretty much guaranteed.

Eat Local

The Wetfish Shop

The Old Watch House, Cobb Square, Lyme Regis, Dorset DT7 3JT • 01297 444205
www.wetfishshop.com
The owners are passionate about supporting local fishermen who fish sustainably, and have an exciting selection of seafood. They run brilliant short courses (1-2 hours) on how to gut a fish, fillet a mackerel or dress a crab.

Millers Farm Shop

Gammons Hill, Axminster, Devon EX13 7RA
01297 35290 • www.millersfarmshop.com
Adored by the locals, this is a fine example of how a good farm shop can replace the need for supermarkets. It stocks everything you'll need for your weekly camping food shop – all from local fields and waters. You can buy Lyme Bay fresh fish, beef, pork, lamb and local dairy and bread here, too.

Washingpool Farm Shop

North Allington, Bridport, Dorset DT6 5HP
01308 459549 • www.washingpool.co.uk
As well as Washingpool's own sausages and vegetables, you can try some of the more interesting local produce here too; the infamous Dorset Naga chilli (until recently the hottest in the world) and Black Cow vodka, the world's first pure milk vodka made entirely from the milk of Dorset cows. It also has an on-site cafe.

Town Mill Bakery

Unit 2, Coombe Street, Lyme Regis, Dorset DT7 3PY
01297 444754

Take away the wonderful breads and pastries or sit down at the communal table for cool soup-kitchen style lunches. Choose your bread – it doubles as your bowl – then add your filling of soup or curry. Great tasting, great value food.

Farmers' Market

Bridport Farmers' Market

Bridport Arts Centre, 9 South Street, Bridport, Dorset DT6 3NR • 2nd Saturday of the month

Eating Out

Hive Beach Café

Beach Road, Burton Bradstock, Dorset DT6 4RF
01308 897070 • www.hivebeachcafe.co.uk

A legend among locals, this beachside cafe serves some of the best seafood dishes in the area.

River Cottage Canteen and Deli

Trinity Square, Axminster, Devon EX13 5AN
01297 631715 • www.rivercottage.net

Well made, imaginative food, embracing the best ingredients in the area. Great atmosphere, location and prices, too.

SMOKED MACKEREL

WITH HORSERADISH POTATOES

Serves 2

A smoked mackerel lunch is really easy, tasty and suitably impressive-looking to the neighbours on the next pitch.

Obviously you can smoke meats or even halloumi cheese if you want, but fish is quick and simple to do.

I place a small triangular smoke box (www.gardengiftshop.co.uk) between the heating elements on my barbecue. Or, it can sit in the glowing coals. Alternatively you can use a very large old saucepan with a lid, put wood dust or chips in the bottom, put in a makeshift grill (use one from a disposable barbecue) then place over a gas hob flame to heat up and start smoking.

Choose your wood chips carefully. I like beech or apple wood, but there are many different types that give subtly different flavours to the food. Just don't use treated wood that might have chemicals on it.

- Soak your wood chips in water for about half an hour before you use them. This gives a longer burning time.

- When that's done, put your wood chips in the smoke box, and place it next to the gas burners on your barbecue, under the cooking grid. Do this before turning your barbecue on!

- If you are using coals, place the smoke box in among the coals when they are glowing hot.

- Now put the lid on your barbecue to allow the smoke to build up from the burning wood chips.

- Make sure all of the bones are out of your mackerel fillets — if you ask nicely, the fishmonger will do this for you.

- Put your new potatoes on to boil with a little salt in the water.

- Cover the bottom of a non-metallic bowl with salt. Lie the fillets skin down on this, then cover them with more salt. This is to draw the excess moisture out, to enable the flesh to take up the smoky flavour. Leave for about 10 minutes then rinse the salt off and pat the fillets dry with kitchen paper.

- Lightly oil a piece of foil, place the fillets on this, then put on to the grid of the barbecue. Close the lid quickly to avoid all the lovely flavoured smoke escaping.

- Mix the crème fraîche with the horseradish and lemon juice and some black pepper.

- When cooked drain the potatoes well, and mix with the horseradish dressing.

- Check your fish. It is cooked when the flesh is opaque and flakes when pressed with a knife. Average-sized mackerel fillets should take no longer than 5-8 minutes to cook.

- Serve the mackerel and potato salad with a green salad - watercress is lovely. Flake the fish to incorporate it into the green salad.

4 fresh mackerel fillets

300g new potatoes

salt (lots of it) and black pepper

vegetable oil

3 tbsp full-fat crème fraîche

1 tsp horseradish sauce or cream

juice of ½ lemon

watercress or salad leaves

FISH TACOS WITH A SUNNY SALSA

This recipe turns a simple fillet of white fish into an exciting mouth-tingling, eat-with-your-hands supper.

Serves 4

- Place the fish on a plate. Finely grate the zest from half of the lime, and put this aside. Cut the lime in half and squeeze the zested half over the fish. Cut the remaining half lime into wedges for serving.

- Mix the paprika, cumin and oregano together in a small bowl, along with the cayenne pepper (if using). Mix in the garlic.

- Sprinkle this spice mixture over the fish fillet, then season well with salt and pepper. Turn the fish in the marinade to coat it evenly. Put it in the fridge for about 10 minutes.

- In a separate bowl, combine the salsa ingredients, but use only half of the coriander. Mix and put to one side.

- Brush a grill pan, or barbecue grid, with some oil and get it medium hot. Place the marinated fish on the grill. Let it cook without moving it for about 3 minutes. Carefully flip it and cook the other side for the same amount of time.

- While you are doing this, place the tortillas on the grid very briefly to warm through.

- Transfer the cooked fish to a plate and gently break it up into bite-sized pieces. Layer some fish pieces and some salsa on the open tortilla. Sprinkle with the remaining coriander, give it a squeeze of lime, and wrap it up to eat.

350g skinless fillet of white fish, like sustainably sourced cod, haddock or pollack

1 lime

½ tsp each of paprika, ground cumin and dried oregano

½ tsp cayenne pepper (optional)

1 small garlic clove, finely chopped

salt and pepper

olive oil

4 flour tortillas, to serve

For the salsa

1 red pepper, seeded and finely diced

4 spring onions, finely sliced

8 cherry tomatoes, quartered

1 tbsp white wine vinegar

1 tsp caster sugar

2 tsp olive oil

½ fresh red chilli, deseeded and finely chopped

THE BISON OF BUSH FARM

A gradual shift in attitudes towards favouring naturally reared food and farming has meant that rare and unusual varieties of cows, pigs and sheep are becoming a more common sight on our rural landscapes. But nestled in a Wiltshire valley, about 25 minutes west of Stonehenge, you'll find a field of livestock that I'll guarantee really does take you by surprise.

In a scene more likely to be found in the Great American Plains than the English countryside, large herds of bison can be found roaming the pastures. In a neighbouring field you'll find elk clashing their antlers, and if you stroll on through the farmyard of Bush Farm you'll come across pens of chipmunks, prairie dogs, racoons and skunk alongside the chickens and ducks. This is the wonderful world that Colin and Pepe Seaford have created at their farm and campsite in the pretty village of West Knoyle.

After turning 40, Colin's midlife crisis took him on a bison fact-finding mission to America that resulted in him buying his own herd. Now Bush Farm has become a focus for British-based Native American Culture enthusiasts, with an annual Pow Wow here each July, when nearly 2,000 people come to dress in Native American garb, sleep in tipis and dance to drum beats amid fields of bison. There is a permanent exhibition space on the farm with pictures, artefacts and information on Native American Culture and the history of bison.

Bison were hunted to near extinction by the first white settlers in America. But, through the efforts of early 20th-century conservationists and ranchers, numbers of wild herds have increased to the point that they are no longer an endangered species. However, work continues to ensure their geographical spread across the Plains once again. Bison meat has increased in popularity in America, so there are also many commercial herds being bred as an alternative to beef. Here in Britain, bison tend to be kept more by enthusiasts, supplying meat in small quantities via farm sales.

Colin and Pepe sell frozen bison and elk meat from their small on-site shop. Perfect for campers are the home-made bison burgers that have won a gold medal in the Guild of Fine Food awards. It is easy to eat local here,

as all the food sold in the shop comes from the farm or from very local producers. It was certainly a shop stocked like no other I had been in; elk in juniper and red wine pie, smoked elk, elk mince, bison burgers, bison sausages, quails' eggs and home-made elderflower cordial – a product of the hedgerows around the farm. And if you don't want to cook, Pepe serves delicious bison chilli and rice or bison burgers from the cafe.

Bison meat is low in fat, high in protein and rich in flavour. At Bush Farm they are raised as naturally as possible and grazed on grass. No growth hormones, steroids or drug residues are used on the stock.

Campers can explore Bush Farm and its menagerie via a wonderful mile-long walking trail that takes visitors past lakes, fields of bison and meadows of elk and on through wooded glens, with oak tree swings along the way. You can get up close to the bison – gigantic beasts with enormous shaggy shoulders and heads and relatively small back legs. Some reach over 6ft in height and can weigh up to 750 pounds, yet despite this they can still reach speeds of 37mph.

As a campsite alone Bush Farm is a wonderful location. Some pitches, perfect for caravans and motorhomes, back on to a wooded area with views across fields. Tent- or tipi-owners can seek out a woodland pitch within the 30 acres of mature oaks. It is a truly enchanting space to explore, full of sudden shafts of sunlight, dream catchers hanging in the trees and 'fairy' toadstools in grassy clearings.

Bush Farm (CS)

West Knoyle, Wiltshire BA12 6AE • 01747 830263 • www.bisonfarm.co.uk

TREE GARDEN

STREAM GARDEN

FARMYARD

BIRCH GROVE

XING

GRILLED BISON STEAK

WITH GREMOLATA AND GRIDDLED POTATOES

I cooked my bison steaks simply on the iron griddle with an accompaniment of griddled sliced potatoes and gremolata, a parsley, lemon and garlic sauce. The texture of the steak is velvety and luscious with a richness of flavour that isn't overpowering. It's unlikely that bison will become a common feature on our farmland, but once you taste the meat from Bush Farm, you might wish the opposite were true.

Serves 2

2 bison steaks of your choice

4 white potatoes, scrubbed and sliced 5mm thick

olive oil

For the gremolata

1 large bunch of flat-leaf parsley, chopped

grated zest of 1 lemon, juice of ½

1 tsp coarsely ground salt

2 garlic cloves, finely chopped

4 tbsp good-quality olive oil

- For the gremolata, grind the parsley, lemon zest, salt and garlic in a pestle and mortar (or weighty bowl). Add the lemon juice and olive oil, and stir well.

- Rub the potatoes with olive oil, and put on the hot griddle. They will need about 4 minutes each side.

- Use the same timings as you would for a beef steak when grilling your bison steak. (I used 2 minutes on each side of a hot grill for medium rare.) Times obviously vary according to personal taste. Keep checking during cooking so as not to over-cook it and let it rest for at least 5 minutes once you have taken it off the grill — it will taste juicier this way.

- Spoon generous helpings of the gremolata over the steak and serve with the potatoes and a salad. Simple and delicious.

SOUTH & SOUTH EAST ENGLAND

Vibrant towns teem with exciting eating places and street food, while the tranquil chalky Downs make the perfect environment for growing vines and hops. So, if you like to sample a local tipple, this is where to come. Kent is one big fertile allotment of fruit and vegetables, so look out for farm shops and gastropubs nestled in picturesque flint and stone villages or with Channel views along the coastline.

08

A PINT AMONG PIGS

When her village inn, The Royal Oak, was threatened with closure a few years ago, farmer Helen Browning and her partner Tim Finney decided to take it over. They saw it as the perfect opportunity to develop a local food community by only serving produce from their farm or grown by local people. So now, villagers bring their home-grown tomatoes, salad leaves and berries to the pub in return for dinner and a pint of ale, and the result is a truly great pub, serving excellent organic food.

Engaging people with food, through the pub or the farm, is important to Helen and Tim. As passionate proponents of organic farming, their friendly approach is a great way of getting people to think about how their food is produced.

The farm on the North Wessex Downs is a combination of dairy, beef, lamb, arable and pigs – which make up the main part of the business. Helen Browning's renowned sausages and bacon are sold by Waitrose and Sainsbury's as well as locally, and it's obvious how happy the pigs are as I watch them rooting around in the large open spaces in a beautiful setting on the Wiltshire/Oxfordshire border.

Tim explains how organic farming benefits every aspect of the land. The only fertilisers used are the ones produced daily by the cows, pigs and sheep. When they've put their natural nitrates and phosphates in the ground the animals are moved on to let wheat, beans and oats grow. No sprays are used, it's all left to the bees and birds that are attracted in the first place by the variety of wild flowers and grasses on offer.

The Royal Oak is the perfect showcase for what Helen and Tim stand for. If you like food, walking, stunning vistas, peace and quiet and the chance to take some exceptionally good sausages back to your campsite, I recommend a visit.

The Royal Oak

Cues Lane, Bishopstone, Swindon SN6 8PP • 01793 790481
www.helenbrowningsorganic.co.uk

Pitch Up

Postern Hill Camping in the Forest Site

Postern Hill, Marlborough, Wiltshire SN8 4ND
01672 515195 • www.campingintheforest.co.uk
I find this site quite magical. The trees around you have witnessed centuries of folk passing beneath their boughs, from royal hunting parties to trysting couples. Along with rare chalk streams and tranquil open downland, this ancient forest forms the unique landscape of the North Wessex Downs.

Don't come here if you want mod cons such as showers and hard standings. Do come here if you want to pitch where you fancy, watch some of the 11 species of bats welcome nightfall, live among rabbits and have direct access to a maze of wonderful walking paths through Savernake Forest, where a number of picnic spots are perfect for a barbecue supper at the end of the day. Marlborough's weekly community market is well worth a visit to get your supplies.

Helen Browning's farm is on the North Wiltshire/Oxfordshire border. The famous chalk Ridgeway, a Stone Age road, runs through the farm – it is described as Britain's oldest road. It extends from Overton Hill in Wiltshire's North Wessex Downs across the Berkshire Downs to the River Thames at the Goring Gap. This part of the Ridgeway National Trail will take you past Bronze Age barrows, Sarsen stones and stone circles. A dry Ice Age valley also sweeps from the Ridgeway down to the village of Bishopstone. The effect is of vast, timeless landscapes.

Farncombe Farm (CS)

Lambourn, Berkshire RG17 7BN • 01488 71833
www.farncombefarm.co.uk
This quiet and low-key campsite is nestled in the Valley of the Racehorse, so named for its 50 raceyards and stables. Farncombe Farm specialises in cows, not horses, and while you camp you can watch the gentle giants that are the Hereford beef cattle grazing in the surrounding fields. The beef is for sale from the farmhouse, so your steak supper will have the lowest food miles possible.

Rough Grounds Farm Campsite (CS)

Lechlade, Gloucestershire GL7 3EU • 01367 253261
www.roughgroundsfarm.co.uk
Situated in the Cotswold Water Park, this secluded Certificated Site has only basic facilities and electric hook-ups so it's great for caravans and motorhomes with their own facilities. It's a big flat field with loads of space for playing and it's walkable to the lovely riverside village of Lechlade.

Devizes Camping and Caravanning Club Site

Spout Lane, near Seend, Melksham, Wiltshire SN12 6RN • 01380 828839
www.campingandcaravanningclub.co.uk
A great club site, with plenty of hard standings, super-friendly managers and all the spotless facilities you'd expect. Yes, it is 50 minutes away from Bishopstone but it's a very comfortable base for exploring the North Wessex Downs.

Eat Local

> **Villagers** bring their home-grown tomatoes, salad leaves and berries to the pub in return for dinner and a pint of ale.

Three Trees Farm

The Ridgeway, Chiseldon, Swindon, Wiltshire SN4 0HT • 01793 741436 • www.threetreesfarm.co.uk
Fifteen minutes north of Postern Hill site is Three Trees Farm, just outside the village of Chiseldon. It's a mixed arable and livestock farm that also runs a one-stop shop for people to buy all the meat they produce: Simmental grass-fed beef, Gloucester Old Spot pork from free-range pigs who've foraged in the woods and lambs who've grazed the fields. Head to the newly built cafe to sample the food. There's a play area outside and a few animals to entertain the children.

Aldbourne Post Office

13 The Square, Aldbourne, Wiltshire SN8 2DU
01672 540255
Buy a stamp, pick up some local deli meats or a tasty pie for your picnic and stop for a piece of cake and a coffee in the cafe while you are at it. They will also make up a veg box for you, and tell you all the local gossip while you're there.

Bloomfields Fine Foods

8 High Street, Highworth, Wiltshire SN6 7AG and 52a High Street, Shrivenham, Oxfordshire SN6 8AA
www.bloomfieldsfinefood.co.uk
This award-winning deli is worth going out of your way for. Big on local produce and great for fresh sandwiches made with the best of the deli counter cheeses, chutneys and charcuterie.

Marlborough Market

High Street, Marlborough, Wiltshire
www.marlboroughmarket.org.uk
Every Wednesday and Saturday, Marlborough's high street bustles with market stalls. On the first Sunday of every month there is the wonderful Marlborough Community Market with plentiful wholesome home-made produce.

SUPER SAUSAGE PASTA SUPPER

This is a 'super' supper because it is so easy to make in relation to its great taste. Can be made on a gas stove or over a campfire.

Serves 4-6

500g fusilli pasta (or whatever shape you prefer)

salt and pepper

For the sauce

6 large pork sausages

1 tbsp olive oil

1 large red onion, finely chopped

1 small red chilli, deseeded and very finely chopped (optional)

2 small garlic cloves, finely chopped

1 tbsp fennel seeds, crushed with a rolling pin or pestle and mortar

2 x 400g tins chopped tomatoes

1 large glass (about 175ml) of red wine

1 tsp dried mixed herbs

salt and pepper

3 tbsp crème fraîche

To serve

grated cheese (why not hunt out a British-made hard cheese?)

fresh salad leaves (optional)

- Carefully cut the skin along the length of each sausage. Remove the sausage meat from the skin, and form it into small balls about the size of a walnut.

- Heat the olive oil in a large frying pan then add the onion and fry gently for 5 minutes.

- Add in the chilli (if using), garlic, crushed fennel seeds and sausage balls and cook for around 8 minutes until the balls start to brown.

- Add the tinned tomatoes, the wine and mixed herbs, season with salt and pepper and simmer gently for about 30 minutes. Keep an eye on the sauce though, as with a large open frying pan it is easy to let the liquid reduce too quickly — add a little water and turn the heat down if it is getting too thick.

- While this is happening, cook the pasta according to the instructions in a large pan of salted, boiling water. Once cooked, drain the pasta and return to the pan.

- In the frying pan check the sausage pieces are cooked and the sauce is well seasoned. Turn the heat off.

- Stir the crème fraîche through the sauce then add the sauce to the pasta. Mix well.

- Serve with cheese sprinkled over the top and a side of fresh salad leaves.

SPICY STUFFED PEPPERS

Serves 4

You can easily adapt this into a vegetarian meal by replacing the sausages with 4 slices of halloumi, cubed, or 2 large chopped portobello mushrooms. If using halloumi, I'd suggest putting it in a glass of very hot water for 5 minutes before using, just to soften it a little.

You'll need a gas or charcoal barbecue with a lid, or a campfire.

- Take a lid off the stem end of the peppers and scrape out the seeds. Parboil the peppers in a saucepan of boiling water for 5 minutes. Remove and leave to cool.
- Heat a splash of oil in a saucepan, and add the rice. Stir it around to coat the grains for about a minute.
- Add in the vegetable stock, and cook the rice. Everyone cooks rice differently. I bring mine to the boil, turn the heat right down, pop on the lid tightly and heat gently for 25 minutes. Take off the heat and leave for another 5 minutes then fork through to fluff it up.
- Meanwhile, in a frying pan, heat a tbsp oil and cook the sausage meat, breaking it up with a wooden spoon as you do. (If using halloumi or mushrooms, cook these in the pan now.) Add in the chopped garlic, paprika and chopped chilli. Cook over a medium heat until the sausage meat is cooked, about 5 minutes.
- Mix the contents of the frying pan in with the cooked rice. Add the spring onions and Tabasco (according to taste), and season with salt and pepper. Stir well.
- Stuff the cooled peppers with this rice mixture. Put the pepper lids back on and then lie each pepper on a large double sheet of foil and wrap it up completely, folding the edges tightly.
- Place the peppers on the barbecue grill or griddle over a low heat, or in the embers of your campfire. If using a barbecue, put the lid down and cook for about 30 minutes until the skin of the pepper is beginning to char. If cooking on the campfire, nestle the packages close to the glowing embers and continue to turn so the peppers cook evenly.
- I find it's easiest to put the foil parcels on everyone's plate and let them unwrap their dinner. The peppers are perfect eaten on their own, or with salad leaves.

4 red peppers

olive oil

200g long-grain or basmati rice

350ml hot vegetable stock (a cube is fine)

2 large good-quality sausages, skins slit and meat taken out

1 garlic clove, chopped

1 tsp smoked paprika

1 small fresh red chilli, very finely chopped

4 spring onions, sliced

½ tsp Tabasco sauce (or 1 tsp sweet chilli sauce for a 'cooler' taste)

salt and pepper

09 NOT JUST A BIT ON THE SIDE

For many of us, watercress is just the green bit on the side of the plate in a posh pub. But as one of the first 'superfoods' it is thought to have all kinds of magical, life-enhancing properties, including curing baldness, inciting wit and enhancing sexual performance. Historians tell how the benefits of watercress have been revered by the great and good from Roman emperors to Napoleon.

Gram for gram, watercress contains more vitamin C than oranges, more calcium than milk, more iron than spinach and more folate than bananas. And where does it get these super powers? Water. Pure, clean, spring water – the kind you'd find in chalk streams. There are only around 200 chalk streams in the world and the UK is home to 85 per cent of them, mostly in the south of England.

The pretty little villages on Salisbury Plain literally sprang up around the springs. One of these is Broad Chalke, 10 miles west of Salisbury, where in 1880, when watercress was in its heyday, Keith Hitchings' great great grandfather set up his watercress farm. Back then, Victorian street sellers sold bunches to passers-by, who ate it like fast food on the go.

For many south of England watercress growers, the arrival of the railway transformed their fortunes. Now it could be picked in the afternoon, taken by horse and cart to the station, then up the Hampshire line to be sold at Covent Garden in the early hours of the morning. The railway line became known as the Watercress Line, inspiring many people to set up watercress beds in the area. Watercress remained popular during the World Wars but Beeching's closure of branch railways in the 1960s and the craving for fancy imported produce led to the watercress industry wilting.

Keith Hitchings' family business stood the distance, and is now enjoying a renaissance. He says, "We still grow it in the same way as my great great grandfather did – harnessing water from the spring deep underground, channelling it through the shallow gravel watercress beds and then letting it flow back into the river."

Chalke Valley Watercress

Slate House, The Marsh, Salisbury, Wiltshire SP5 5HJ • 01722 780142
www.chalkevalleywatercress.co.uk

Pitch Up

Salisbury Camping and Caravanning Club Site

Hudson's Field, Castle Road, Salisbury, Wiltshire SP1 3SA • 01722 320713
www.campingandcaravanningclub.co.uk
This site gets a thumbs-up for easy access to the wonderful city of Salisbury along a traffic-free riverside route to the centre. The two open camping fields are overlooked by Old Sarum castle, a mighty Iron Age hill fort that you can walk to from your pitch.

Summerlands Caravan Park

College Farm, Rockbourne Road, Coombe Bissett, Salisbury, Wiltshire SP5 4LP • 01722 718259
www.summerlandscaravanpark.co.uk
Large pitches with pretty views over the adjacent farmland. It's mainly an open field, but tents can be pitched in the shelter of trees. It's peaceful and secluded, but close enough to all the local highlights of Salisbury, Stonehenge and Old Sarum.

Riverside Lakes (CS)

Slough Lane, Horton, near Verwood, Dorset BH21 7JL
01202 821212 • www.riversidelakes.co.uk
An eco-lover's delight, this site has a series of separate camping areas according to your camping mood – you can choose to be on a little island in the middle of a lake, in the woods or among the long grasses in a field. Enjoy the communal fire pits, swim and fish in the lakes and leave the stress of the modern world behind. Five pitches for caravans, the rest is for tents.

Verwood Camping and Caravanning Club Site

Sutton Hill, Woodlands, Wimborne, Dorset BH21 8NQ • 01202 822763
www.campingandcaravanningclub.co.uk
This large Club site is in a great location on the edge of the New Forest, and near the pretty little village of Cranborne, where watercress grows in the streams that run through the middle. It's a fantastic site that is well run and has all the amenities you need for a comfortable and easy camping trip.

Eat Local

Chalke Valley Stores

URC Chapel, High Road, Broad Chalke, Wiltshire
SP5 5EH • www.chalkevalleystores.co.uk
A fabulous community-run shop in village chapel.
The focus is set firmly on local and homemade
produce. You can buy local smoked trout here to go
with your watercress.

Coombe Bissett Village Stores

Homington Road, Coombe Bissett, Wiltshire SP5 4LR
01722 718852 • www.coombebissettstores.co.uk
A good old-fashioned traditional village shop. You can
get watercress and smoked trout for your recipe here
(see page 87), draught cider or just a cup of tea, get
your shoes mended, clothes cleaned, a fishing licence
and a stamp ... you get the picture.

Ansty PYO and Farm Shop

Ansty, near Salisbury, Wiltshire SP3 5PX • 01747
829072 • www.anstypyo.co.uk
With a fully stocked farm shop and tearooms, this
PYO has a long season of strawberries, redcurrants,
loganberries, blackcurrants and raspberries right up
until October.

Britford Farm Shop

Bridge Farm, Britford, Salisbury, Wiltshire SP5 4DY
01722 413400 • www.britfordfarmshop.co.uk
This farm shop's owner Robert Lewis' speciality is
high-class cakes, ice-creams, sorbets and chocolates.
The cafe menu is all about indulgence.

Futurefarms Shop

Martin, Fordingbridge, Hampshire SP6 3LD
07005 805519 • Monday to Friday 9-11am and 5-6pm
Saturdays 9:30am-12:30pm
The village of Martin set up an experiment in 2003
to see if they could come together as a community
to grow and produce all the food they needed. Their
initiative – Futurefarms – is still thriving.

Cranborne Stores

1 The Square, Cranborne, Wimborne, Dorset
BH21 5PR • 01725 517210
Excellent local stores selling fresh breads and an array
of the best local foods including smoked trout, meats
and seasonal veg.

Farmers' Markets
Wiltshire Farmers' Market

Poultry Cross, Salisbury, Wiltshire • 07541 762497
www.wiltshirefarmersmarkets.co.uk • Every
Wednesday (call to confirm market is running)
There's also a Farmers' and Artisan Market here on
the 1st Sunday of the month, with over 50 stalls of
artisan breads, local meats, smoked goods, street food
and music.

The Charter Market

Market Place, Salisbury, Wiltshire • Tuesday
and Saturday
The Charter Market has been running since 1227. It
has some local food stalls as well as clothes, gifts, etc.

Wimborne Farmers' Market

The Square, Wimborne, Dorset • 3rd Saturday of
the month

Blandford Farmers' Market

Market Place, Blandford, Dorset • 2nd Friday of
the month

Verwood Farmers' Market

Ferret Green, Verwood, Dorset • 4th Saturday of
the month

SMOKED TROUT, AND APPLE SALAD
WATERCRESS

Serves 4

The hot peppery tang of the watercress, the delicate smokiness of the trout and the crisp sharp bite of the apple combine to make a simple salad that is exploding with flavour. Trout thrive in the chalky streams and rivers of the area, making it a perfect and natural match with the watercress. There are two trout farms close to the campsites.

You can add extra vegetables to this salad according to what you can lay your hands on. Quartered beetroot and thinly sliced fennel would be fantastic additions, or even just grated carrot. You can leave the potatoes out if you fancy a lighter meal.

- Put the watercress and potatoes in a shallow serving dish. Scatter over the spring onions and apple sticks (and beetroot or fennel if you are using them).
- Flake the trout into large pieces over the top.
- Put the yoghurt and horseradish in a bowl, and add the lemon juice. Mix well.
- Drizzle the dressing over the salad and toss very gently. Divide between 4 plates and enjoy.

300g hot-smoked trout fillets, skinless

1 large bunch of watercress, long stalks removed

12 small new potatoes, cooked, cooled and halved

4 spring onions, sliced

1 crisp apple, cored, quartered and cut into thick matchsticks

2 tbsp plain yoghurt

1 tsp horseradish sauce

juice of ½ lemon

10 HOPPY DAYS

A non-scientific survey conducted in my local beer garden revealed that the wine drinkers were able to name a considerable amount of grape varieties. The beer drinkers couldn't name a single variety of hop. A little strange perhaps, considering we produce far more beer than wine in this country.

It was the Romans who introduced hops to us. They ate them rather than brewed them though. Cooked a little like asparagus, young hop shoots were considered a luxury. But only when Flemish settlers showed us you could make alcohol with them in the 1500s did we Brits really begin to take notice. The Flemish had discovered that hops could both flavour and preserve the beer. We soon got a taste for it and became dedicated hop growers. By the 1870s over 75,000 acres of Kent was devoted to hop growing. Proof enough, if it were needed, that we like our beer.

Kent is the perfect location for hops, with its mild climate and well-drained fertile soil. And, at the height of the Victorian hop industry, it was near enough to London to ensure a plentiful supply of labourers at harvest time. Hoards of hop pickers relocated from the city every September. For many families, this was their 'holiday', a chance to leave the city smog for the fresh air and fields of Kent. It was hard work and poorly paid, but the countryside, camaraderie and atmosphere made it worth it. Families met year after year, creating lasting friendships. The arrival of the hop-picking machines in the 1930s brought this exciting seasonal exodus to an end. And while the inevitable decline of hop growing has been compounded by foreign imports and changing tastes, Kent remains a hub for beer-making in Britain.

Evidence of the county's connection to hops and brewing can still be seen across the landscape. Those ubiquitous oasthouses with their white cowl tops remain worthy of a pointed finger as we drive past. Built in the 19th century to make quick work of drying the hops, most are now converted into luxurious homes. The crops themselves are distinctive. Fields of 16ft-high hop poles, cat-cradled with wires, support the climbing plants and can still be spotted in parts of the county.

Shepherd Neame in Faversham is the oldest brewery in the country, founded in the 17th century, and in continuous production ever since. Shepherd Neame only uses Kentish hops, with barley from Kent or East

Anglia. They grow their own yeast and the water they use comes from a nearby well of chalk-filtered water. It would be tough to find a more local brew than this one.

There are many other small, artisan brewers based in Kent. Recent years have seen a resurgence of interest in British brewed ales, so it's worth seeking them out while you are here. I've noted a few in the Eat Local listings, alongside some totally unique drinking holes in which to sample them.

Shepherd Neame Visitor Centre

11 Court Street, Faversham, Kent ME13 7AX • www.shepherdneame.co.uk

Pitch Up

Santon Farm Cottages (CS)

Lower Santon Lane, Preston, Canterbury,
Kent CT3 1JF • 01227 721495
www.campingandcaravanningclub.co.uk
Camp among the apples, pears and plums in this
orchard campsite and take your shower in the old
barn. It's rustic all the way at Santon Farm, but all the
better for it. The pitches are huge, made more private
by the shelter of fruit trees, and the owners are very
friendly. This is a little piece of rural paradise shared
with just a handful of other campers, the birds and
rabbits. The local butcher and village shop are great
and there are some fine pubs within walking distance.

Canterbury Camping and Caravanning Club Site

Bekesbourne Lane, Canterbury, Kent CT3 4AB
01227 463216 • www.campingandcaravanningclub.
co.uk
Just a couple of miles south of Canterbury, this
Camping and Caravanning Club site offers a mix of
grass and hardstanding pitches with electric hook-ups
and sparkling clean amenities. There is also a small
play area for the children. It's in a great location for
city, coast or countryside so is the perfect base for
exploring the best bits of Kent – including the food.
The Goods Shed (see page 92), a food hall of dreams,
is only a 10-minute drive.

The Plough Inn (CS)

Stalisfield, Faversham, Kent ME13 0HY
01795 890256 • www.theploughinnstalisfield.co.uk
A pitch and a pint anyone? This campsite is in a pub
garden. Even better, it is in a great pub's garden. The
food is outstanding and the beer is proudly local. The
four traditional hand-pumps feature an ever-changing
selection of Kent ales. The campsite is basic. The only
facilities are the pub's toilets – available during pub
opening hours, so you'll need your own loo.

Eat Local

Gibsons Farm Shop

Crockshard Lane, Wingham, Kent CT3 1NY
01227 720262 • www.gibsonsfarmshop.com
Gibsons Farm Shop is a family-run business. Their
fabulous store is the culmination of the whole family's
love of farming life, the countryside and their belief
in the importance of the rural economy. This shop is
a platform for their farm produce and the talents of
producers around them. You can stock up on plenty of
camp-friendly food here such as barbecue meat packs
and fantastic sausages – try the ever-popular Old
English variety. The farm is self-sufficient – all of the
livestock is fed on home-produced feed so you can be
guaranteed you are buying the purest, highest quality
meats. The modern cafe serves English breakfasts
every day, cream teas for summer days and filling
roasts in the autumn.

Perry Court Farm

Canterbury Road, Bilting, Ashford, Kent TN25 4ES
01233 812302 • www.perrycourtfarm.co.uk
This shop has been running for over 50 years and has
slowly expanded from a small fruit stall to the food
hall it is today. It's worth going just for the astounding
displays of fruit and vegetables in the summer months
and the free tasting of the home-grown fruit, including
their apple juice and 'apple crisps'. An exciting cheese
room stocks over 100 English cheeses including a
selection from Kent, there is freshly baked bread every
morning, and if you're still not convinced there are
beautiful walks, farm animals to see and a tea room
with healthy home-made refreshments.

Twenty different varieties of hops (the female flowers or 'seed cone' of the hop plant) are grown in Britain, each one of them giving a distinct flavour and aroma to the beer.

The Barn Shop

Canterbury Road, Challock, Kent TN25 4BJ
01233 740237 • www.thebarnshopchallock.co.uk
The Barn Shop is an independent store in the heart of Challock village that prides itself on sourcing its food from local farms and producers. During harvest time, the vegetables are on the shelves within a couple of hours of being picked. You can get a great selection of local beers here, too.

Pluckley Farm Shop

Weeks, Smarden Road, Pluckley, Ashford, Kent TN27 0RF • 01233 840400 • www.pluckleyfarmshop.co.uk
Making the most of fruits and vegetables from the fertile fields and laden orchards of the 'Garden of England', Pluckley Farm Shop also has fresh baked bread every day, local dairy and meat, home-made pies, cakes, cheeses and deli goods as well as beers from Kent.

The Goods Shed

Station Road West, Canterbury, Kent CT2 8AN
01227 459153 • www.thegoodsshed.co.uk
I challenge anyone not to be bowled over by The Goods Shed in Canterbury. It's a converted railway shed that has a six-day-a-week farmers' market selling fresh bread, meats, vegetables, cakes and local drinks. The cheese stall has at least 12 varieties of Kentish cheese while the veg stallholder visits farms around Kent early every morning to collect the freshest produce. Their **Whitstable Larder** restaurant serves delectable vegetarian meals for eating in or to take away (try the Kentish Land Girl Homity Pie).

Old Dairy Brewery

Tenterden Station Yard, Station Road, Tenterden, Kent TN30 6HE • 01580 763867
www.olddairybrewery.com
Some really interesting ales are coming out of this brewery, including Wild Hop – an outstandingly fruity pale ale using stacks of the finest local wild hops. The brewery is housed in two old World War II Nissen huts next to the Kent & East Sussex Steam Railway, just off the high street of the picturesque town of Tenterden.

Goody Ales

Bleangate Brewery, Braggs Lane, Herne, Kent CT6 7NP • 01227 361555 • www.goodyales.co.uk
Goody Ales are producing some award-winning tipples using traditional methods and Kentish hops. They run themed events and host film screenings, Morris Dancing and live music.

The Butchers Arms

29A Herne Street, Herne, Kent CT6 7HL
01227 371000 • www.micropub.co.uk
It may only be tiny, but the front room of this former butchers shop is big on atmosphere most nights of the week. The 'try before you buy' policy certainly adds to the whole experience.

The Thirty-Nine Steps Alehouse

5 Charlotte Street, Broadstairs, Kent CT10 1LR
www.thethirty-ninesteps.co.uk
A popular little ale house, just off Broadstairs seafront, with at least three real ales and a selection of wine.

The Bouncing Barrel

20 Bank Street, Herne Bay, Kent CT6 5EA
07777 630685 • www.thebouncingbarrel.com
Kent-made cheese with crackers served alongside the local real ales adds a nice touch in this great little drinking hole.

SAUSAGE AND ALE SUPPER

This is a simple and rustic big pan feast that can be plonked on the table to serve a group of hungry campers. The addition of the ale provides an extra depth of flavour to the dish.

You'll need a two-ring gas stove, a large frying pan and a saucepan for the rice.

Serves 4

300g short-grain rice

salt

1 tbsp olive oil

8 fine butchers' sausages (pork and apple, or pork and chilli would be good)

4 rashers smoked bacon

1 onion, sliced

1 red pepper, deseeded and sliced

2 garlic cloves, crushed

1 tbsp harissa paste

250ml Shepherd Neame ale – something slightly citrussy and malty like Goldings Ale

1 x 400g tin chopped tomatoes

1 x 400g tin cannellini beans, drained and rinsed

a small bunch of parsley, chopped (optional)

- Put the rice on to cook in salted water before you get going on the rest of the meal. It will need about 12 minutes.

- Heat the oil in a frying pan. Snip each sausage and each bacon rasher into three pieces using scissors and fry in the oil for 5 minutes.

- Add the onion and pepper and continue to cook until browned.

- Add the garlic, harissa paste and ale and simmer for 2-3 minutes before adding the tomatoes and cannellini beans. Heat through for 5 minutes.

- Once the rice has cooked, drain it well, rinse it in hot water, and let it steam for a couple of minutes, with a tea-towel over the top of the pan.

- Stir the cooked rice into the contents of the frying pan, making sure it is combined well.

- Take off the heat, season well and sprinkle with some fresh parsley if you have it. If not, just plonk the pan on the table and serve in bowls along with a few bottles of the same fine ale!

CHICKEN BALTI PARCELS

Serves 2

- Preheat your barbecue, hotplate or frying pan, keeping the heat quite low.

- Cut the skinned chicken breasts into bite-sized pieces no bigger than 2.5cm.

- Put the crème fraîche in a bowl, add the curry paste and mix well. Put the tomatoes and the pepper into the bowl and mix so that both ingredients are well coated. Add the chicken and mix again.

- Cut out 2 large rectangles of double-thickness foil, just a bit bigger than A4 paper. Put these double-thickness rectangles on a flat surface and spoon half of the mixture into the centre of each. Fold the longest two sides of the rectangle up to meet in the middle and fold it over several times, almost making a seam across the middle rather like a Cornish pasty. Fold the shorter two edges over a couple of times towards the middle to seal the parcel.

- Place the parcels on the barbecue, hotplate or frying pan and, still keeping the heat quite low, cook the parcels for about 15 minutes. Turn halfway through.

- After 15 minutes, carefully open a parcel to check that the chicken is cooked through. If not, cook for a few more minutes.

- While the parcels are cooking, cook your rice in some salted water for about 12 minutes. Drain when tender, and stir in the fresh coriander leaves (if using). Then leave to steam in the pan under a tea-towel.

- Divide the rice between 2 plates, and lay the parcels next to the rice. Let everyone open their own parcels. Serve with a cool lager.

These aluminium foil 'parcels' are a neat way to cook individual curry portions. You can make them on a conventional barbecue grill, a hotplate or even in a large heavy-bottomed frying pan.

I've used curry paste in the recipe. Sure, you could cook this curry from scratch using about 10 different spices, but let's get real, this is camping. There are times when taking the short-cut is the right thing to do – and this is it. Campsite cooking is about making great-tasting food with as little fuss as possible. Most farm shops stock a range of hand-made curry pastes or sauces, so you can try something a little different and local at the same time.

Use 'proper' chicken for this recipe, by which I meant at least free-range and ideally organic. It really will make the difference to the flavour: you will taste the chicken as well as the curry.

This recipe also works really well with prawns.

2 small chicken breasts, skinned

200g (about ⅔ of a standard tub) full-fat crème fraîche (low-fat is friend to no-one in this dish!)

3 tbsp balti curry paste

6 cherry tomatoes, halved

1 red pepper, seeded and cut roughly into 1cm cubes

150g basmati rice

salt

2 large handfuls of fresh coriander leaves (optional)

11 A MARQUED MEAL

I'm sure the New Forest was designed with picnics in mind. Every glade, stream bank and fallen tree seems to shout 'picnic spot!' In truth it was created for William the Conqueror to hunt boars and deer in 1079, and although it remains largely unchanged since then, it would appear that picnicking is now the more popular pastime.

A glance at most of the food laid out on my picnic rug reveals that it has been grown, reared, caught, brewed or produced within the National Park boundary. I know this thanks to a small blue logo called the New Forest Marque.

The New Forest is certainly a place worth marking out as special. The swathes of open heath and beautiful woodland have been preserved for centuries by an ancient system of land management which allows 'commoners' (authorised local inhabitants) to graze their cattle and ponies on the land. The commoners also famously let their pigs run through the forest during the pannage season in autumn. By scoffing the fallen acorns they protect the 3,000 semi-wild ponies from poisoning themselves on an excess of the fallen nuts. Obviously the pigs love it and the farmers benefit too as acorn-fed pork is a highly desirable product.

Maintaining this unique landscape for future generations relies on the survival of these ancient systems, and of course the people who make their livelihoods in the area. This is why a collection of food producers established the New Forest Marque in 2004. In order for a food producer to be awarded a marque, part of their production process must take place within the boundaries of the National Park and they must undergo stringent assessments to ensure that the highest standards of animal welfare and husbandry are met.

Even just the food I've chosen for my picnic would reveal a wealth of fascinating food stories about where it's from and who's made it. For example, the tangy Old Sarum blue cheese in my sandwich is from Loosehanger Farmhouse Cheeses. This small-scale producer on the northern edges of the Park is run by Ness and Gwyn Williams, who came to cheesemaking only 13 years ago but have already won many awards. Ness started making cheese in her kitchen to use up spare milk from her job as a relief milker and became so good at it that Gwyn gave up his office job to join her. "I think handcrafting our cheese in the time-honoured way on a small scale is the secret to its quality," says Gwyn.

According to my husband, you can't have a picnic without a pork pie. So how about a hand-made one filled with tasty pannaged pork encased in perfect pastry? **Owls Barn Farm** (see page 102), on the southern side of the Park, make their great range of pies on-site. They also raise their own pigs right outside the shop, alongside sheep and beef cattle. Owner Ron is a thoroughbred New Forester, so is especially proud to display the blue logo on his products. His family have used their 'commoners rights' here for generations, letting their pigs pannage in the forest.

I've also got wine from **Setley Ridge Vineyard** (see page 102), smoked trout from the **New Forest Smokery and Trout Farm**, ham from **Hale Pig n' Poultry** and strawberries and salad from **Sopley Farm**, 'grown for taste not shelf life'.

This feast of kings is a mere sliver of the produce being baked, brewed, cured, and created in this ancient landscape. So, if you are lucky enough to be camping, or just picnicking in the forest, I'd suggest making a food trail of your own by following the blue logo.

> The New Forest is certainly a place worth marking out as special.

Pitch Up......

The sites I have picked here are run by Camping in the Forest, many of which also provide ranger-led activities from the campsites.

Holmsley Caravan and Camping Site

Forest Road, Thorney Hill, Bransgore, Christchurch, Dorset BH23 8EB • 01425 674502
www.campingandcaravanningclub.co.uk
Holmsley is a lovely campsite steeped in history. Occupying part of what used to be Holmsley Airfield in World War II, it is one of 12 wartime airfields in the New Forest. The site has won many awards, has a well-stocked shop and is close to the lovely villages of Burley and Bransgore.

Hollands Wood Camping in the Forest Site

Lyndhurst Road, Brockenhurst, Hampshire SO42 7QH • 01590 622967
www.campingintheforest.co.uk
Pick your own patch of forest to pitch your tent; a secluded spot under an oak tree perhaps or maybe next to a stream – the choice is yours. The ponies, cattle and deer wandering through the site just add to the magic – although the friendly site managers are pretty special, too. It's a short walk to Brockenhurst village and **Setley Ridge Farm Shop** is close by for local supplies.

Setthorns Camping in the Forest Site

Wooton, New Milton, Hampshire BH25 5WA
01590 681020 • www.campingintheforest.co.uk
For a real back-to-nature experience Setthorns is a good choice. There are no toilet and wash facilities so you'll need your own, but the pitches are big and you can choose to 'upgrade' to one with electric hook-up and your own picnic bench. Other than that, it's just you and the forest...

Ashurst Camping in the Forest Site

Lyndhurst Road, Ashurst, Hampshire SO40 7AR
023 8029 2097 • www.campingintheforest.co.uk
A big, lively site, perfect for a sociable family holiday. There is plenty of space to choose from, with a pitch-where-you-like policy. There is more open grassland here than some other forest sites, but you can still hide away in the trees if that's what you fancy. On the eastern side of the park, you are in a good position for local attractions beyond the forest experience. For the kids, Paulton's Family Theme Park and Longdown Activity Farm (with farm shop) are nearby.

Eat Local·····

Owls Barn Farm

Derritt Lane, Sopley, Christchurch, Dorset
BH23 7AZ • 01425 672239
The farm is run on organic principles by a family who have commoners rights, having lived in the New Forest for generations. The small farm shop sells meat from the farm and a fantastic array of pies, faggots, sausages and seasonal game.

Setley Ridge Vineyard

Lymington Road, Brockenhurst, Hampshire S042 7UF
01590 622020 • www.setleyridge.co.uk
Right at the heart of the National Park. The farm shop sells the five varieties of wine that they grow and make in the winery (you can try before you buy!) as well stocking a boozer's bounty of other locally brewed ales and ciders. The shop also caters for great picnics and campers' meals with local meats, venison, eggs, chocolates, cheeses and chutneys, all sourced from a 30-mile radius. There are plenty of New Forest Marque products to choose from, including Loosehanger Cheese.

Longdown Farm Shop

Deerleap Lane, Ashurst, Southampton, Hampshire SO40 7EH • 023 8029 2837 • www.longdownfarm. co.uk

This well-priced shop stocks a large range of New Forest produce including meat, sausages, pies, cakes, fruit and veg, free-range eggs, and dairy.

Acres Down Farm Shop

Minstead, Lyndhurst, Hampshire SO43 7GE
023 8081 3693 • www.acresdownfarm.co.uk

The shop started life in 1978 as a gateside cart selling a few eggs and potatoes. It's now a lovely old converted barn and cowshed selling the farm's home-grown beef, pork and lamb, sausages, eggs, bread and seasonal home-grown vegetables, alongside plenty of other New Forest produce. While you are here, it would be rude not to stop off for one of the legendary cream teas served in the idyllic tearoom and garden. They've been serving them here for over 35 years!

Farmers' Markets
Ringwood Farmers' Market

The Furlong, Ringwood, Hampshire BH24 1AT
www.hampshirefarmersmarkets.co.uk • Last Saturday of the month

ALI'S EAT LOCAL PICNIC LOAF

Half-sandwich, half-pie, this picnic loaf crams the best of the local farm shop into one easy-to-carry meal that can be enjoyed at any beauty-spot stop-off. Prepare it the night before you go so the flavours have time to soak in – and as it uses griddled or grilled veg, you can use them in a barbecue supper and just cook extra for your picnic loaf.

You can chop and change the ingredients according to the flavours you like and what is available in the local deli/farm shop/market. I've gone for Mediterranean-type flavours with the pesto, but you could substitute a tapenade or even a mustard pickle if you are using a rustic ham.

Serves 6

- Carefully cut the top off the cob loaf (save this for later) and hollow out the middle to leave a shell. Don't make the walls too thin or it won't stay crisp.

- Toss the courgettes and peppers in the olive oil and put on a preheated griddle or barbecue grid. Cook for 4-5 minutes on each side until soft and lightly charred. Put to one side to cool.

- Rub the cut garlic clove over the insides of the bread shell, before using a spoon to spread the pesto all around the inside walls and under the lid.

- Blot the grilled veg, and slices of mozzarella (if using) with kitchen roll. Season both well with salt and pepper, then start building up layers of veg, cheese, meat and salad leaves. Finish with a layer of basil leaves. The hollow in the bread must be filled well.

- Put the top of the bread back on, then wrap the whole thing tightly in clingfilm. Put a plate on top and weigh down with something heavy to let the flavours fuse together for at least 2 hours, preferably overnight, in the cool-box.

- Cut into thick, cake-style slices to eat now or pack in your lunch-box.

1 cob loaf (the crusty round one)

1 garlic clove, halved

2 tbsp or so of pesto from a jar

For the filling

2 courgettes, sliced lengthways

2 red and 2 yellow peppers, seeded and sliced in thick lengths

2 tbsp or so olive oil

about 200g of an interesting local cheese – a soft-rind/mozzarella/goat's cheese

salt and pepper

about 200g sliced charcuterie meats or ham

a good handful of salad leaves

2 tbsp fresh basil leaves

12 HIGH WEALD HALLOUMI

Halloumi cheese is funny stuff. In its uncooked state it's pretty tasteless, rubbery to the point of chewing an inner tube, and it squeaks. But show it a marinade and this ugly duckling of cheeses becomes a swan. A simple swipe of sweet chilli sauce, a few minutes on the grill and it has a crunchy caramelised outside and a gorgeously gooey inside.

From being almost unknown in Britain a couple of decades ago, we now eat more halloumi than any other European country outside of Cyprus. This salty, brined cheese gets its texture from the fact that no 'starter cultures' are used to make it. Most other cheeses are developed with special acid-producing bacteria which create the 'cheesy' textures. The low acid content also means the cheese doesn't melt easily. Halloumi is a diet staple for many of my vegetarian friends.

I've discovered a wonderful British-made halloumi from the Weald in deepest Sussex. Mark Hardy of High Weald Dairy diversified from sheep farming to become an award-winning cheesemaker and halloumi isn't the only star of this dairy. Mark and his small team produce 15 different varieties of cheese, including a new blue-veined cheese called Brighton Blue.

Having given up sheep farming in favour of cheesemaking, Mark now gets his organic sheeps' milk from farmers around Sussex and Kent. The cows' milk for his other cheeses comes straight from the cattle I can see in the field outside the window. "We are talking food metres, not miles here," explains Mark. "We pump the cows' milk straight from the parlour into the creamery."

The rustic appearance of the old converted grain shed belies the slick, hi-tech set-up inside. From weighing and wrapping to curd cutting, a collection of shiny machines enable Mark to keep to his traditional principles and techniques, while maintaining his output with just a small team of cheesemakers.

Outside in the yard, I spot a wonderfully battered old smoking shed that imbues some of those finished truckles with a delicate smoked flavour. "Not everything is high-tech," smiles Mark.

If you are camping in the area, you'll find that many local shops, delis and restaurants stock High Weald Cheese. "We do local farmers' markets too – it's a great chance to meet the customer and give them recipe ideas for how to cook with halloumi. I get lots of repeat customers like that," grins Mark.

High Weald Dairy

Tremains Farm, Horsted Keynes, West Sussex RH17 7EA • 01825 791636
www.highwealddairy.co.uk

Pitch Up

The Old Dairy Farm (CS)

Sliders Lane, Furners Green, Uckfield,
East Sussex TN22 3RT • 01825 790517
www.theolddairyfarmshop.co.uk

Follow a pretty winding Sussex lane to find this treasure of a site. It's basic, just grass pitches and no electric, but it has a small toilet block and two showers, and offers a wonderful secluded spot in the heart of this beautiful High Weald landscape. Best of all is the diminutive yet delightful on-site farm shop.

Crowborough Camping and Caravanning Club Site

Goldsmith Recreation Ground, Eridge Road,
Crowborough, East Sussex TN6 2TN • 01892 664827
www.campingandcaravanningclub.co.uk

Set within the High Weald Area of Outstanding Natural Beauty yet just moments from Crowborough town centre, this well-kept site has colourful floral displays and a choice of different sheltered camping zones. The tent field has far-reaching views across the Downs towards the south coast. If you are feeling active, the site backs on to a large park and leisure centre with a swimming pool.

> The area around the dairy is known as the Weald – once a heavily wooded swathe of the country separating the North and South Downs. Now it is dotted with traditional picturesque villages of red brick and tiled houses centred around manicured village greens.

Idle Hours (CS)

Owlsbury Park, Hadlow Down Road,
Crowborough, East Sussex TN6 3SA • 07787 945667
www.campingandcaravanningclub.co.uk

This simple Certificated Site is an adults-only option. There are no electric hook-ups, but the amenable owners loan out solar panels, which do the job nicely. There are other friendly features too, such as picnic benches and a communal fire pit.

Eat Local

Perryhill Farm Orchards Farm Shop

Edenbridge Road, Hartfield, East Sussex TN7 4JJ
01892 770595 • www.perryhillorchards.co.uk

You can get High Weald Cheese here and some rather decent cider to go with it. Perryhill Farm produces a large selection of single variety apple juices, some ciders and perry – all from their own fruit – and they offer free tastings in the shop. Add in honey from their own hives and home-made cakes, along with fruit, vegetables, breads, biscuits and ready meals – and you've got quite a selection for your camping cook-up. There is a butcher too. **The Orchard Tea Room** has far-reaching views across Ashdown Forest, and is open seven days a week for a cuppa and cake.

Denniker Farm Shop

Fletching, East Sussex TN22 3SH • 01825 722038
www.denniker.co.uk

A neat supply of Sussex producers' wares here, including the High Weald dairy cheeses. The farm itself produces free-range lamb and pork and supplies The Griffin Inn, in the village – one of my all-time favourite food pubs!

Wapsbourne Manor

Sheffield Park, Uckfield, East Sussex TN22 3QT
01825 723414 • www.wowo.co.uk

This is actually a campsite shop (on a corking little campsite), but the secret is out among the locals who also shop here, and now I'm passing it on (with the owners' blessing). It's a small shop, but it epitomises the best of 'eat local'. The seasonal veggies are from the manor's own vegetable patch, the organic bread is from a local artisan baker (**Flint Owl**) and the cheese is from the **High Weald Dairy**.

The Old Dairy Farm

Sliders Lane, Furners Green, Uckfield,
East Sussex TN22 3RT • 01825 790517
www.theolddairyfarmshop.co.uk

Small but fab, this farm shop is manned for a few hours a week, and the rest of the time it runs on an honesty box policy. The food is fresh from the farm: rare breed pork, lamb and poultry raised free range, naturally and slowly. The vegetables are grown by local residents in a swap scheme or from a nearby farm, and the cakes are ... well, just marvellous.

Farmers' Markets
Crowborough Farmers' Market

Social Club Car Park, Croft Road, Crowborough, East Sussex • www.abmarkets.org • 4th Saturday of the month

Uckfield Farmers' Market

Luxford car park, Library Way, Uckfield, East Sussex
www.uckfieldtc.co.uk • 1st Saturday of the month

Lewes Farmers' Market

Cliffe Precinct, Lewes, East Sussex
www.commoncause.org.uk • 1st and 3rd Saturday of the month

Lewes Farmers' Market was one of the first certified farmers' markets to be set up, back in 1997 (Bath being the very first). Many of the producers have won local, regional and national awards for their produce. It's lively and packed with great food.

> "I've certainly witnessed many a disgruntled vegetarian bring their halloumi to the barbecue only to watch all the carnivore guests digging in and raving about it!"

SWEET CHILLI HALLOUMI

WITH SUMMER COUSCOUS SALAD

Putting sweet chilli sauce on halloumi before barbecuing it produces the most fantastic crispy, caramelised outside, to contrast with that absurdly soft and squeaky inside. This is such a tasty dish, I bet you'll it make again and again.

Serves 2

200g quick-cook couscous

1 vegetable stock cube

2 courgettes, sliced on a slant

1 fennel bulb, sliced lengthways

1-2 tbsp olive oil

8 cherry tomatoes, halved

2-3 tbsp sweet chilli sauce

1 x 250g pack halloumi cheese thickly sliced grated zest of ½ lemon

salt and pepper

For the dressing

125ml olive oil

3 tbsp lime juice

2 large garlic cloves, finely chopped

2 tbsp chopped mint

½ tsp caster sugar

- Put the couscous into a large bowl and crumble in the stock cube. Add 300ml of boiling water. Mix and cover and leave it to do its thing.
- Heat up your barbecue.
- Drizzle the courgette and fennel pieces with olive oil and lay them on the barbecue grill or hotplate. Keep a close eye and turn them occasionally until they have softened and got lovely char-grilled marks on them. When they are nearly cooked, put the halved tomatoes flat-side down on the grill too, to heat for a minute.
- While the vegetables are cooking, drizzle some sweet chilli sauce on each halloumi slice, and spread it so that it covers both sides. Lay the halloumi slices on the grill and cook until they start to caramelise and brown on the outside.
- Put the dressing ingredients in a bowl and mix together well, then add the cooked vegetables and mix gently to cover them with the dressing.
- Sprinkle the lemon zest over the couscous, season well with salt and pepper and fluff up with a fork.
- Put a serving of couscous on a plate, pile on the griddled veg and finish by putting the sweet chilli halloumi on the top.

SOUTH DOWNS NATIONAL PARK

13 ROTHER VALLEY ORGANICS

Brothers Shon and Simon Sprackling run Rother Valley Organics, an organic farm near Petersfield. They farm over 3,000 acres in the South Downs National Park, from the chalky downlands in the north to the coastal grazing marshes around Chichester in the south.

"We converted the entire farm to organic in 2000 because we wanted to manage every part of the process from 'pasture to plate', so that customers could be certain that what they were eating is of the highest quality," says Shon.

"We farm extensively, not intensively," he explains, as we sit watching a herd of his Aberdeen Angus cattle grazing in the sunshine. "Big isn't always beautiful when it comes to meat. An animal that is fed intensively and confined within a small area will not taste anywhere near as good as an animal that has walked the landscape and grazed naturally on grass all year round. Our cows have worked up strong muscle fibre, making the meat denser and with more flavour and goodness."

But extensive grazing needs lots of land. Luckily, since converting to organic status, the Spracklings have been approached by many landowners in the region, including the National Trust, Chichester Harbour Conservancy and the council's Queen Elizabeth Country Park, inviting the cattle to graze on their land as a method of naturally maintaining the environmentally sensitive areas.

Grazing is often the most effective and sustainable way to manage a huge variety of plants and other wildlife such as insects and birds. Cows such as the Aberdeen Angus choose the more dominant plant species to eat, which allows the less competitive plants to become established and increases biodiversity. Behaviour like rolling around in or flattening areas of grass provides an ideal place for birds like lapwings or snipes to nest and rear their young. And, on a practical level, grazing animals can access areas that machinery can't, enabling tricky and difficult terrains across the Downs to be maintained.

So it's a win-win situation. The customers get fantastic-tasting, high-quality meat, the animals have the most natural, free-ranging life it is

112 | South & South East England

possible to have, the farmers have a large, diverse, organic area of land on which to graze their livestock, the landowners have their land maintained with little intervention, the environment gets to flourish and develop a varied range of plant and wildlife ... and we the visitors to this newest National Park get to enjoy it in its beautiful and natural state.

And you thought you were just buying a steak.

Rother Valley Organics

Sandilands Farm, Rogate, Petersfield, Hampshire GU31 5HU
01730 821062 • www.rothervalleyorganics.com

Pitch Up

Graffham Camping and Caravanning Club Site

Great Bury, Graffham, Petworth,
West Sussex GU28 0QF • 01798 867476
www.campingandcaravanningclub.co.uk
In the heart of the South Downs, 90 pitches nestled
in secluded woodland glades and dappled sunlight
make for a wooded wonderland of a campsite. Paths
and tracks weave through the site and out onto the
heath and downs. This is wilderness with facilities.
It may not be the usual offering from a Camping and
Caravanning Club Site, it's a little wilder and more
'free-form', but it is a very magical place to stay.
Night-times are particularly special in a 'hoot', 'snap'
and 'rustle' kind of way...

Brocklands Farm Caravan Site (CS)

Brocklands Farm, West Meon, Petersfield,
Hampshire GU32 1JN • 01730 829325
This is simple escapism. No frills. No tents and
15 huge pitches. You may need your own facilities
but what you get in return is a perfect little summer
hideaway, tucked alongside a golden cornfield on
this working farm. A great base for walking the Downs
or just heading into the village for a great meal in **The
Thomas Lord** freehouse (www.thethomaslord.co.uk),
where they have their own kitchen garden and free-
range chickens in the pub grounds.

The Sustainability Centre

Droxford Road, East Meon, Hampshire GU32 1HR
01730 823549 • www.sustainability-centre.org
This campsite is a good choice for those interested in
the environment, sustainability and green and ethical
living. The Centre runs day courses for families:
wild wood walks, seasonal cooking and woodland
crafts. Naturally the facilities are sustainable, too:
solar heated showers in the bale-built shower block
and compost loos. You can pitch your own tents (no
caravans) or hire a tipi or yurt. Campers can use the
wood-fired pizza oven and the fire pits. The on-site
Beech Cafe offers organic, Fair Trade, vegetarian and
vegan food, ranging from home-made soup or a hearty
ploughman's to chickpea and spinach curry.

···Eat Local

Graffham Village Shop

The Street, Graffham, West Sussex GU28 0QA
01798 867700 • www.graffhamvillageshop.co.uk
As well as the usual convenience stock, the shelves
show a good range of Sussex and Hampshire
products, including local meats, fish from East
Wittering every Tuesday and Sussex cheeses. If you
are lucky you may find fresh cakes made by residents
of the village and surplus garden produce in season.

Cowdray Farm Shop and Cafe

Cowdray Park, Easebourne, Midhurst, West Sussex
GU29 0AJ • 01730 815152 • www.cowdray.co.uk
The food on offer here is exceptional, artisan and
at the higher end of the budget, but the quality is
extremely high. Try the Boerworz or lamb sausages
from the butchery for a real treat or get into
conversation with the very knowledgable fromagier
at the cheese counter. There's fresh fish available on
Tuesday and Fridays and artisan breads, too.

Durleighmarsh Farm Shop PYO and Tea Barn

Durleighmarsh Farm, Rogate Road, Petersfield,
Hampshire GU31 5AX • 01730 821626
www.durleighmarshfarmshop.co.uk
The fresh produce on sale here comes from just
outside the door. The farm grows 12 fruit crops, and
20 different types of veg. You can go and pick them
yourself if you fancy. Beyond vegetables you can get
everything you need for a fabulous campsite cook-up.
Rother Valley Organics lamb, beef, pork and chicken
are sold here, as are the smoked meats, fish and local
cheeses. The views from the tea barn stretch out
across the produce fields that grew the food on your
plate. There's a real sense of 'keeping it real' about this
place – and I like it.

Farmers' Markets

Rother Valley Organics sell their wares at the following
farmers' markets:

Petersfield Farmers' Market

The Market Square, Petersfield, Hampshire
GU32 3HQ • www.hampshirefarmersmarket.co.uk
1st Sunday of the month

Winchester Farmers' Market

Middle Brook Street Car Park, Winchester, Hampshire
SO23 8DQ • www.hampshirefarmersmarket.co.uk
2nd and last Sunday of the month
Often voted in polls as the best farmers' market
in the country.

THAI BEEF SALAD

I made this many times during the year I travelled around Australia in Custard, my campervan. The steaks in Oz were so good and the Asian influence in their cuisine must have rubbed off on me, too. It tickles all aspects of the tastebuds from sweet, to sour to salty, with a bit of zesty zing for good measure.

Serves 4

500g rump steak

coarse salt and pepper

1 tbsp olive oil

For the salad

a few spinach leaves

4 spring onions, sliced thinly lengthways

1 cucumber, cut in half, then cut into batons lengthways

1 red pepper, seeded and sliced thinly lengthways

a handful each of fresh coriander and mint leaves, roughly chopped

½ fresh red chilli, very finely chopped

Dressing

juice of 2 limes

2 tbsp soy sauce

1 tbsp fish sauce (if you don't have this, use 2 tinned anchovies)

1 tbsp sweet chilli sauce (or ½ finely chopped red chilli and a squidge of honey)

2 tbsp each of chopped fresh coriander and mint

1 garlic clove, crushed

- Prepare the salad first. Put the spinach, spring onion, cucumber, pepper, herbs and chilli in a bowl and gently mix together then lay out on a large plate.

- Make the dressing. Put all the ingredients in a jar or small bowl and shake/mix well.

- Season the steak with plenty of salt and pepper on both sides.

- Get the oil hot in a frying pan or on a griddle and cook your steaks to your liking. As a guide about 3 or 4 minutes on each side — until a nice crust forms on the meat.

- Once cooked, take the steak off the heat, loosely cover it in foil and leave to rest for 5 minutes.

- Slice the beef into thin slices (on a bit of a slant) and add to the salad, then drizzle with the dressing and gently toss together.

14 SUSSEX
VIN IN THE VAN

From the Barossa Valley in Australia to the Champagne region of France, Custard my campervan is no stranger to international wine routes. So now that English wine is making its name on the world stage I thought it was high time we set off to discover what an English wine route has to offer.

I decided to explore the fine wines of Sussex with my established wine-buddy and friend Amanda. There are around 30 vineyards and wineries in the county, producing a mix of white, red, organic and sparkling wines, although they aren't all open to the public. Sussex has chalky soil similar to the Champagne region of France, and a 'semi-continental' climate – ideal for wine making.

Our first stop was at the Bolney Estate, reached via the picture-perfect Bolney village – all red-brick houses, roses and hollyhocks. The vineyard was equally attractive, with 39 acres of vines and ancient woodland.

The hour-long tour taught me that the Romans brought vines to Britain over 2,000 years ago and that Roman soldiers often drank a litre of wine before heading into battle. It was uncomfortable to hear that only two per cent of people on these tours have tasted English wine. I felt duty bound to increase that percentage.

Our tour ended with a guided tasting of three wines. As I was driving, I was restricted to small sips, but enough to establish my favourite was the Cuvée Rosé, a vintage sparkling wine made with a pinot noir grape. I was told the flavours I was enjoying were a 'mix of cherry and toasted brioche'. I can tell you it was good wine, made all the more enjoyable by the terraced setting and taster plates of local cheeses.

Back in the van we headed south to Highdown Vineyard, nestled on the southern slopes of the South Downs, in close proximity to the coast. Frost is the winemakers' enemy, but being so far south, Highdown staves off the late frosts more than most. Much smaller than Bolney, Highdown's 10 acres are planted with eight varieties of grape including Pinot Noir, Dornfelder, Bacchus and Chardonnay. The chalky soil and salt deposits from the coast make these varieties distinctive to the vineyard.

The fantastic tearoom in a bright and airy glass-fronted building serves an inventive menu of local ingredients. I recommend The Vignerons – a plate of the best Sussex cheeses, warm crusty bread, pickles and a glass of Highdown wine. Amanda informed me the South Downs Red was 'effortlessly drinkable'. It certainly appeared to be. Highdown runs guided tours and informal tasting sessions as well as themed tasting nights focusing on different wine regions.

With a satisfying chink of bottles in a bag, we drove on to the attractive flint village of Ditchling. As no girls' weekend would be complete without bubbles, we were heading to Ridgeview, whose multi-award-winning sparkling wines have been known to beat the finest champagnes in international blind tastings. Theirs was the wine served at the Queen's Jubilee and regularly served to visiting dignitaries. The owners, two generations of the Roberts family, work hard to keep up with demand.

Visitors can turn up during the week for tastings, or pre-book one of Ridgeview's hugely popular tours on a Saturday. Ridgeview's Fitzrovia Rosé certainly got my seal of approval in a tasting.

It's high time I got over my sense of surprise that the wines from the best English vineyards are not just enjoyable, but can be truly world class.

Bolney Wine Estate

Foxhole Lane, Bolney, Haywards Heath, West Sussex RH17 5NB
01444 881575 • www.bolneywineestate.com

Ridgeview Wine Estate

Fragbarrow Lane, Ditchling Common, East Sussex BN6 8TP
0845 345 7292 • www.ridegeview.co.uk

Highdown Vineyard

Littlehampton Road, Ferring, West Sussex BN12 6PG
01903 500663 • www.highdown-vineyard.co.uk

"It was uncomfortable to hear that only two per cent of people on these tours have tasted English wine. I felt duty bound to increase that percentage."

Pitch Up

Norman's Bay Camping and Caravanning Club Site

Norman's Bay, Pevensey, East Sussex BN24 6PR
01323 761190 • www.campingandcaravanningclub.co.uk
A big, wide and open campsite with views straight across the Channel. The 200-pitch site is a literal stone's throw from the pebbly beach where William the Conqueror landed before the Battle of Hastings in 1066. Battles aside, this is also a good spot to base yourself for touring the wineries of the area. **Carr Taylor Vineyard** (www.carr-taylor.co.uk) and **Sedlescombe Organic** (www.englishorganicwine.co.uk) are within striking distance.

Oakside Farm Campsite (CS)

Green Lane, Ringmer, East Sussex BN8 5AD
01273 483685 • www.oaksidefarmcampsite.co.uk
Campsites located even vaguely close to the party town of Brighton are few and far between, but this is a good option – if you have your own facilities. The gorgeous town of Lewes is a bike ride away, packed with great places to eat and a castle for good measure. Back on site you can hire fire pits to sit round on a summer's evening and sample the spoils from your wine tour.

Sumners Ponds Campsite & Fishery

Chapel Road, Barns Green, Horsham, West Sussex RH13 0PR • 01403 732539 • www.sumnersponds.co.uk
A campsite with spacious pitches and plenty of home comforts. Enjoy piped music while you shower and underfloor heating in the state-of-the-art loo block, or relax with a morning coffee and English breakfast in the on-site cafe overlooking the fishing lake. The site is close to two of the best vineyards in the region, **Nyetimber** (www.nyetimber.com) and **Nutbourne** (www.nutbournevineyards.com)

Eat Local

Sharnfold Farm

Hailsham Road, Stone Cross, Eastbourne,
East Sussex BN24 5BU • 01323 768490
www.sharnfoldfarm.co.uk
The shop's shelves and baskets are overflowing with
just-picked produce, plus there are store cupboard
goods and a butchers' counter, too. You can head out
to PYO in the fields, walk the farm trail, use the fishing
lake, tire the kids out in the play area then kick back in
the cafe.

Middle Farm

Firle, Lewes, East Sussex BN8 6LJ • 01323 811411
www.middlefarm.com
A truly lovely farm shop based on this 625-acre
working family farm at the foot of Firle Beacon on
the South Downs. This farming family have been
selling their produce from the farm for over 40
years. You can shop for meat, cheese, dressings,
pickles and preserves, ice-cream, seasonal fruit and
vegetables from local small-scale producers. Much
of it is organic. The traditional butcher specialises
in additive-free meat and poultry, including Middle
Farm's own home-produced beef, pork and lamb.
The National Collection of cider and perry is based
here too, with over 100 draught varieties.

New House Farm Shop

Old Crawley Road, Faygate, Horsham,
West Sussex RH12 4RU • 01293 851890
www.newhousefarmshop.co.uk
A rather chi-chi converted 16th-century Sussex barn
on an arable and pick-your-own farm. The farm shop
and tea room source their stock and ingredients from
nearby butchers, bakers and nurseries and sell a good
range of Sussex wines.

Farmers' Markets

Hailsham Farmers' Market

Market Street, Hailsham, East Sussex
BN27 2AG • www.southeastmarts.co.uk
2nd Saturday of the month

Lewes Farmers' Market

Cliffe Precinct, Lewes, East Sussex
www.commoncause.org.uk • 1st and 3rd Saturday
of the month

Pulborough Farmers' Market

Village Hall, Brooks Way, Pulborough, West Sussex
RH20 2BF • Last Saturday of the month

Horsham Local Produce Market

Carfax, Horsham, West Sussex RH12 1EB
Every Saturday (main market) and every Thursday
(smaller number of stalls)
Horsham market offers a brilliant alternative to
supermarket shopping. It's on every week for a start,
and it runs all day, plus all the traders and their
produce come from within a 40-mile radius of the
town. And if you can't make it then Crates, a shop
just off the market area, is open the rest of the week.
It's stocked with the market traders' produce and has
a great little coffee shop at the back. An exciting hot
street food market runs every Thursday, too.

CHOOK AU VAN

Serves 2

As a campervan camper, 'chook au van' is my take on the old coq au vin classic. It's easy to make, with simple ingredients that you'll find in a local farm shop or market: chicken, bacon, mushrooms, cream and, of course, an English wine. Serve it with mashed potatoes or thick crusty fresh bread to mop up all the wine-flavoured juices.

- Use a heavy-based pan. Melt the butter then pour in the oil. Fry the thick cubes of bacon until they start to brown a little.

- Add the onions and cook over a lowish heat until they are beginning to soften. Scoop out the bacon and onions, using a slotted spoon, and put to one side.

- Put the chicken in the pan and fry skin-side down first. When golden, turn over and fry the other side.

- Now add the sliced mushrooms and cook for a few minutes, then add the garlic for a minute then return the bacon and onions to the pan.

- Pour in the wine, bring to the boil then turn it down to bubble away for about 25 minutes. Turn the chicken occasionally. When the chicken is cooked, lift it out of the pan and put to one side.

- Pour the cream into the pan, season with salt and pepper and add the chopped parsley.

- Let the sauce bubble away until the cream starts to thicken. Put the chicken back in the pan and bubble until it is thoroughly hot.

- Serve with mini mountains of mash and a large glass of English wine.

50g butter

1 tbsp olive oil

100g smoked bacon or pancetta, thickly diced

10 small onions or shallots, or 1 large onion, chopped

4 free-range chicken joints on the bone

250g brown or field mushrooms, sliced

2 garlic cloves, finely chopped

500ml medium-dry white wine

300ml double cream

salt and pepper

2 heaped tbsp chopped parsley

EAST ANGLIA...

Endless blue skies, swathes of wild coastline, wetlands riddled with birds ... It may be flat but East Anglia is epic. And so fertile. In windmill-flecked Norfolk samphire grows along the saltmarshes and seafood comes fresh off the boat. In Suffolk, bucket-and-spade villages dot the coastline and smokehouses season the air. Bustling farmers' markets feature locally reared pork and plump game birds, and the field-to-fork ethos is commendable.

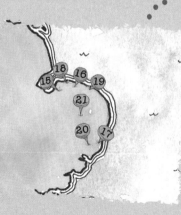

FIT FOR A KING

Sandringham is famous for being Her Majesty The Queen's house in the country, and no less than four generations of British monarchs have used it as their rural retreat since 1862. The elegant house is at the heart of the 8,000-hectare Sandringham Estate, 240 hectares of which constitute the heath and woodland of the Country Park, open to visitors every day without charge. The thriving mixed landscape of the Estate includes the tidal mudflats of the Wash, woodland and wetland. It is also a productive farm that includes livestock, arable farmland growing wheat, rye and barley and organic vegetables, but is probably best known in a farming sense for its apples and apple juices.

Apple orchards were first planted here by King George VI after World War II and they now stretch over 65 acres of Norfolk countryside. Varieties such as Egremont Russet, Laxton Fortune, Worcester Pearmain and Cox's are pressed and bottled on the estate, producing 14 different varieties of very local juice. Branch to bottle can take as little as 48 hours. If you are camping here in September and October, you can visit the orchards and pick your own apples.

Apples are not the only commercial crop to be grown on the estate. Vegetables raised in the old Walled Garden are used in the visitor centre restaurant. Blackcurrants grown at Sandringham are supplied to the makers of Ribena and the '150-minute peas' (so called because they take 150 minutes at the most to transfer from the vine to the freezer, retaining their flavour and goodness) are sold in bulk to frozen food companies.

The next diversification plan is organic truffles. The grounds have been found to be ideal for hazel and oak trees infected with truffle spores, so the estate's dog kennels are planning to train the dogs to find the truffles – which will be used in the Royal kitchens.

With a farmers' market here on the fourth Sunday of every month and a well-stocked campsite shop, you have no need to eat anything but local.

The Sandringham Estate

Estate Office, Sandringham, Norfolk PE35 6EN • 01485 545408
www.sandringhamestate.co.uk

Pitch Up

Sandringham Camping and Caravanning Club Site

The Sandringham Estate, Double Lodges, Sandringham, Norfolk PE35 6EA • 01485 542555
www.campingandcaravanningclub.co.uk

You can enjoy a taste of royal life here at this rather special wooded site. It's a Camping and Caravanning Club Site, which means you'll have access to pristine loos (with cut flowers by the sinks), hot showers, electric hook-ups and daily paper delivery, but the secluded woodland pitches add that at-one-with-nature feeling at the same time. The campsite is set within the Sandringham Estate, and a woodland walk from the site will take you to the visitor centre.

Eat Local

Walsingham Farm Shop

Lynn Road, Heacham, Norfolk PE31 7JE
01485 570002 • www.walsinghamfarmsshop.co.uk

Housed in a converted lavender distillery, this is a slick set-up running alongside its sister shop in Little Walsingham. The shelves are a window into the scores of artisanal food producers hidden throughout the county; their jars, packets and boxes of interesting sauces, spices and bakes will stretch your willpower. **The Lavender Kitchen Café-Restaurant** offers menus using farm shop food.

Knights Hill Farm Shop

South Wootton, King's Lynn, Norfolk PE30 3HQ
01553 674212 • www.knightshillfarmshop.net
Using three main local growers, Knights Hill stocks
mud-covered spuds and focuses on seasonal veg
plucked from the north Norfolk landscape.

Farmers' Markets

Docking Local Produce Market

The Ripper Hall, High Street, Docking, Norfolk
PE31 8NG • 01485 576233 • www.dockingmarket.com
Every Wednesday
Punching well above its weight, this market does the
small village proud. Its weekly local produce market in
the village hall covers all the bases, with wet fish stalls,
butchers, cheeses, fresh bread and fresh fruit and
vegetables. There's a cafe, too.

Snettisham Farmers' Market

Memorial Hall, Church Lane, Snettisham, King's
Lynn, Norfolk PE31 7LX • 2nd Friday of the month
Pork, beef, lamb, fish, shellfish, home-made cakes
and chocolate, plants and flowers, cheese, seasonal
vegetables, mushrooms, old-fashioned puddings,
bread, Norfolk apple juices from the Sandringham
Estate and much more.

Eating Out

King William IV Country Inn

Heacham Road, Sedgeford, Hunstanton,
Norfolk PE36 5LU • 01485 571765
www.thekingwilliamsedgeford.co.uk
The 'King Willy' manages to retain its atmosphere as
a great local pub while keeping visitors happy, too. It's
busy, but it deserves to be – the food is great and the
prices are good. Keeping with the apple theme, try
their apple and cinnamon puff.

The Rose and Crown

Old Church Road, Snettisham, Norfolk PE31 7LX
01485 541382 • www.roseandcrownsnettisham.co.uk
A charming coaching inn devoted to offering food
from local suppliers. They've won lots of awards and
stay on top of their game with daily changing specials
and good service.

The White Horse

Brancaster Staithe, Norfolk PE31 8BY • 01485 210262
www.whitehorsebrancaster.co.uk
Seafood is their strength, and it tastes particularly
good when you can enjoy sea views over Brancaster
while eating it.

CAMPERS' CHICKEN

APPLE, POTATO

AND FENNEL ONE-POT SUPPER

This one-pot dish is perfect proof that just because you are camping it doesn't mean it always has to be hot dogs for supper. A bowl of this makes a flavoursome and impressive (not to mention cheap!) campsite supper that uses ingredients which are easy to come by in any farm shop. I think chicken thighs have more flavour than breast, and the smoky bacon adds saltiness to counter the sweetness of the apple juice. Fresh parsley to finish is a must!

Serves 2

olive oil

½ onion, cut into thin wedges

2 garlic cloves, lightly crushed, skin left on

100g smoked bacon lardons

4 chicken thighs, boned, skin on

1 heaped tsp fennel seeds

salt and pepper

2 tsp plain flour

250ml dry apple juice
(you can use cider if you like)

4 baby new potatoes, quartered

½ apple, peeled and cored

a small handful of parsley leaves, chopped

- In a large saucepan, heat a glug of oil. Add the onion, crushed garlic and the lardons and cook slowly until the onions have softened, about 10 minutes. Remove the onions, garlic and bacon from the pan and keep to one side.

- Turn the heat up a little, and add the chicken pieces, skin-side down, and the fennel seeds. Season the chicken generously with salt and pepper and cook for a few minutes until the skin is golden and beginning to crisp. Turn it over and cook for another minute.

- Tilt the pan to one side so the oil and juices pool together. Add the flour and mix quickly into a paste. Swiftly add the apple juice, stirring all the time.

- Now put the onions, garlic and bacon back into the pan, along with the quartered new potatoes. Pop the saucepan lid on and let the whole dish bubble gently for 25 minutes. Check and stir occasionally, turning the chicken over once or twice.

- Cut the apple half into 8 wedges and add them to the pan after 15 minutes of cooking.

- Once the chicken is cooked (check there are no pink juices) and the potatoes are soft, take the pan off the heat and sprinkle chopped parsley over the top. Spoon into two bowls and enjoy.

16

REAL ALE

The irrepressible Teddy Maufe, tenant farmer on the vast Holkham Estate in North Norfolk, bubbles with infectious energy and sees adversity as just another word for opportunity. So, when the crippling farming recession hit in the 1990s he took a gamble and opened an ale shop slap bang in the middle of his farm.

"It was my son who gave me the idea. He had been travelling and had noticed how wine regions exploited their 'terroir' and successfully marketed their produce as being of its place," Teddy explains. Knowing that there were a number of micro-breweries in the area making amazing beers, Teddy made a deal with his favourites to stock and promote their beers in his shop if, in turn, they purchased his barley for their beer-making process. "So now we have a wonderful situation whereby the brewers deliver their beers to the shop and collect their supplies of malted barley at the same time. You can't get much better than that for traceability." Almost on cue, I watch a supply of bottles being delivered to the shop by a small van.

Sixteen brewers now supply the shop with its honey-coloured flagstones and views out to the hustle and bustle of the farm. Bottles of every shade of gold and brown line the shelves and the colourful artwork on the labels makes choosing your beer akin to strolling through an art gallery.

The shop's staff know every beer inside and out: the history of the producers, the stories behind the labels and the methods and recipes used. They'll even match you to your perfect beer. The fact that I left with a large bottle containing 'a fiery kick of chilli and ginger' needs no further comment.

The Real Ale Shop

Branthill Farm, Wells-next-the-Sea, Norfolk NR23 1SB
01328 710810 • www.therealaleshop.co.uk

Pitch Up

High Sand Creek

Vale Farm, The Greenway, Stiffkey, Norfolk
NR23 1QP • 01328 830235

If you like festival camping, this one is for you. It's
tents and campervans only, and as much bunting
and colourful camping kit as you can muster. The
pitches aren't big, but the location and atmosphere
make up for it. A gate at the bottom of the camping
field leads directly on to the marshes. Walk across
beds of samphire and sea lavender to get to the sea.
It's a simple site, although there are modern facilities,
shower blocks, a washing-up area and laundrette,
and a pile of beach toys and crab lines to borrow
at reception.

Creake Meadows (CS)

The Common, South Creake, Fakenham,
Norfolk NR21 9JA • 01328 823656
www.creakemeadows.co.uk

As much as I enjoy the company of my exuberant
children, I can still appreciate the desire for some
'adults only' campsites. Not in the naughty 'adults
only' sense you understand, but in the long, quiet
lie-ins with no fear of being mowed down by bikes
outside the toilet block sense, and for the generally
low-key vibe. This is a good one. It's a simple, small
site but each pitch has a water supply and light, TV
point and picnic table. There are free-range eggs,
bacon, home-made cakes and pies stocked in the
fridge freezer for campers to enjoy (honesty box).

Sunnydene Farm (CS)

The Common, South Creake, Fakenham,
Norfolk NR21 9JB • 01328 823301

A small, simple, well-kept Certificated Site with very
friendly owners. There's a play area for children, a
duck pond, electric hook-ups and sparkling facilities.

Eat Local

Walsingham Farm Shop

Guild Street, Little Walsingham, Norfolk NR22 6BU
01328 821877 • www.walsinghamfarmsshop.co.uk

Housed in an impressively converted flintstone barn,
the shop is packed with tempting goods produced by
the tenant farmers on the Walsingham Estate along
with heaps of other fresh, bottled, plucked, picked
and chopped delights. The open kitchen area shows
off the skills of the chefs busily creating the pies, tarts
and pasties. Don't leave without buying the barbecued
pulled pork pasty.

Arthur Howell

51 Staithe Street, Wells-next-the-Sea, Norfolk NR23
1AG • 01328 710228 • www.arthurhowell.com

A bit of a legend in these parts, Arthur and the meat
he sells are well trusted by the locals. He says, "We
only use farms that look after their animals and
have the same attitude to standards and service as
ourselves. In our opinion North Norfolk's beef, pork
and lamb are some of the best in the land. The rolling
mists from the sea give nutrients to the land which
give our meat wonderful flavours." There's a bakery
and deli here, too.

J & D Papworth

16 Miller's Walk, Fakenham, Norfolk NR21 9AP
01328 855039 • www.papworthbutchers.co.uk

Customers of Papworths can be reassured that
the meat they buy here is the result of high welfare
husbandry. The beef and lamb come from their
own farms, pork is from nearby, and they also stock
seasonal game.

Farmers' Markets

Fakenham Farmers' Market

Market Square, Fakenham, Norfolk NR21 9AF
www.fakenhamfarmersmarket.co.uk • 4th Saturday
of the month

This vibrant market has over 20 stalls selling organic
meats, cheese, fresh bread and vegetables. Street
entertainment adds to the atmosphere.

Malting barley has been grown in this area of Norfolk since Shakespearian times, and ale brewing in the region has always been popular due to the access to such great arable crops including barley. Sandy loam over chalk, coupled with micro-climate conditions, sets the scene for wonderful real ales.

Creake Abbey

North Creake, Fakenham, Norfolk NR21 9LF
www.creakeabbey.co.uk • 1st Saturday of the month
(excluding January)

An award-winning farmers' market with more than
55 stallholders selling fresh local meat including rare
breed pork, Aberdeen Angus beef, chickens reared
with no antibiotics, fresh vegetables, fruit and flowers
in season, cheeses, cakes, tarts (savoury and sweet),
artisan breads, local ales, juices and plants. Held
in two newly roofed old Norfolk barns and outside
by the picturesque pond with music and cookery
demonstrations throughout the year.

BACON, EGGS AND ALE

Serves 4

I actually call this my 'beery Mexicanny brunch thing'. I cook it when camping with friends, and everyone is still on 'go-slow', sitting around mid-morning in their pyjamas. The chilli puts a bit of zing in their tails. It is great as a brunch or evening supper dish and it's lovely with fresh, chopped coriander sprinkled over the top.

If buying your light ale in The Real Ale Shop in Wells-next-the-Sea, you could try Beeston Brewery's The Squirrel's Nuts or The Why Not Brewery's Norfolk Honey Ale.

1 tbsp olive oil

1 onion, roughly chopped

1 red pepper, deseeded and roughly chopped

8 rashers unsmoked streaky bacon, snipped into 2cm pieces

200ml light ale

1 x 400g tin chopped tomatoes

¼–½ tsp chilli flakes

2 garlic cloves, finely chopped

1 tbsp caster sugar

salt and pepper

4 eggs

50g mature Cheddar, grated

4 flour tortillas, warmed

- In a frying pan, heat the oil, and cook the onion, pepper and bacon until the onion and pepper are soft and golden, about 10 minutes.

- Add in the light ale, tomatoes, chilli flakes, garlic and sugar and cook for a further 15 minutes until quite thick. Have a quick taste and season accordingly.

- Make four wells in the tomato sauce and crack an egg into each well. Sprinkle over the cheese and cook with a lid on for 4–5 minutes until the eggs are just cooked.

- Season and serve on warmed tortillas, with an accompanying bottle of Norfolk ale.

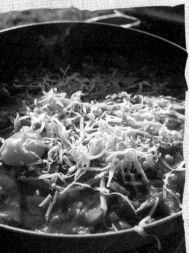

FISH SHEDS

The first rule of seafood for me is 'the closer to the sea you can eat it the better', so a plateful of fresh crab, oysters and prawns served from a knackered old beach shack would win hands down over a fussy sauced plate in a restaurant any day.

The fish shack is a familiar sight along the entire Suffolk coastline. Whether it's a black tarred wooden shed on the shingle, a reclaimed beach hut, or a simple deli-chiller in a seafront garden, the equation is the same: boat goes out in the morning, brings back the catch a few hours later, sells it straight to the customer. It is a centuries-old ritual along this coast.

Aldeburgh beach front retains its timeless charm. Now loved by nautically attired ladies and men wearing raspberry-coloured shorts, this landscape of sea, sky and shingle is furnished with colourful wooden fishing boats seemingly arranged on the beach by someone with an artistic eye.

It's the long line of black-tarred wooden huts selling wet fish, shellfish and plates of simply prepared smoked fish that keeps the place 'real' though. I like the way that fresh produce, eaten in the place it is cut, caught or reared can do that. It's a process that keeps us humble.

You'll be spoilt for choice as you wander along the promenade past the huts enticing and informing you with their hand-painted signs: 'We Smoke Here' (fish not fags) or 'Potted Lobster with Tarragon, Skate Wings, Rock Eel, Flounder, Dabs'... It's a veritable guide to the East Coast's wonderful and varied marine life.

Then there's the fish-and-chip shop in stylish Aldeburgh High Street, which has developed such a reputation for greatness that the queue winds down the road. The White Hart next door (owned by Suffolk-based Adnams brewery) invites folks to eat their fish and chips in the pub on the condition that they buy a pint. A fair arrangement I'd say, and as food matching goes, this is a winning pairing.

> " Black tarred wooden huts selling wet fish keep the place 'real'... "

Pitch Up

Beach View Holiday Park

Sizewell Common, Leiston, Suffolk IP16 4TU
01728 830724 • www.beachviewholidaypark.co.uk
A big site, with all the holiday-park trimmings, that also happens to have direct access to a long, sweeping pebble and sand beach. Yes, you can see Sizewell Nuclear Power Station from this part of the coast but that doesn't seem to bother any of the happy campers, so it probably won't bother you. With a cafe and bar serving local ales and a children's play area, games and TV room this isn't really a back-to-nature place, but it will certainly provide a streamlined family camping holiday without too much effort.

Bailiffs Cottage (CS)

Lodge Road, Hollesley, Woodbridge, Suffolk
IP12 3RR • 01394 411275
A quiet site where you can reconnect with nature. There are great walks and cycle rides, including one into Hollesley village with its excellent village store. A mile away is the village of Shottisham and its village-owned pub **The Sorrel Horse**, which supports East Anglian breweries such as Adnams, Woodforde's, Calvors and Aspalls (www.thesorrelhorse-shottisham. co.uk).

Shrubbery Farm (CS)

Hasketon, Woodbridge, Suffolk IP13 6HR • 01394 383106 • www.campingandcaravanningclub.co.uk
Rural yet just a mile from Woodbridge, rustic but with clean and tidy amenities, just a few pitches but with plenty of space – the balance is just right here at Shrubbery Farm Certificated Site. Friendly owners Gordon and Molly also sell chicken and goose eggs, pies, ice-cream and apple juice from the small shop by their back door. All food scraps are given to the chickens, so there's no waste and plenty of recycling bins on site.

Eat Local

Fish Sheds

Aldeburgh beachfront
A range of fish sheds, all lined up on the shingle, sell an astounding variety of fresh wet fish and shellfish on a daily basis. **The Fish Shack** is a great one; their potted crab with fennel, dill and peppercorns is a speciality.

Maximus Sustainable Fishing

Unit 1, Friday Street Farm Shop, Farnham, Saxmundham, Suffolk IP17 1JX • 01728 603854
www.maximusfish.co.uk
Chris Wightman has been committed to using sustainable and ethical fishing practices throughout his 20-year career in the industry. He supplies all the best restaurants in the area with the catch of his fleet of small boats, but luckily for us he also runs a great little unit at Friday Street Farm (see page 145). He was trying out his new coffee cure on salmon when I visited. Delicious.

Brinkleys' Fish Shed

Orford Foreshore, Orford, Suffolk IP12 2NU
07530 911458

Preserving Orford's tradition as a working fishing port, this small fish shed on the quay is run by the local fishermen selling their locally caught fish and shellfish. The village of Orford is a haven for food lovers; the village store has a deli and cafe and the award-winning Pump Bakery is here, too.

Pinney's of Orford

The Old Warehouse, Quay Street, Orford, Suffolk IP12 2NU • 01394 459183 • www.pinneysoforford.co.uk

This revered smokery and fresh fish shop is one of the many reasons people head to Orford. There's a tempting selection of freshly landed fish, rollmops, pâtés and oysters from their own oyster beds in nearby Butley Creek. They have a restaurant too, in Market Hill. The simple dishes let the flavour of the fish speak for itself and offer refreshingly fuss-free fish lunches.

> " Aldeburgh beach front retains its timeless charm ... this landscape of sea, sky and shingle is furnished with colourful wooden fishing boats ... "

Friday Street Farm Shop

Farnham, Saxmundham, Suffolk IP17 1JX
01728 602783 • www.farmshopsuffolk.co.uk
Okay, I'm shallow. I like this farm shop because it's pink. Luckily for me it's also incredibly worthy of recommendation and a heartfelt plea – please don't go to a supermarket when you could go somewhere like this. It's a meeting place for all of the local small producers, and has plentiful deliciously fresh home-grown stuff like soft fruits and vegetables pulled from the fields next door.

Farm Cafe and Food Market

Main Road (A12), Marlesford, Woodbridge, Suffolk IP13 0AG • 01728 747717 • www.farmcafe.co.uk
I had the most fantastic lunch in this bright, relaxed and welcoming cafe. It is on the busy A12, which makes it the best roadside cafe I have ever had the pleasure of experiencing. Once in the conservatory area at the back, you can look across the fields and enjoy a wonderful menu made with local ingredients served by happy and helpful staff. The cafe has over 100 local suppliers. Next door is a small but well-stocked food market selling the ingredients for you to use yourself.

Aldeburgh Market

170–172 High Street, Aldeburgh, Suffolk IP15 5AQ
01728 452520 • www.thealdeburghmarket.co.uk
A fishmonger, deli and cafe all in one that's a great place to be.

The Sorrel Horse

The Street, Shottisham, Suffolk IP12 3HD • 01394 411617 • www.thesorrelhorse-shottisham.co.uk
A village-owned pub supporting the local breweries.

Snape Maltings

Snape, Aldeburgh, Suffolk IP17 1SR
01728 688303 • www.snapemaltings.co.uk
This place is all very 'lifestyle darling', with a mix of tasteful home-ware shops, galleries, holiday homes and a concert hall all attractively developed from a vast Victorian maltings complex. Regardless of your feelings towards heritage hues, the food is so fantastic in the shops, pantry and cafes, that Snape Maltings is a must for all kinds of food lovers.

All beautifully presented and packaged, much of the food here is proud to be local. Artisan breads are from the local **Pump Street Bakery**, the pantry is packed with seasonal produce, there's smoked fish and pâtés from the renowned (and local) **Pinney's of Orford** and Revetts Sausages from **Wickham Market**, renowned as the best sausage-makers in Suffolk. Suffice to say, it showcases the best of Suffolk's food industry. There's also a monthly farmers' market here, on the first Saturday of the month.

FLIP FLOP POP
FISH
AND CAMPERS' COLESLAW

Serves 4

- Make the coleslaw first. Slice the cabbages and red onion as thinly as possible. Put in a large bowl. Grate the carrots into the bowl. Add the plain yoghurt and mustard and mix well.

- Sprinkle at least 6 tbsp plain flour all over a large plate and mix in the paprika, grated lemon zest, salt and pepper.

- Crush the Rice Krispies® in a freezer bag and pour on to a separate plate. Have your beaten egg next to this.

- One at a time, flip the fish fillets over in the flour, then flop in the egg, then flip back into the flour. Pop into the Rice Krispies®, making sure the fish fillets are well coated.

- Heat up a slug of olive oil in a large frying pan. Put the coated fish fillets in the pan, and fry for about 4 minutes on each side. Resist the temptation to push the fish about with the spatula as it might disintegrate. Check the fish is cooked.

- Put the fish fillets and a heap of coleslaw in a soft bread bun. Enjoy.

This is a super-simple recipe for cooking fish when camping.

It is also a very child-friendly recipe. In fact it was my five-year-old who suggested the Rice Krispies® coating. It works brilliantly, providing a satisfying crunch. You could try breadcrumbs, rolled oats or even cornflakes in place of the cereal.

The coleslaw is low-cost, quick and easy and very tasty.

4 skinless fish fillets (use a white, firm, flaky-fleshed fish like pouting, whiting or sustainably caught cod or pollack)

olive oil

4 soft bread buns

For the coating

plain flour

2 tsp paprika

grated zest of 1 lemon

salt and pepper

3 large handfuls of Rice Krispies®

1 large egg, beaten in a wide bowl

For the coleslaw

½ red cabbage

½ white cabbage

½ red onion

3 carrots, peeled

4 tbsp plain yoghurt

1 tbsp wholegrain mustard

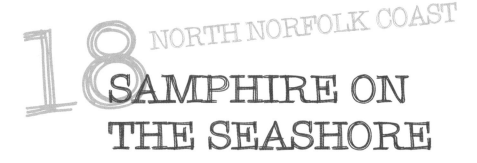

18 SAMPHIRE ON THE SEASHORE

Being a lover of rolling surf, it took me a while to tune in to the beauty of East Anglia's coastline. It's flat, it's vast and, well, it's often a long way across the beach to the sea. In fact I seemed to be walking over marshland, heath and a bit of shingle rather than beach on my way for a dip. But as I picked my way through the greenery of the Brancaster Marshes, concentrating on where I was putting my feet, I realised what I was walking on: samphire. This saltmarshy coastline's version of asparagus was stretched out like a big green shag pile carpet towards the sea. My trip to the beach had been transformed. I sat down and started to harvest my supper, and never made it as far as the water.

Samphire is only around for a few weeks of the year, from mid-June to the end of August, giving it that 'get it or it's gone' excitement. During much of the camping season it will be on every menu, roadside stall and farm shop shelf. But you can't beat picking your own.

This is marsh samphire (*Salicornia europaea*), not to be confused with rock samphire (*Crithmum maritimum*), which is more of a Mediterranean plant that grows on cliffs or shingle. Marsh samphire thrives around the Norfolk and Suffolk coastline and estuaries, both wetland areas which are rich in minerals.

It has a fresh and slightly salty taste, and is a perfect side to fish dishes as well as crab. They live in the same environment, in the same season, so my rule of thumb is that it means they'll often work well together on your plate. I treat samphire as I would asparagus: I boil it (or steam it) for a couple of minutes then heap it on my plate, squidge some lemon juice on top, a big wodge of real butter and oodles of black pepper. For a more substantial meal, you can toss hot samphire into pasta with butter and garlic, or stir some fresh cooked crab meat through hot buttered samphire, add a few chilli flakes and a squeeze of lime. Perfect.

So there I was, gathering my supper before the tide came in. I wasn't alone. In scenes from a forager's dream there were others, of all ages, harvesting this uncultivated crop across the mudflats.

I suspect the same scenes have been repeated across the decades up and down this coastline. Kneeling on the mudflats, and picking the emerald spears gives a vaguely spiritual appreciation of the uncultivated wilderness of this coastline. It echoes the unspoilt and unassuming vibe that keeps East Anglia so different from the rest of the country. And I hope it never changes.

Pitch Up

The Paddocks (CS)

Fakenham Road, Stanhoe, King's Lynn, Norfolk
PE31 8PX • 01485 578657

Scott and Katie run this fabulous little Certificated
Site effectively in their front garden. It's spacious,
has countryside views, spotless facilities and free fire
baskets to use for campfires. You can hire the tipi or
shepherd's hut, too. It's just 10 minutes drive to the
coast and close to two great local produce stores. The
Duck Inn in nearby Stanhoe is fabulous for food.

Deepdale Backpackers

Burnham Deepdale, Norfolk PE31 8DD
01485 210256 • www.deepdalebackpackers.co.uk

Deepdale is a way of life as much as it's a campsite.
This arable farm offers eco-friendly accommodation
in the form of a backpackers' hostel, glamping tipis,
shepherd's huts and a campsite that takes tents and
campervans only. Camping fields stretch across five
paddocks and there's a modern solar-heated facilities
block. You can hire a bike from the site, although the
Coast Hopper bus service picks up from the campsite
entrance. The popular **Deepdale Cafe** is just around
the corner. Be prepared – it gets super-busy in
high season.

The Rickels Caravan & Camping Site

Bircham Road, Stanhoe, King's Lynn, Norfolk
PE31 8PU • 01485 518671

This is an adults-only site that is beautifully
maintained. If you like things 'just so' this will be
great for you. The facilities are spotless and you have
all that you'll need for your stay – washing, drying
and freezer facilities. There is even a TV room with
sofas and a dining table. It's a short drive out to the
coast for some bracing walks and wonderful bird-
spotting opportunities.

Eat Local

Gurneys Fish Shop

Market Place, Burnham Market, Norfolk PE31 8HF
01328 738967 • www.gurneysfishshop.co.uk

Oh, if only every high street had a Gurneys! Set up by
Mike Gurney 40 years ago, the passion for fabulous,
locally landed fresh fish has never faded. This shop
is a delight. As well as a wonderful range of wet fish,
Mike and his staff produce fish pâtés, soups, pies,
chowders and curries. You can buy all your ingredients
for your Eat Local recipe here (see page 152).

Remember to follow the basic rules of foraging:
• Seek permission from landowners before entering private land
• Don't collect plants from nature reserves or Sites of Special
  Scientific Interest
• Only collect as much as you know you can eat
• Avoid collecting from areas that are popular with dog walkers!
• Never pull up plants by their roots; pinch out or snip off the tops,
  leaving the stems in the ground to continue to grow

> *When picking samphire, pinch out or snip off the tops of the plants, leaving the stems in the ground to continue to grow.*

Walsingham Farm Shop

Lynn Road, Heacham, Norfolk PE31 7JE
01485 570002 • www.walsinghamfarmsshop.co.uk
It's a 15-minute drive from the campsites to this top-class farm shop. You can stock up on all of your weekly groceries here in the knowledge that the contents of your basket have mostly come from local companies, fishermen and farmers.

Docking Local Produce Market

The Ripper Hall, High Street, Docking, Norfolk
PE31 8NG • 01485 576233 • www.dockingmarket.com
Every Wednesday
This weekly local produce market in the village hall covers all the bases with wet fish stalls, butchers, cheeses, fresh bread and fresh fruit and vegetables. There's a cafe too.

Bircham Windmill

Great Bircham, King's Lynn, Norfolk PE31 6SJ
01485 578393 • www.birchamwindmill.co.uk
This one is great for a morning out with the children and you can get your freshly baked bread at the same time. Although the mill no longer grinds the flour, the bakery is still open for cakes and bread. There's a mill museum, gallery and teashop and children's baking corner for budding bakers to make and bake their own mini-loaf.

Top spots to find samphire

Norfolk
- Holkham Bay
- The creeks north of Blakeney
- High Sand Creek, near Stiffkey
- Burnham Overy Staithe

Suffolk
- On many of the unspoilt creeks and inlets of the Suffolk coast
- The marshland around Snape and Orford
- Along the banks of the estuary in Blythburgh

Eating Out
Sculthorpe Mill

Lynn Road, Sculthorpe, Fakenham, Norfolk
NR21 9QG • 01328 856161 • www.sculthorpemill.com
Another mill, but this one is less flour-focused, more 'food fabulous'. Serving the seasonal Norfolk greats such as Cromer crab and Norfolk mussels, there is also an enticing daily specials board. The setting is stunning, with great views out on to the River Wensum and the surrounding beautiful Norfolk countryside. The river flows through the large rear garden, under the mill and out into the mill pond at the front of the pub. Definitely one for a holiday treat meal.

PAN-FRIED SEA BASS
WITH CHORIZO AND
SAMPHIRE

Serves 2

You can chop and change the fish in this dish. Lemon sole works well or even a piece of cod. This dish has crispness, crunch, zest and a spicy little kick from the chorizo. Don't forget that the samphire is naturally salty, so you don't really need extra salt. Just add more black pepper!

To prepare the samphire, remove any tough stems and rinse thoroughly to get rid of any sand, grit or dirt. Now trim into manageable-sized pieces: small bunches of about 3cm.

Serve with some cooked new potatoes, slightly crushed, with plenty of butter, black pepper and lemon juice.

about 200g samphire (if you can't weigh it, hold it in your hand – you need a decent handful per person)

butter

olive oil

100g chorizo (dry-cured), sliced

2 x 150g sea bass fillets, skin on

coarsely ground black pepper

a little grated lemon zest

- Rinse the samphire well, several times, and discard any woody or damaged stems. Boil for 2 or 3 minutes. Drain, top with a knob of butter and put to one side.

- Add a little oil to a large frying pan, heat and add the chorizo. You need to cook it until it starts to go a little crispy on the edges and that wonderful red oil begins to show in the pan. Once that is done, remove the chorizo from the pan and keep warm but make sure you leave the flavoured oil in the pan.

- Add the fish to the pan, skin-side down. Season the flesh with black pepper, and grate a little lemon zest over the top.

- Fry the fish until the skin is nice and crispy (about 4 minutes) then reduce the heat and flip it over to cook the flesh on the other side (this should only take a minute depending on the thickness of the fillets).

- Remove the fish from the pan and cover with foil to keep warm. Quickly return the chorizo and the samphire to the pan to heat through for a minute or so.

- Divide the samphire and chorizo between two plates. Serve the fish on top.

19 CRAB COAST

I tend to rate my holidays on the standard of crab sandwiches I can find. My trip to Norfolk fared rather well. The North Norfolk coastline is renowned for good crab, especially around Cromer, where the crab is said to contain more white meat than the brown crabs 'down south'. Locals say the meat tastes sweeter because of the chalk shelf below Cromer bay where they are caught. Others say that the crabs grow slower here, making the flesh more tender. Whatever the reason, it tastes good, and there are plenty of memorable shacks and sheds to buy it from. Cromer has long been associated with crabs, so I was surprised to learn that there are only around a dozen crab boats working out of Cromer now, catching them traditionally in the 200 pots that lie on the seabed a few miles out.

The crab are brought back to shore, washed, checked and boiled for around 25 minutes and then 'dressed'. This means the legs and shell are removed, including the 'dead man's fingers' (the gills). The meat is picked out and the white and brown meat is carefully separated then packed back into the cleaned top shell, with attractively arranged white meat through the middle and brown meat either side.

Wedged incongruously between two amusement arcades in a narrow backstreet off Cromer seafront, is a tiny fisherman's cottage with a chiller cabinet in the front porch. Here you'll find eighth-generation Cromer crab fisherman John Lee selling the eponymous crustaceans caught on his daily 4am fishing trips. At just £3 per crab it's a steal. If you crave a little more comfort with your crab then head off to the **Jetty Cafe** (see page 157) and sit inside to sample one of the best crab sandwiches you'll ever taste.

Cookies Crab Shop (see page 157) in the tiny village of Salthouse on the north Norfolk coast has been selling fresh crab for over 60 years. It now serves huge platters of lobster, crab, prawns, cockles and smoked fish from a tiny cottage on the village green overlooking the Cley Marshes nature reserve. It has become so popular that its size struggles with its reputation. On my last visit I witnessed two well-dressed old gents having a ruckus over the last empty chair in the lean-to gazebo on the side of the cottage. If you come here, as well as taking your own wine, my advice is to either take a picnic rug and sit on the green, or instead head to the wonderfully unaffected **Blakeney Crab Shed** (see page 157) just down the road where Andy Randall catches, prepares and sells his freshly caught crabs and lobsters.

Pitch Up

West Runton Camping and Caravanning Club Site

Holgate Lane, West Runton, Cromer,
Norfolk NR27 9NW • 01263 837544
www.campingandcaravanningclub.co.uk
Nestled in a wooded valley, the lovely West Runton
Camping and Caravanning Club Site is still close
enough to the atmospheric North Norfolk coastline
that you can smell the salt in the air. The sandy beach
in West Runton village is walkable from the site. Take
your crab lines for the rock pools.

This 200-pitch site is surrounded by trees and
feels suitably secluded from the hustle and bustle of
the world outside. With a variety of camping areas,
electric hook-ups, a playground and immaculate
facilities, the coast in one direction and countryside in
the other, it's a great all rounder.

The on-site staff are dedicated to promoting local
produce to their campers. The site shop sells bacon,
hand-made burgers and sausages from the butchers'
shop in Sheringham and jars of local honey. Enormous
double-yolked eggs and milk are provided by the local
farm. A big whiteboard outside reception gives details
of great local produce shops and times of local food
markets. **Cookies Crab Shop**, the **Blakeney Crab
Shed** and Cromer are all close by for a fish supper.

Kelling Heath Holiday Park

Weybourne, Norfolk NR25 7HW • 01263 588181
www.kellingheath.co.uk
If you want a bit more action out of your camping
holiday this is a good option. It's set among 270
acres of woodland and open heathland in an Area of
Outstanding Natural Beauty on the North Norfolk
coast. There is a bit of a Center Parcs type feel to it in
that there are both indoor and outdoor pools, tennis
courts, cycle hire and cafes. They also have woodland
lodges. It's pricier than your average pitch but the
extras may be worth it.

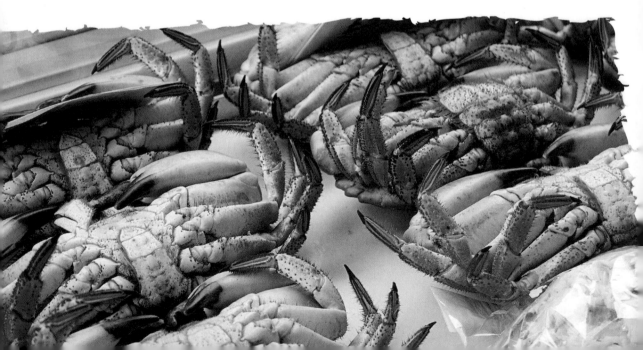

> **The North Norfolk coastline is renowned for good crab, especially around Cromer, where the crab is said to contain more white meat than the brown crabs 'down south'.**

Baconsthorpe Meadows Campsite

Pitt Farm, Baconsthorpe, Holt, Norfolk NR25 6LF
07884 432412 • www.baconsthorpemeadows.co.uk
With a name like this, I can't ignore it. Baconsthorpe is a traditional tents-only campsite on a working farm just five miles from the North Norfolk coast. Best of all you can have a campfire. You can pitch where you like in the five acres of meadow set aside for campers. There are toilets, showers, washing-up sinks, laundry facilities, chemical waste, a small shop and tourist information on site.

Eat Local

Cookies Crab Shop

The Green, Salthouse, Holt, Norfolk NR25 7AJ
01263 740352 • www.salthouse.org.uk

Blakeney Crab Shed

63 New Road, Blakeney, Norfolk NR25 7PA
01263 740988
Fresh local crab, lobster and delicious home-made crab cakes.

John Lee's Crab Stall

New Street, Cromer, Norfolk (between two arcades)
Fresh dressed crab straight out of the sea a few hundred yards away.

Jetty Cafe

11 High Street, Cromer, Norfolk NR27 9HG
01263 513814
This little high street cafe is well known for its fabulous crab sandwiches – a whole crab in each one, no mayo, just lemon juice, served on fresh brown bread and with home-made coleslaw. Yum.

Groveland Farm Shop

Thorpe Market Road, Roughton, Norfolk NR11 8TB
01263 833777 • www.grovelandfarmshop.co.uk
Located in a traditional Norfolk flint barn, the Groveland Farm Shop is part of a bigger complex that includes a garden centre, gift shop, craft shop and car wash! It's definitely the place to come for an enormous range of fresh local fruit, vegetables and deli goods. The meat is from **Blythburgh Free Range Pork** and **Great Grove Poultry**, both respected free-range, ethical farms. Ring ahead and time it right so you come on one of the free tastings days.

CHILLI CRAB SHELLS

Serves 4

With the minimum of effort, these attractive little mounds of fresh crabmeat with punchy, zingy flavours make an impressive and tasty snack. For a twist, you can replace the mayonnaise with a couple of tablespoons of coconut milk (should you happen to have any with you!), or you can add slices of avocado to the lettuce shells to make them more substantial.

- Put the crabmeat, mayonnaise, chilli, herbs, cucumber, salt and plenty of black pepper into a bowl.

- Squeeze in the juice of the lime and mix it all together quite roughly.

- Spoon the crab mixture into the lettuce leaf 'shells' and top each one with a few fresh torn coriander leaves.

400g fresh white crabmeat

1 tbsp mayonnaise

¼ fresh red chilli, deseeded and finely diced (can be increased if you like it hot!)

4 tbsp chopped fresh coriander and dill, plus extra fresh coriander to serve

½ cucumber, sliced and quartered

salt and pepper

1 lime

2 baby gem lettuces, leaves separated

20 MELLOW YELLOW

Butter, vegetable oil, sunflower, olive … what you fry your egg in in the morning can be charted on a culinary timeline. At the time of writing, we are about to take another oily step forward. Rapeseed is the new olive oil. It's the leaner, meaner alternative. This nutty, buttery golden oil is lower in saturated fats, has more omega 3, 6 and 9 and has a higher 'smoking point' than olive oil, meaning it holds its flavour and nutrients for longer as you heat it.

Another obvious 'plus' for me is that we grow rapeseed here in Britain. Traditionalists may disagree, but I love seeing the vibrant, near-neon yellow patchwork of rapeseed fields. Along with apple blossom and rippling corn, it has become a familiar part of our food production landscape. East Anglia's vast, flat fields, good soil and agreeable climate suit the crop.

Just over ten years ago, Sam Fairs of Hillfarm Oils in Suffolk discovered a friend was taking rapeseed oil tablets as a health supplement. Although Sam was growing it as a crop, he was selling it to refineries that processed it at high temperatures, used chemicals and solvents to bleach the life out of it then sold it on as cheap vegetable oil. Intrigued about the health benefits, Sam researched whether it was a crop worth processing himself, in a way that retained all the goodness.

Positive results inspired Sam to buy a press and by 2004 he had launched his first range of cold-pressed rapeseed oils for cooking. In taking this step to press and bottle their own virgin oil rather than ship out the seeds and let other companies add the value, the Fairs became the first producers of cold-pressed extra virgin rapeseed oil in the country. Since then Hillfarm Oils have become ever more popular – sales have doubled in the last year alone.

I watched as the tiny black seeds were delivered from the fields, gently squeezed through a small screw press and the saffron yellow oil dripped out. It was piped directly into bottles and labelled. Liquid gold, like sunshine in a bottle.

Hillfarm Oils

Heveningham, Suffolk IP19 0ED • 01986 798660
www.hillfarmoils.com

Pitch Up

Mill Hill Farm Caravan and Camping Park

Westleton Road, Darsham, Saxmundham,
Suffolk IP17 3BS • 01728 668555
www.suffolkcamping.webs.com
With far-reaching views over the yellow rapeseed
fields in season, the folk at Mill Farm really enjoy
their surrounding landscapes, which is why they are
keen to run their business using recycled, natural and
sustainable materials wherever possible.

The pristine shower and toilet blocks have all the
eco features: solar-assisted hot water, motion-sensitive
and low-energy lighting and water-saving flushing.
Pitches are large. Choose from a secluded tent
meadow, an open field or hedge-lined spaces next to
a flower meadow that has paths mown into it for dog
walking. For entertainment there is a boules pitch,
fishing lake, football field and a sheltered area for
communal feasts.

Orchard Cottage (CS)

Mill Lane, Weybread, Harleston, Suffolk IP21 5RS
01379 586411 • www.orchardcottagecamping.co.uk
Utterly magical. Pitch in the orchard among the
damsons, plums, apples and quinces, choose your
own private glen in the wood or try the cosy nook
amphitheatre-type space near the pond. Wherever you
pitch, you'll love it here. Chickens wander around the
site reminding you that you can buy their freshly laid
eggs for breakfast. Then again you could have toast
spread with jams and jellies made with the orchard
fruit by owner Ann. Decisions, decisions.

Kessingland Camping and Caravanning Club Site

Africa Alive Wildlife Park, Whites Lane, Kessingland,
near Lowestoft, Suffolk NR33 7TF • 01502 742040
www.campingandcaravanningclub.co.uk
This immaculate flower-filled site of 90 pitches,
all with electric hook-ups, makes a welcoming and
comfortable base for exploring the area. You are
well positioned for both the Norfolk Broads and the
picturesque Suffolk coast, or you could stay on site
and walk next door to the Africa Alive Wildlife Park.
It's not often I have fallen asleep in my campervan to
the sound of roaring lions and chattering monkeys.

Eat Local

Emmerdale Farm Shop

Westleton Road, Darsham, Saxmundham, Suffolk
IP17 3BP • 01728 668648 • www.emmerdalefarmshop.
co.uk
A pleasant walk along the lane from Mill Hill Farm
campsite is a fuss-free shop selling great home-reared
beef, with a 'fresh veg corner' and multiple chillers
containing ready meals and barbecue-ready foods.
You can also stop at the on-site cafe for a slab of
proper home-baked cake.

The rapeseed plant is part of the brassica
family, like broccoli and mustard. The seed
part is small and black, a bit like a poppy
seed. Inside the black outer shell there is
an oily yellow middle, hence the beautiful
yellow colour of the oil.

Darsham Hamper

London Road, Darsham, Suffolk IP17 3QR
01986 784679

Not really a farm shop at all but an East of England
Co-op convenience store. It's brilliant. All the
products have clear on-shelf signage telling the story
of where and who the item came from, including
the food miles used to get it to the store. The prices
are competitive, the stock is fresh, interesting, local
and seasonal but presented in a familiar convenience
store set up. There's an on-site cafe, too and plentiful
parking for those with big vans. They sell chorizo and
Hillfarm Oils here.

Middleton Farm Shop

Reckford Farm, Leiston Road, Middleton, Suffolk
IP17 3NS • 01728 648936 • www.middletonfarmshop.
co.uk

Inside this pretty wooden building with chickens
scratching around outside are carefully sourced
products from speciality producers in Suffolk
including Hillfarm Oils, artisan breads, Stokes sauces
(a favourite of mine) and wonderful ice-creams. I
bought the most delectable freshly picked plums, a
fresh juice and stunning bread cooked in the wood-
fired oven. The compact cafe is charming and does
great coffee and light lunches.

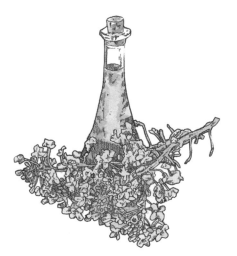

Metfield Stores

The Street, Metfield, Harleston, Suffolk IP20 0LB
01379 586204

A shop to make you smile. This village shop was
saved from closure by its community in 2006. Now
volunteers serve you Suffolk-made pies, excess veg
from the allotments, breads and sausages made down
the road from the Metfield herd. A friendly welcome
is all part of the service.

D A Browne & Son

35 The Thoroughfare, Harleston, Suffolk IP20 9AS
01379 852235

If you are staying at Orchard Cottage camping site
then it's worth visiting this fabulous family butchers
in nearby Harleston. Meat is from local farms, they
smoke and cure their own bacon and hams and also
stock chorizo for the recipe (see page 165).

SUFFOLK CHORIZO
& CANNELLINI BEANS

This delicious one-pan dish, courtesy of the folk at Hillfarm Oils, can be made in 15 minutes. All ingredients can be bought from Middleton Farm Shop or Darsham Hamper.

Serves 2

- Heat 2 tbsp oil in a pan and add the finely chopped onion and chorizo. Cook on a medium heat until the onions are soft, about 10 minutes, and the chorizo is crisp around the edges.

- Add the cannellini beans and cook for 1 minute.

- Add the remaining ingredients and simmer for about 7-8 minutes.

- Remove from the heat, and put into individual serving dishes. Drizzle with a little Hillfarm Rapeseed Oil, and serve with crusty bread.

Hillfarm Rapeseed Oil

6 spring onions, sliced

150g chorizo, sliced about 5mm thick
(the Suffolk Salami Company one is delicious)

1 x 400g tin cannellini beans, drained and rinsed

1 x 400g tin chopped tomatoes

1 tbsp tomato purée

3 garlic cloves, crushed

½ tsp crushed dried chillies

2 tsp paprika

1 tsp coarsely ground black pepper

salt to taste

The **HOME of the NORFOLK BLACKS**

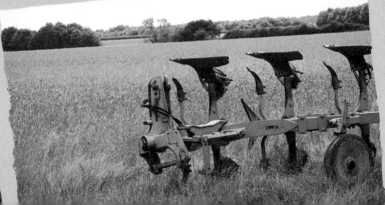

THUX

21 TALKING TURKEY

It wouldn't be stretching it to say that James Graham, fifth-generation turkey farmer and breeder, is a world authority on Norfolk Black turkeys. He can even talk turkey — a warbley yodel that is immediately answered by the loudest, funniest, strangest cacophony of a thousand gobbling turkeys. Spending a morning with him at his farm in Thuxton, Norfolk was a privilege and a chance to see that, along with his turkeys, he is a rare breed himself. James is passionate about protecting this heritage breed through traditional, sustainable farming methods.

It was Henry VIII that first singled out the breed as special. Norfolk then secured its reputation as a poultry area due to the abundance of corn and arable crops to feed them. For centuries East Anglian turkey breeders hired drovers to walk the turkeys to London, setting off in November so they arrived in time for Christmas. The turkeys' feet were tarred and feathered to protect them from all the walking.

In 1932 James' grandfather Frank came across some of the last surviving Norfolk Blacks and dedicated himself to conserving the breed. James continues to rear them using the same additive- and antibiotic-free methods, allowing them to mature slowly on a diet of home-grown wheat, barley and corn.

Most commercially reared turkeys are bronze turkeys. The black turkey has a unique textured meat and tastes slightly gamey, and of course has the glossy jet-black plumage. In fact, the beautiful black feathers plucked from James' turkeys have played starring roles on the silver screen as Kevin Costner's arrow flights, as period costume decorations in *Downton Abbey* and they have also been invited to several Royal weddings atop an elegant hat.

Peele's Norfolk Black Turkeys
Rookery Farm, Thuxton, Norwich, Norfolk NR9 4QJ • 01362 850237
www.peeles-blackturkeys.co.uk

Pitch Up

Thetford Forest Camping and Caravanning Club Site

Puddledock Lane, Great Hockham,
Thetford, Norfolk IP24 1FJ • 01953 498455
www.campingandcaravanningclub.co.uk
Wonderfully friendly and attractive site on the edge
of Thetford Forest – a low-lying pine forest. There
are electric hook-ups, pristine showers, a family
bathroom, a laundrette, children's play area and a
site shop. 150 pitches are split over three different
camping areas, giving an opportunity for different
camping moods. I like the small but pretty fishing
lake overlooked by wooden camping pods (available
for hire), and also love the fact there are plentiful fruit
trees around the site. Staff actively encourage campers
to pick the fruit for themselves.

Local food options are great here. An excellent
burger van comes on a Wednesday. It's run by local
farmers Geoff and Kate who rear the pigs and lamb,
then make all the burgers and sausages themselves.
Geoff is always trying new flavour combinations: pork
and chilli, Moroccan lamb, lamb and mint ... Kate
delivers fresh eggs to the site throughout the week,
but Saturdays are hog roast day. There's a fish and
chip van on Fridays and a produce market in nearby
Watton every Wednesday.

Church Farm (CS)

Carbrooke Road, Ovington, near Watton, Thetford,
Norfolk IP25 6SD • 01953 885019
www.campingandcaravanningclub.co.uk
Hidden away down a country lane, Church Farm
site is one large (slightly sloping) field sheltered by
trees. Run by the wonderfully friendly Marie-Ana,
who'll point you in the direction of local markets and
good pubs, it's a simple site but offers electric, toilets
and a shower. There's also plentiful peace and quiet.
In season you'll find excess allotment produce sold
by a neighbour just up the road, while Wednesday's
Watton market will enable you to fill your basket with
essentials from nearby farms, bakeries and kitchens.

The Garden House (CS)

Quidenham Road, Kenninghall, Norfolk NR16 2EF
01953 887128 • www.campingandcaravanningclub.
co.uk
Angela and Ian are great hosts at this quiet and
secluded site. The flat field is sheltered by trees and
has a pretty old flint wall with glimpses of pastoral
delights on the other side. The simple facilities consist
of loo, shower and washing-up sink. More importantly
it's an easy walk to **The Red Lion** pub in the village
that serves a good selection of local ale. What more
could you want? A giant communal fire pit? Done.

Eat Local

Steven Smith

23 High Street, Watton, Thetford, Norfolk IP25 6AB
01953 885467
Locally sourced turkey steaks are available all year
round at Smith's butchers, who are also renowned
locally for their hot meat counter. Hot turkey
baguettes are the popular choice. Steven also rears
his own turkeys for Christmas.

Yallops

St Leonards Street, Mundford, Thetford, Norfolk
IP26 5HG • 01842 878287
This village butchers sells turkey mince and turkey
steaks throughout the year.

Elveden Estate Food Hall

Brandon Road, Elveden, Thetford, Norfolk IP24 3TQ
01842 898068 • www.elvedencourtyard.com
The label 'food hall' immediately gives an indication
of the class of this place. The estate owners support
around 50 small local artisan food producers by
showcasing them in their shop where you'll find a
delightful array of fresh meats and cheeses, breads,
fruit and vegetables, pickles, jams and chutneys, cakes,
biscuits, chocolates and sweets – and an impressive
wine cellar. The butchers' counter sells turkey steaks
and turkey mince for the recipe. Spend the morning
browsing food, home ware and garden shops then
recover in the cafe.

J Jones Butchers

King Street, Thetford, Norfolk IP24 2AP
01842 752218
This well-respected butcher tempts high street
shoppers by cooking sausages outside his shop.

Farmers' Markets

Wyken Vineyard

Wyken Road, Stanton, Bury St Edmunds, Suffolk
IP31 2DW • 01359 250262 • www.wykenvineyards.
co.uk • Every Saturday
A hugely popular Saturday market with tables
straining beneath the best of the area's produce.
The Vineyard is a perfect day out for any food lover.

Diss Farmers' Market

Market Place, Diss, Norfolk IP22 4AB
www.disscouncil.com/market.php • 2nd Saturday
of the month
There is also a weekly general market on a Friday
with a few local food stalls including a fishmonger
and greengrocer.

Watton Village Market

High Street, Watton, Norfolk • Every Wednesday
Although not a certified farmers' market there is
good attendance from local producers at this weekly
Wednesday market. Look out for fresh fish, just-baked
bread and a great pie man.

TURKEY AND APPLE BURGERS

These make a lighter change from your usual beef burger on the barbecue. You can vary the herbs you use.

Serves 4

350g turkey mince

4 spring onions, finely sliced

1 apple, peeled, cored and grated

75g white breadcrumbs
(roll up 3 thick slices and grate them)

1 tsp dried mixed herbs

salt and pepper

1 medium egg, beaten

olive oil

To serve

4 baps

2-3 tbsp farm shop fruit chutney, mango chutney or sweet chilli sauce if you like a bit of heat

1 extra apple, cored and sliced into rings

- Place the turkey mince in a mixing bowl and stir in the spring onions, grated apple, breadcrumbs and mixed herbs. Add seasoning to taste — lots of pepper — and mix the ingredients together.

- Bind together really well with the beaten egg and form into 8 round patties of about 1.5cm thick

- Put the patties on a plate and stick into a cool-box or fridge for about 30 minutes to firm up. Let them come back up to normal temperature for 10 minutes before you want to cook them.

- Heat up your barbecue. Brush your barbecue hot plate or grill (or large frying pan) with a little oil, and then cook the burgers. Depending on your heat source this should take about 5-6 minutes on each side. Turn the burgers only once, halfway through cooking, to prevent them falling apart. When they are cooked just cut into one to check there are no pink juices.

- Split the baps and place, split-side down, over the hot coals for 1-2 minutes or until lightly toasted.

- Spread one side of the bap with a little fruit or mango chutney. Top with the cooked turkey burgers, lay a slice of apple on each burger, and cover with the lid.

HEART OF ENGLAND

A gastronomic tour around England's heartland offers an intoxicating fusion of traditional dishes rooted in the region's industrial past mixed with new cooking styles. Bakewell and Melton Mowbray are well known for their eponymous dishes and you'll find fantastic new cheeses, glorious Herefordshire ciders and hearty bakes and cakes in the Derbyshire villages. It's a region of contrasts, from gritty urban landscapes to honey-hued villages – and the variety of food is just as exciting.

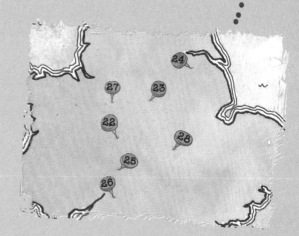

22 PIGS IN SPACE

Two of our most distinct regional foods, Stilton cheese and the Melton Mowbray pork pie, hail from the Midlands – an area usually thought of in terms of its industrial heritage. But beyond the sprawl of urban hubs are pockets of rural oasis and productive farmland.

A brief account of the area's food story might go like this … The fertile pasturelands in the East Midlands provided great dairy, which in turn inspired cheesemaking, giving us some legendary regional cheeses, Stilton and Red Leicester. The whey (that's the by-product from the cheesemaking) provided good fodder for pigs, thus a thriving pork industry developed. The off-cuts of pork couldn't be wasted so were encased in pastry to make a conveniently transportable pork pie in the pockets of agricultural workers. And so it goes round …

The area remains big on pigs. Hunted by William the Conqueror, large numbers of wild boars once ran through Cannock Chase, now a designated Area of Outstanding Natural Beauty just north of Birmingham.

Woodland pigs were eventually herded and penned (making them fatter) and interbred to become prime meat producers. By the 18th century Staffordshire, Northamptonshire and Leicestershire became key areas for pig breeding. Tamworth, a town just south of Cannock Chase, gives its name to a distinctive ginger pig of lean body and long snout, which was revered for its bacon. Having never been crossbred with Asian pigs, like so many other breeds in this country, its pork tastes quite different, and it's considered by some to be the original English pig.

Rob and Alec Mercer are fourth-generation pig farmers at Packington Free Range, a pork farm known for its ethical farming practices. "There is too much emphasis on speedy results at ever lower cost in food farming today," explains Alec, "and this impacts on animal welfare and the environment as much as on the quality of the meat."

In partnership with Natural England they take part in schemes such as planting grass margins around their fields to protect hedgerows and encourage wildlife. Many of their field corners are planted with wild bird seed mixes or pollen and nectar mixes to supply insects and farmland birds with vital food sources. Their pigs have plenty of space to graze and forage completely naturally, so the pork is additive-, hormone-, and growth promoter-free and there's no water added. So, if you are partial to a decent sausage or a proper bacon sandwich – this is where to find it.

www.packingtonfreerange.co.uk

Pitch Up

Reindeer Park Lodge

Kingsbury Road, Lea Marston, Warwickshire
B76 0DE • 01675 470811 • www.reindeerpark.co.uk
You can camp with reindeers in 100 acres of parkland
just 10 minutes away from Birmingham city centre.
Strange, but true. Reindeer Park is a picturesque
hideaway with a tiny campsite. The pitches overlook
pristine parkland roamed by reindeer, pygmy
goats and mini-pigs. The facilities are modern and
immaculate, plus there is a washing machine and
drying facilities. Each pitch has hard standing, electric,
WiFi and water supply.

Cannock Chase Camping and Caravanning Club Site

Old Youth Hostel, Wandon, Rugeley, Staffordshire
WS15 1QW • 01889 582166
www.campingandcaravanningclub.co.uk
Location wins out over fancy facilities here. You have
direct access out onto the Chase from this site, one
of the Midlands' most popular beauty spots. It's a
pretty little campsite sheltered by trees and visited by
wildlife, and you can choose between hard standing or
grass pitches. There is a shop for basic provisions.

Sealwood Cottage Campsite (CS)

Sealwood Lane, Linton, Derbyshire DE12 6PA
01283 761371 • www.sealwoodcottage.co.uk
You can sit by your pitch and sup wine from this
campsite's own vineyard – book a tour around the
vines if you are keen. Set in a pretty pocket of the
National Forest, the simple site is a long grass strip
backed by trees and bushes and fronted by beautiful
countryside views. The facilities are new and spotless
and it's just a short walk to the local village.

Eat Local

The Butcher, The Baker, The Ice Cream Maker

Barton Marina, Barton-under-Needwood,
Staffordshire DE13 8DZ • 01283 711002
www.bbicm.co.uk
Great name for a great farm shop. You can buy
Packington pork here, and all the other meats
are sourced from within the National Forest and
surrounds. They hand-bake their own range of
delicious meat pies, pasties, sausage rolls and
turnovers. For the barbecue there's home-produced
sausages, burgers and great home-smoked bacon.

Manor Farm Fruits

Manor Farm, Hints, Tamworth, Staffordshire B78
3DW • 01543 483308 • www.manorfarmfruits.co.uk
This is one of Staffordshire's longest established soft
fruit growers and one of the few remaining pick-
your-own farms in the area. With over 85 acres of
strawberries, raspberries and other soft fruit to choose
from, you can fill your punnets and have a decent
fruit-filled picnic then grab a cuppa while the children
exhaust themselves in the play area.

Bradshaw Bros Farm Shop

Ironstone Road, Burntwood, Staffordshire WS7 1YL
01543 279437 • www.bradshawbros.co.uk
The farm rears traditional breeds such as Hereford
beef, Gloucester Old Spot pork and Suffolk lamb.
To try before you buy from the shop, head to the cafe
for a great breakfast sandwich, hot steak baguette or a
proper farmers' ham, egg and chips. Perfect.

Packington Moor Farm Shop

Packington Moor Farm, Jerrys Lane, Packington, Lichfield, Staffordshire WS14 9QB • 01543 481223
www.packingtonmoor-farmshop.co.uk
Bakery, butchery and grocery come together to make this a great one-stop shop for a basket full of quality local goods. Packington pork and chicken is sold here alongside other local meats and game. There are fresh daily bakes of pastries and pies, cold meats, pâtés and a cheese counter to make the region proud. Veggies are homegrown.

P Coates & Son

100 Main Street, Alrewas, Staffordshire DE13 7AE
01283 790205 • www.coatestraditionalbutchers.co.uk
If you like a proper traditional butcher's shop – this is it. Antony Coates knows pretty much everything there is to know about great meat and animal welfare and is happy to provide any cut of meat along with cooking advice and recipes. You can buy Packington pork here.

Chase Farm Shop

Weeford Road, Roughley, Sutton Coldfield, West Midlands B75 5RL • 0121 308 1946
www.chasefarmshop.co.uk
Pedigree Limousin cattle are the focus of the farm, but the shop also offers a wonderful selection of fresh, baked and chilled delights. The meat counter is outstanding. The cakes are made by the farmer's wife and the cafe serves great English breakfasts and hearty roasts.

Farmers' Markets
Lichfield Farmers' Market

Market Street, Lichfield, Staffordshire WS13 6LH
1st Thursday of the month
The last man to be burnt at the stake in England met his untimely end here in Lichfield's market place in 1612. These days the square bustles with happy farmers and marketgoers. General markets are held weekly on Tuesday, Friday and Saturday.

Cannock Farmers' Market

Market Place, Cannock, Staffordshire WS11 1BP
3rd Friday of the month
This market has over 35 stalls.

Tamworth Farmers' Market

The Town Hall, Market Street, Tamworth, Staffordshire B79 7LU
www.staffordshirecountrymarkets.co.uk
Every Friday

Moseley Farmers' Market

Village Green, Moseley, West Midlands B13 8HW
www.moseleyfarmersmarket.org.uk • Last Saturday of the month
Moseley Farmers' Market's 60 stalls cater for everyone's needs, whether it be fruit and vegetables, cheeses and wine or pies and beer. Everything available is guaranteed to be local and reared, grown or processed by the people selling.

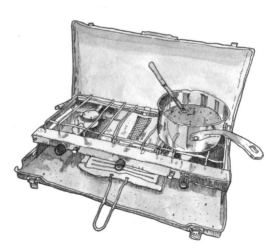

PORK BELLY BITES

AND ITALIAN BREAD SALAD

Pork belly is most often used for long, slow roasting. This, however, is a quick pan-fry recipe that will become a good-value family favourite. The flavours in this dish remind me of the Italian porchetta I had on my honeymoon. The fennel seeds make this dish – don't leave them out.

Serves 4

4 strips of pork belly

olive oil

1 tsp fennel seeds

1 tsp paprika

grated zest of 1 lemon

1 tsp caster sugar

1 large garlic clove, skin on

1 large bunch of spring onions, sliced diagonally

1 tbsp sweet chilli sauce

4 tbsp full-fat crème fraîche

4 wraps or soft buns, to serve

For an Italian-inspired salad

8 ripe tomatoes (they have to be ripe)

1 small stale ciabatta loaf (or any good stale white loaf), torn into 2cm chunks

½ cucumber, diced

½ red onion, very thinly sliced

4 tinned anchovies (optional), broken into pieces

salt and pepper

2 tbsp balsamic vinegar or red wine vinegar

6 tbsp olive oil

a handful of basil leaves, torn

a little lemon juice

- Cut any skin off the pork and discard. Cut the pork belly strips into 1cm dice.

- Heat a glug of olive oil in a large frying pan. Put the pork pieces in the pan, along with the fennel seeds, paprika and lemon zest. Add the sugar, just to caramelise the edges.

- Add the garlic clove, which you lightly crush first. No need to peel it, as you'll take the clove out at the end. Then add the spring onions.

- Stir everything about to stop it sticking, and do keep an eye on it.

- While it's cooking, prepare the salad. Cut the ripe tomatoes into eighths. Put in a bowl along with the bread, cucumber, red onion and anchovies. Season well with salt and pepper.

- Pour the vinegar and olive oil over the top, then put your hands in and give it a good mix. Top with shredded basil leaves if you have them and a squeeze of lemon juice.

- For your sauce, mix the sweet chilli sauce into the crème fraîche.

- Now, check your pork. If in doubt, cut a cube open; there should be no pink juices. Remove the garlic clove.

- Spoon the pork and spring onions into a wrap or soft bun, add a dollop of sauce then serve with the tomato salad.

FLASH IN THE PAN PORK

WITH CIDER AND CREAM

Serves 2

I call it flash-in-the-pan because it's quick, easy and can be cooked in one large frying pan. It's perfect if you are camping alone, or just have a single gas burner. All of the ingredients can be sourced in your average farm shop – pork tenderloin, a bottle of locally made cider, cream, apples, an onion and some fresh bread. Six basic ingredients can be turned into a tremendous supper.

- Cut the tenderloin into slices (medallions) of about 1.5cm thick. I allow about 4 per person.

- Using a large frying pan, melt the butter and add a splash of olive oil to stop the butter burning too quickly.

- As it starts to foam, put in the apple and onion pieces. Cook for about 5 minutes until they start to soften and brown slightly. Once that has happened, remove the apple and onion from the pan, using a slotted spoon, and set to one side.

- Keep the pan on the heat. Season the pork medallions and put them in the fat remaining in the pan. Cook for about 2 minutes on each side.

- Now pour in the cider — make sure the cider is a dry one, otherwise the dish becomes too sweet — and let it bubble until reduced to about half. This will probably take about 4 minutes.

- Return the apple and onion to the pan and pour in the cream. Turn the heat right down and stir the cream through until it has heated.

- Take the pan off the heat, and serve the pork on a large piece of thick rustic toast, with the apple, onion, cider and cream sauce poured over it. You could use mashed potato and salad, instead of the bread, for a more substantial meal.

1 pork tenderloin (about 200g)

a generous knob of butter

olive oil

1 large apple, skin on, cored and chopped into wedges (something medium-tart like a Braeburn)

1 large onion, cut into wedges

salt and pepper

100ml dry cider

3 tbsp single cream

2 thick slices rustic or country bread, toasted

23 CHATSWORTH FARM SHOP

For all the priceless artwork and gilded artefacts in Chatsworth House, the lavish Derbyshire stately home of the Duke and Duchess of Devonshire, I rate the farm shop more highly. Not just because of the food (although that is first class) but because of what it represents. The produce in the shop has a greater impact on the surrounding economy and landscape than any of the Old Masters in the house ever could.

One of the country's original farm shops, and certainly the first ever set up on an estate, it was the inspired decision of the then Duchess of Devonshire (née 'Debo' Mitford) who became a bit of a trailblazer in the local food movement in 1977. She wanted the tenant farmers on her estate to have more control over their financial futures and get a fair price for their produce and saw that cutting out the middle man and selling directly to the customer would go some way to helping out.

The late Duchess was proud of the 'food yards, not food miles' status of her shop, with meat from the cows and sheep you see in the fields as you drive towards the house and venison and pheasant from the estate, too. One of the first things she did was to put a baker in the shop, so all the cakes, breads and pies are also made in-house.

From cheese to yoghurt and ice-cream, a lot of the shop's produce comes from the tenanted farms as well as artisan food producers in the area, some of whom have been suppliers for 30 years. The shop runs regular 'Meet your suppliers' events including free tastings.

It was also the Duchess's idea to open an educational working farmyard on the estate where children can meet farmers and watch cows being milked to help them make the connection between the animals on the farm and the food on their plate.

And that is exactly what a proper farm shop does. You buy the food from the place that produced it, and in doing so support the farmer who looks after the countryside around you. The late Duchess just saw the sense in that earlier than most.

Chatsworth Farm Shop
Pilsley, Derbyshire DE45 1UF • 01246 565411 • www.chatsworth.org

Ready when you are

It takes just minutes to get the cakes from our bakery onto the shelves.

Pitch Up

Heathy Roods Farm (CS)

Butterton, Staffordshire ST13 7SR • 01538 304397
www.heathyroodsfarm.co.uk

Take a deep breath, then breathe out slowly. You'll do this many times as you stand on top of the hill that is Heathy Roods campsite and survey the utter beauty around you. It won't be long before the magic of this place has eradicated every bit of modern-day stress from your body (and all the signal from your phone!). Campfires, hot showers, lovely owners and did I mention the views?

Laneside Caravan Park

Hope, Hope Valley, Derbyshire S33 6RR
01433 620215 • www.lanesidecaravanpark.co.uk

If you like your campsites well-ordered, neat and tidy then Laneside will appeal. The welcome is always warm and the owners work hard to keep the place immaculate – the floral displays are very impressive. The site has static caravans and a small shop. A small river runs through the site providing a focal point for both campers and kingfishers. The views across the Peaks are fabulous, as is the location for exploring this beautiful part of the world. Castleton caves and the Pennine Way are walkable and Chatsworth is 15 minutes away.

Bakewell Camping and Caravanning Club Site

Hopping Lane, Youlgreave, Bakewell, Derbyshire DE45 1NA • 01629 636555
www.campingandcaravanningclub.co.uk

Bakewell campsite enjoys a peaceful, rural setting with stunning views over the Derbyshire countryside. The attractive site is excellently maintained and its 100 pitches are spacious, some benefitting from the shelter of the trees that dot the site. It's worth being aware that this is a basic site with no toilets or showers so it is suited to campers with their own facilities. Bakewell town is just five miles away – go there and try the authentic pudding (not tart!).

Eat Local

Chatsworth Farm Shop
Pilsley, Derbyshire DE45 1UF • 01246 565411
www.chatsworth.org

Watson's Farm Shop
Leacroft, Edale Road, Hope, Hope Valley, Derbyshire
S33 6ZF • 01433 620223 • www.watsonsfarmshop.co.uk
A carnivorous camper's dream – this small family-run farm on the slopes of Losehill in the heart of the National Park is a great place to come to stock up on delicious meats for your barbecue. For a champion campers' breakfast you can have home-cured bacon and choose from an impressive selection of sausages. The black pudding is the signature product not to be missed.

The Farmers' Market Shop
3 Market Street, Bakewell, Derbyshire DE4 1HG
01629 815814 • www.thefarmersmarketshop.co.uk
This attractive little shop sources as much as possible within a 30-mile radius, although the rules are extended somewhat on teas and coffees. Regardless, the central philosophy of knowing the source of their products results in shelves stocked with unique, varied and distinct cheeses, deli meats and store-cupboard essentials.

The Old Original Bakewell Pudding Shop
The Square, Bakewell, Derbyshire DE45 1BT
01629 812193 • www.bakewellpuddingshop.co.uk
This is your chance to sample the famous eponymous pie.

Thornbridge Riverside Brewery
Buxton Road, Bakewell, Derbyshire DE45 1GS
www.thornbridgebrewery.co.uk
The multi-award-winning Thornbridge Brewery offers tours and tastings. Cask, keg and bottled beers cover

> "You buy the food from the place that produced it, and in doing so support the farmer who looks after the countryside around you."

an eclectic range of styles: Vienna-style lager, Bavarian beers, creamy vanilla and raspberry stout and Scotch Ale matured in whisky casks are just for starters.

Farmers' Markets
Bakewell Farmers' Market
Agricultural Business Centre, Agricultural Way, Bakewell, Derbyshire DE45 1AH • Last Saturday of the month.
A huge, fantastically vibrant market with over 70 stalls. Many sell out before closing so make sure you get there early. There is plenty of parking.

Leek Fine Food Market
Market Place, Leek, Staffordshire ST13 5HH
3rd Saturday of the month
Great food, entertainment, live music and cookery demos.

Buxton Farmers' Market
St John's Road, Buxton, Derbyshire SK17 6XN
1st Thursday of the month
This lovely indoor market is always well attended. As well as the range of meats, cheeses and locally brewed drinks, you can buy freshly made pizza and pies.

STICKS AND DIPS
SWEET AND SOUR PORK

Serves 4

A meal on a stick is a culinary novelty, loved by adults and children alike. My children whinge about eating meat or vegetables served on a plate but give them the same meal piled on a skewer, and it seems that different rules apply.

You can adapt your stick contents according to what you have found in the market or farm shop that day: a nice piece of beef or a tasty pork steak, along with some seasonal veggies, and you've got a easy and exciting dinner in the bag.

Master a few dips and you can mix and match until the cows come home. This sweet and sour pork dish can also be made with child-friendly sausages.

- A couple of hours before you are ready to cook, cut the pork steaks into 3cm cubes. (By the way, don't pick the leanest pork as it will dry out too quickly; a bit of fat is good here.)

- Mix all the dip ingredients except for the cornflour together in a cup or bowl.

- Put the pork pieces in a freezer bag and add 3 tbsp of the dip mixture to the bag. Mix to coat well, then leave in a cool-box to marinate the meat for 2 hours if possible.

- When you are ready to cook, cut your pineapple rings into pieces roughly the same size as the pork.

- Do the same with the peppers — cut them roughly into squares of 3cm.

- Thread the marinated pork pieces alternately with the pieces of pepper and pineapple on to 4 skewers (soaked if wooden). Leave enough room at one end for you to hold.

- Put the kebab sticks on to the barbecue or hotplate and cook for about 12 minutes, turning them attentively.

- While they are cooking, make your dip. Put the remaining dip mixture into a small pan, or little frying pan, along with the cornflour and mix it together well. Then put the pan on the heat and keep stirring until the sauce thickens. Take off the heat immediately and decant the dip into a bowl to cool a little.

- Check that the juices run clear on your pork pieces to confirm that it is cooked. Don't feel afraid to cut a piece open and check to make sure.

- Serve the pork skewers with your sweet and sour dip. You could also serve this with rice, or keep it simple and have it in a wrap.

300g pork steaks

1 small (220g) tin pineapple rings in natural juice

1 red pepper, 1 yellow pepper and 1 green pepper

For the sweet and sour dip

2 tbsp soy sauce

3 tbsp tomato ketchup

3 tbsp rice wine vinegar

3 tsp caster sugar

75ml pineapple juice from the tin

1½ tsp cornflour

CHILLI
CORN ON THE COB

A corn on the cob on the barbecue is a classic campsite favourite. This adds chilli butter for a bit of a kick, although you can make up all sorts of butter flavours from a simple garlic to fresh herb butter or even a pesto one. If this is for children, you can leave out the chilli and use a teaspoon of smoked paprika instead.

If you can't find corn cobs with their leaves on, you can still make this dish by wrapping the cobs up in foil and putting some of the butter mixture inside. You shouldn't put raw kernels directly on to the heat as they won't cook properly and will just taste burnt.

Serves 4

4 corn cobs, outer leaves still on

100g butter (leave it out for a while to go soft)

2 garlic cloves, finely chopped

1 tbsp runny honey

juice of ½ lemon

1 small mild, fresh red chilli, very finely chopped

black pepper

- Heat up the barbecue and place the corn cobs, in their outer leaves, on to the griddle. They will need to cook for about 30 minutes and you will need to turn them intermittently to cook evenly.

- In a metal bowl, aluminium tray or small saucepan, put the butter, garlic, honey, lemon, chilli and a few shakes of black pepper.

- When the cobs have been cooking for about 20 minutes, mix the bowl or saucepan of the chilli butter mixture on the edge of the barbecue so that it begins to melt — but not bubble!

- Once the corn has cooked, the outer husk will have charred and the kernels will have gone soft. Take it off the heat, strip back the leaves and then baste the corns with the chilli mixture. Put back on to the barbecue for another 5 minutes.

- Then put the corn cobs on a plate, with the pulled back husks facing outwards so that people can use them as a handle, then drizzle more of the butter over the top and add extra black pepper.

- Let everyone serve themselves. Just remember to hand out kitchen paper to catch the butter dribbles.

24 LINCOLNSHIRE
SAIL AWAY

If you buy a postcard on your Lincolnshire holiday, I bet it will have a windmill on it. Standing tall and proud on an otherwise flat landscape, these graceful icons offer a reassuring reminder of times past: a time when the pace of life was slow enough to wait for the wind to grind your flour, and gentle folk spent their morning making the daily bread.

Mount Pleasant Windmill in North Lincolnshire is one of the few working mills left in the county. It was restored in 2000 by Mervin Austin, a baker who had worked in London for 30 years and wanted to run his own organic bakery, despite never having milled before. "I knew everything there was to know about flour so I was halfway there," he laughs. "Modern roller mills grind the wheat at tremendous speed which damages the starch and heats up the flour, destroying the vitamins and nutrients in the wheatgerm. Grinding it traditionally gets a better product."

Mervin now stonegrinds 10 different organic flours, which he sells in the tearooms. He also sells 30 varieties of bread, baked in his 18-ton wood-fired oven, in his True Loaf Bakery next door.

Mervin is continuing a long-held tradition of millers and bakers in Lincolnshire – a county perfectly suited to both activities. The flat, fertile fields (Lincolnshire is one of the most productive areas for home-grown produce in the UK), are perfect for growing wheat and corn, and being a famously low-lying region, windmills take the full impact of the wind.

At its peak the county had more than 500 windmills in operation. Even when other areas of the country started to abandon windmills in favour of engine-powered mills, Lincolnshire persevered with wind power. Only 136 mills now remain, many converted into quirky houses, tearooms or visitor attractions and just a handful continuing as working mills producing flour which can be bought by the public.

A discussion of milling and baking in Lincolnshire is not complete without a mention of Plum Bread – the region's speciality loaf. It's a rich and heavy bread made with dried fruits – no actual plums, strangely. Secret recipes for the loaf are passed down through generations, with one of the best coming from **Myers Bakery** in the village of Horncastle (see page 193), where the Myer family have made and sold plum loaf in their bakery since 1969.

Come here to sample a slice of Lincolnshire history. Buy plum bread and perhaps a wedge of Lincolnshire Poacher Cheese in Myers Deli next to the bakery, sit beneath those huge Lincolnshire skies and take a few minutes to taste a slower pace of life.

Mount Pleasant Windmill and True Loaf Bakery

North Cliff Road, Kirton-in-Lindsey, Lincolnshire DN21 4NH
01652 640177 • www.trueloafbakery.co.uk

Pitch Up

Woodhall Spa Camping and Caravanning Club Site

Wellsyke Lane, Kirkby-on-Bain, Woodhall Spa, Lincolnshire LN10 6YU • 01526 352911 www.campingandcaravanningclub.co.uk
This is a pretty, rural campsite bordered by trees and favoured by rabbits and wild birds such as woodpeckers and moorhens. The site has its own lake. There are 90 pitches and a choice of both open field pitches or secluded wooded ones and grass or hard-standing areas. There's a charming children's play area and lovely walks through the woods. Get fresh eggs just up the road at Brackenside Farm.

Lincolnshire Lanes

Manor Farm, East Firsby, Lincolnshire LN8 2DB
01673 878258 • www.lincolnshire-lanes.com
Hidden among a grove of Christmas trees this friendly, homely site caters for all breeds of campers. There is a quiet field, a family field and a rally field as well as a little play area for children with some rabbits and guinea pigs. Showers and toilets are spick and span. For an alternative stay you can hire a log cabin, tipi or gypsy caravan. The Roman city of Lincoln and pretty Market Rasen are nearby, as is the **Mount Pleasant Windmill** and the wonderful **Uncle Henry's Farm Shop** (see page 194).

Willow Farm Campsite (CS)

Willow Farm, North Drove, Martin Dales, Woodhall Spa, Lincolnshire LN10 6XN • 01526 353206 www.campingandcaravanningclub.co.uk
Tucked away down a country lane, this serene and secluded site is an excellent base for some easy cycling as it's surrounded by lots of quiet, flat, back roads. Willow Farm is listed as one of Camping and Caravanning Club's 'Hideaway' sites, a claim that it certainly lives up to. Wonderfully quiet with lovely pitches, there's a water tap and electric point with each pitch but no showers or toilets.

Eat Local

Maud Foster Windmill

Willoughby Road, Boston, Lincolnshire PE21 9EG
01205 352188 • www.maudfoster.co.uk
At over 80ft tall, with sails that are 37ft long, Maud Foster is the tallest working windmill in England. Energetic visitors can climb its seven floors, watch flour being made in the traditional way and step out onto the viewing platform to take in the surrounding views. Bags of organic flour and porridge oats can be bought in the mill shop.

Five Sailed Windmill

32 East Street, Alford, Lincolnshire LN13 9EH
01507 462136 • www.alford-windmill.co.uk
This beautiful mill on the edge of the market town of Alford welcomes visitors and sells its stoneground wholemeal organic flour and oats.

Sibsey Trader Windmill

Frithville Road, Sibsey, Boston,
Lincolnshire PE22 0SY • 01205 750036
www.sibseytraderwindmill.co.uk
Built in 1877, this is one of the few six-sailed mills left
in England. It is open for visitors and has a convenient
tearoom in which to rest your legs after the five-storey
climb. Stoneground organic flour can be bought from
the mill shop.

Myers Bakery

20 The Bullring, Horncastle, Lincolnshire LN9 5HU
01507 522234 • www.myersbakery.co.uk
As well as the bakery there's a cafe serving delicious
cakes, morning coffees, lunches using local produce
and afternoon teas. The deli is packed with regional
specialities including a great cheese selection with
award-winning Lincolnshire Poacher and the tasty
mature cheddar known as The Dambuster. You can
buy flour from the Maud Foster mill. Even the crisps
are from Lincolnshire.

Field Farm Shop

High Toynton, Horncastle, Lincolnshire LN9 6NL
01507 523934 • www.fieldfarmshop.co.uk
Everything produced on this poultry, livestock and
vegetable produce farm is sold through the shop.
This is where to come for true Lincolnshire sausages.
Using only five ingredients – pork, sage, bread, salt
and pepper – they taste fantastic. The pork is from the
farm's pedigree Berkshire herd who spend their time
clearing the past year's vegetable beds.

Leagate Farm Shop

Leagate Road, Tumby, Boston, Lincolnshire
PE22 7SY • 01526 344092
Packed with home-grown summer fruits, Myers Plum
Bread, the locals' favourite 'Lymn Bank' Cheese and
Maud Foster organic flour, it's just 10 minutes from
Woodhall Spa campsite.

Mountain's Boston Sausage

13 High Street, Boston, Lincolnshire PE21 8SH
01205 362167 • www.bostonsausage.co.uk
Lincolnshire is a stronghold for artisan butchers and
the wonderfully named Mountain's Boston Sausage
specialise in the finest-quality handmade Lincolnshire
sausages and other locally sourced meat. Alongside
traditional cuts are regional specialities such as stuffed
Chine, a traditional dish of salt pork stuffed with
herbs, and Haslet, a ball of pork mince seasoned with
sage, salt, white bread and pepper.

Sunnyside Up Farm Shop

Poplar Farm, Tealby Road, Market Rasen,
Lincolnshire LN8 3UL • 01673 843840
www.sunnyside-up.co.uk
Farming along organic principles with their rare breed
pigs and pedigree lamb, the folk at Sunnyside apply
equally high standards to sourcing other produce. You
can do a full food shop here for a week of seasonal
fresh veggies, breads, snacks and dairy. The cafe serves
great home-made food.

Uncle Henry's Farm Shop & Coffee Shop

Grayingham Grange Farm, Grayingham,
Gainsborough, Lincolnshire DN21 4JD
www.unclehenrys.co.uk
Focusing on 'fresh, local and seasonal' Uncle Henry's
showcases products from their own farm, Lincolnshire
producers and small local businesses. The shop has
won over 50 awards, the butchery has over 100 – so
you should be in no doubt as to its standards. The
cafe is a real treat. The 'special' boards change daily,
so you might find yourself making repeat visits. How
about Lincoln Red Beef with Tom Wood's Ale Pie or
home-reared gammon with Lincolnshire seasonal veg?
There's a log fire for cold days and a playhouse for
the children.

Farmers' Markets

Good produce markets have always been a way of life
here. Many markets date back hundreds of years and
have an unrivalled reputation for quality and value.
The city of Lincoln runs a great farmers' market where
you can pick up Plum Bread, Lincolnshire Poacher
Cheese and a variety of award-winning meats from
producers such as Redhill Farm and smoked eels from
Smith's Smokery. The market takes place several times
a month in three different locations in Lincoln:

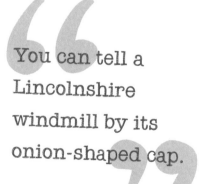

You can tell a
Lincolnshire
windmill by its
onion-shaped cap.

High Street, Lincoln
LN5 7DW • 1st Friday of the month

City Square, Lincoln
LN1 3AA • 2nd Wednesday of the month

Castle Hill, Lincoln
LN1 3AA • 3rd Saturday of the month

Boston Farmers' Market
Wide Bargate, Boston, Lincolnshire PE21 6RX
3rd Wednesday of the month
There have been markets held in this historic market town for over 450 years. As well as the monthly farmers' market, there's a weekly market every Wednesday and Saturday with over 120 stalls, some of which sell local meats and vegetables.

Horncastle Farmers' Market
Wharf Road, Horncastle, Lincolnshire LN9 5HL
4th Saturday of the month

SUMMER BERRY PANCAKES

For my children, a meal isn't complete without a pudding, and that includes when we are camping. These berry pancakes are a perfect Lincolnshire campsite pud, using local flour and any summer berry of your choice. There are plenty of pick-your-own farms around the county. Also pancakes are great for camping – flour, eggs and milk are basics from the local shop. I've added a bit of a twist here, using fruit yoghurt for a denser pancake and also some bicarbonate of soda for a rise.

Makes 10 small pancakes

1 large handful of fresh berries of your choice (raspberries, strawberries, blueberries), cut into small pieces, plus extra to serve

plain yoghurt, to serve

For the pancakes

150g plain flour

½ tsp bicarbonate of soda

½ of one of those big pots of strawberry or raspberry yoghurt (about 200g)

a generous splash of milk

1 large egg

1 tbsp vegetable oil

a knob of butter

- Make the pancakes. Put the flour, bicarb, yoghurt, milk and egg into a big bowl, and whisk them up, giving them a good beating. It will be lumpy at first, and you can add a little more milk if you need to. But remember your mixture needs to be pretty thick, just enough to 'gloop' off your spoon.

- I like my pancake mixture to sit for a bit. I'm not sure why — I think it just feels right after it has had such a beating.

- So while it's resting, heat your griddle or frying pan so it's quite hot. Add the oil and butter.

- Drop some of the batter on, enough to make a circle about the size of a crumpet. Sprinkle some of the fruit on the top of each pancake and cook until the batter starts to bubble.

- Turn over until cooked through, then pop on a plate. Continue until you have used all the batter.

- Serve the pancakes with a dollop of plain yoghurt and extra berries.

GROWING, GROWING, GONE

For some, the first sign of summer is a swallow. For food lovers it's asparagus, supposedly the first vegetable of the summer. It's actually a spring vegetable – the official asparagus season gets going around 23 April, St George's Day, and lasts for just eight weeks.

It is said that asparagus arrived on our shores from Southern Europe in the 16th century. Once we got the taste for it, we started to grow it everywhere, and for a while we grew more than any other country in the world. In 2012 we Brits spent £22 million on asparagus during the British season. And while you can get asparagus all year round, flown in from abroad, there is absolutely *nothing* like British asparagus, freshly picked, in season.

The Vale of Evesham in Worcestershire became the centre of asparagus growing in the 1930s, until the growers had to dig up their asparagus fields to make way for other crops at the beginning of World War II. While it never quite regained its prominence, the area is once again laying claim to being the epicentre of asparagus, with an annual festival dedicated to the vegetable.

Growing asparagus is labour-intensive stuff. Once the cutting process starts, harvesting is continual. An asparagus spear grows a couple of inches every day so whole fields must be harvested on a daily basis. It grows best in flat, well-drained sandy soils. Cutting stops after about six weeks and certainly would not go on beyond 21 June, as the plants need plenty of time to recover before producing another crop the following year. It takes three years from planting to cutting your first crop, but a plant can continue to yield for up to 20 years.

The fresher you can get it the better. Choose asparagus with tightly closed heads and bright green stems. Old asparagus tends to be bendy and a duller green. As soon as it is cut, the sugars in the vegetable start turning to starch and make the spear tougher – another reason not to buy it from the supermarket.

You can't fail to catch asparagus fever if you are travelling through the Vale during the season. Stalls at the end of driveways offer their wares and the local farm shops celebrate the crop, but for a true carnival, time your camping trip to coincide with the Asparafest music and food festival. As well as a packed schedule of bands and performers, recipe exchanges and asparagus-eating competitions, there is a busy local produce market selling asparagus pies, flans and other delights… and plenty of local real ales to wash it down. **www.asparafest.co.uk**

And if you are wondering what to do with the armfuls of asparagus that you'll inevitably take back to the site, they are brilliant on the barbecue. Just brush them with olive oil and sprinkle with sea salt then cook them over medium-hot coals or on a griddle plate for 6-8 minutes. A family favourite is our 'spears in blankets' – wrap a couple of spears in good smoked streaky bacon then cook them over the coals until the bacon is cooked through.

Pitch Up

Winchcombe Camping and Caravanning Club Site

Brooklands Farm, Alderton, near Tewkesbury, Gloucestershire GL20 8NX • 01242 620259
www.campingandcaravanningclub.co.uk
When there are fresh flowers in the men's toilets you know that this is a site that goes the extra mile. With views over the surrounding countryside and a pretty carp pool at the centre, the site shop sells a variety of local produce from nearby farms, dairies, butchers and bakers and there are several local farmers' markets.

Adam Henson's Cotswold Farm Park

Guiting Power, Cheltenham, Gloucestershire GL54 5UG • 01451 850307 • www.cotswoldfarmpark.co.uk/camping
This site is as much loved as the TV presenter and rare breed farmer it's named after. In a field next door to the fabulous Cotswold Farm Park, this is a peaceful and child-friendly campsite. Sixteen of the 40 pitches on the 2-acre level, grassy site have electric hook-ups, and with all the usual washing-up facilities, showers, toilets and so on, all forms of camping are catered for. The site shop is a good one, with everyday provisions including freshly baked home-made bread and local farm produce. You can also take advantage of having 'Adam's Kitchen' on the doorstep, offering delicious home-made cakes and lunches.

Blackmore Camping and Caravanning Club Site

No. 2 Hanley Swan, Worcestershire WR8 0EE
01684 310280 • www.campingandcaravanningclub.co.uk
On the edges of the Vale, this Worcestershire site is well positioned for the Malvern Hills in one direction and the Vale of Evesham in another. Wild camping this isn't, but if you like cleanliness and order, along with friendly staff, you'll love it here. A great local dining pub, **The Bluebell Inn** at Ryall, is good for treat nights.

Eat Local

Chadbury Farm Shop

Chadbury, Evesham, Worcestershire WR11 4TD
01386 446705 • www.chadburyfarmshop.co.uk
This new addition to the Evesham Farm Shop landscape was set up in 2011 in response to the thriving fruit and vegetable industry here. Being fifth-generation farmers of 600 acres of Evesham arable land, they are familiar with the excellent qualities of the soil – and the fantastic foods that grow in it. Keen to support other local growers and producers they stock a wealth of produce from the region.

> **"** There is absolutely nothing like British asparagus, freshly picked, in season. **"**

Hayles Fruit Farm

Winchcombe, Cheltenham, Gloucestershire GL54 5PB • 01242 602123 • www.haylesfruitfarm.co.uk
Set in an Area of Outstanding Natural Beauty, this 100-acre farm offers a range of seasonal PYO fruit such as tayberries and raspberries, and cob nuts. The farm's apple press produces delicious single-variety apple juices made from Greensleeve, Bramley, Red Pippin and Blenheim Orange varieties. The shop also sells seasonal veg including asparagus, locally sourced beef, free-range pork and fresh breads and cakes. The tea shop serves cream teas with strawberry jam or the trademark fruit crumble at your table overlooking the strawberry fields.

Clive's Fruit Farm

Upper Hook Road, Upton upon Severn, Worcestershire WR8 0SA • 01684 592664
www.clivesfruitfarm.co.uk
Clive's Fruit Farm is the real deal. Pioneers of the Pick Your Own concept in the 1960s, the farm continues to be a popular place to come and spend an afternoon filling punnets. Cherries, berries, plums and pears and of course Worcester apple varieties are ripe for the picking (in season, naturally!). Cider and apple juice made on the farm can be bought in the farm shop and, while you are there, why not visit the butchery to pick up some bacon for tomorrow's breakfast?

Revills Farm Shop

Bourne Road, Defford, near Pershore, Worcestershire WR8 9BS • 01386 750466
www.revillsfarmshop.co.uk
In 2003, Isabel Revill started to sell her asparagus from a trestle table with an old cash tin set up in the stables. She gradually introduced other produce from the farm and word got out that a new farm shop had opened. Using networks of other farmers and growers that she met at the local farmers' markets, she began to stock their food, too ... and still does, in this very lovely example of an authentic local farm shop.

BARBECUED AND PINE NUT SALAD ASPARAGUS, ROCKET, GOAT'S CHEESE

This recipe, perfect for a light campsite lunch, was donated to us by the British Asparagus Association at www.british-asparagus.co.uk

Serves 4

- Trim the asparagus as necessary. Place on a baking sheet or in a bowl and toss with the oil, making sure all the asparagus is coated. Season with sea salt and black pepper.

- Put the asparagus on the grill rack of the barbecue and cook for approximately 2 minutes each side, until it is lightly charred. Remove from the barbecue and set aside.

- Make the dressing: mix together all of the ingredients and whisk well. Season to taste.

- Divide the rocket between 4 plates. Top with the barbecued asparagus, crumble over the goat's cheese, sprinkle with the toasted pine nuts and drizzle over the dressing.

- Serve immediately with warm, crusty bread.

2 bundles of British asparagus

2 tbsp olive or rapeseed oil

salt and pepper

100g rocket leaves, washed

150g goat's cheese

1 tbsp pine nuts, dry-toasted

warm crusty bread, to serve

For the dressing

3 tbsp olive or rapeseed oil

juice of 1 lemon

2 tsp grainy mustard

1 tbsp runny honey

26 GLOUCESTERSHIRE

AN APPLE
A DAY

How many varieties of British apple can you name? I'm ashamed to say that I can count the ones I know on two hands and still have a couple of fingers left over. "You could eat a different variety of apple every day for six years and still not come to the end of the list we grow in Britain," says Angela King, founder of Common Ground, the charity that campaigns to save our traditional orchards. That makes well over 2,000 varieties, not including all the cider apples.

The names alone are worthy of our attention, ranging from the romantic-sounding Beauty of Bath and Fair Maid of Devon to the curious Jackets and Waistcoats or the rather off-putting Kill Boys and Hens' Turds. Yet the reason that so many of us have never heard of them is because of how we buy our fruit these days – in plastic bags from the supermarkets. Faced with knobbly and perhaps misshapen forms of our traditional varieties, it seems we'd all rather play it safe with the likes of imported Golden Delicious and Gala.

"I have older people tasting apples from my market stall with tears in their eyes," says Helen Brent-Smith of Day's Cottage, near Stroud, who sells 'heritage variety' juice and apples picked from her Gloucestershire orchard. These customers remember the smell, colours, taste and texture of the lovely old varieties from trees they had in their gardens as children. To them, apples like this are evocative of a time when a piece of fruit was a treat, something of value and, most importantly, something local.

Helen and her partner Dave Kaspar are passionate promoters of old apple varieties. They left jobs in London and moved to a cottage on the family farm in 1989 to find a more gentle pace of life. The old orchards surrounding their cottage produced such abundant crops that Helen and Dave decided to try and make juice out of them. They now produce 25,000 bottles of juice a year and 15,000 gallons of cider and perry.

I tried some apple juice on a visit to their orchards and was amazed how different one variety can taste to another. My taste buds went into overdrive as I tried to keep up with Dave, who was handing me glass after glass. Names and apple facts were coming even faster. It was a good thing we weren't discussing ciders. My favourites were Pipmaston Pineapple, a curious apple that tastes like, well, pineapple and the unusual Taynton Codling, a variety unique to Gloucestershire.

As well as the many varieties of juice, they sell apples in the traditional way; from baskets on their weekly market stalls in Bristol and Stroud Farmers' Markets. Home-grown apples aren't just for autumn as most people think. The apple season runs from July to December. "Week by week we sell different varieties on our stall. We have people coming back asking for the same apples they bought last week, but we have to explain that that's it for another year – or maybe two years in the case of some heritage varieties."

It was a quintessentially beautiful British countryside scene as I walked around the Day's Cottage orchard. There were trees of every shape, size and contortion imaginable. Mist-covered spider's webs were suspended between gnarled old branches, birdsong, bees and butterflies filled the air. Dave points out, "Traditional orchards, where the trees are planted far enough apart, are hugely beneficial for the landscape and wildlife. They encourage biodiversity."

He and Helen have planted a 'museum orchard' to preserve many of the 99 varieties native to Gloucestershire. Re-creating a variety involves grafting, a skill that involves connecting the tissues of a twig from the desired variety onto a root stock of another tree. New varieties are 'invented' by trial, error and years of patience.

There are huge benefits to seeking out local varieties of apple. The range of wonderful flavours, hardiness, shapes, colours and aromas is vast. Buying the fruit and the locally produced juice and cider will help our traditional orchards survive. As campers who take an interest in the countryside around us, we are in the perfect position to do our bit.

Day's Cottage
Upton Lane, Brookthorpe,
Gloucestershire GL4 0UT
01452 813602 • www.dayscottage.co.uk

Pitch Up

Apple Orchard Camping

Whitehouse Farm, Adsett, Westbury on Severn, Gloucestershire GL14 1PH • 01452 760618
www.appleorchardcampsite.co.uk

A brilliant family-run site at the corner of the Forest of Dean surrounded by spirit-lifting views of the Severn Vale and forest landscape. Apples from the on-site orchard are used to make some (rather strong!) cider, which is sold in the little campers' bar in the converted cowshed. Clear that head in the morning with a decent coffee and breakfast served in the cafe, where all the cakes are home-made. The facilities block is top notch, and for even more luxury you can hire the Wishbone Glamping Pods – all you have to bring is your bedding and cooking facilities.

Bracelands Camping in the Forest Site

Bracelands Drive, Coleford, Gloucestershire GL16 7NP • 01594 837258
www.campingintheforest.co.uk

Bracelands is popular with families and groups of friends who are looking for space to run and a forest to explore. The wonderful Wye Valley is your playground and if you are lucky you might spot deer and wild boar on the edges of the site. You can book ranger-led activities from the site or just head off onto the many cycle trails.

> "You could eat a different variety of apple every day for six years..."

Rectory Farm (CS)

Lawn Road, Ashleworth, Gloucestershire GL19 4JL • 01452 700664 • www.rectoryfarm-caravanandcamping.com

Small and simple is sometimes all you need when you want a relaxing break. At Rectory Farm you can enjoy peace and quiet in a sheltered paddock. There isn't electric hook-up but there are toilets and showers. It's a pleasant mile's walk to the local bakery and you can buy eggs and meat from the farm.

Eat Local

Severn and Wye Smokery

Chaxhill, Westbury on Severn, Gloucestershire GL14 1QW • 01452 760190 • www.severnandwye.co.uk

The Rivers Severn and Wye are synonymous with wild salmon and eels. Between the two rivers, this outstanding smokery specialises in both fish. Along with a wealth of delicious smoked goods, the on-site shop sells fresh produce, cheeses, meats and wonderful fresh fish – perfect for the barbecue. It's walkable from Apple Orchard campsite.

Primrose Vale Farm Shop & PYO

Shurdington Road, Bentham, Cheltenham, Gloucestershire GL51 4UA • 01452 863359
www.primrosevale.com

This is a lovely spot to spend a morning hidden among the fruit plants, harvesting some ripe berries. If you don't want to pick your own, the on-site farm shop sells them ready-picked alongside an enticing range of goods, each with local stories. The ethically produced and tasty beef and pork is from **Adey's Organic Meats** in Berkeley, Gloucestershire. There's game from local estates and the most delightful cheese selection, including Mrs Smart's authentic Double Gloucester – famous for the annual cheese rolling just down the road at Coopers Hill.

> ## British Orchards
> Since the 1950s we have lost around 75 per cent of our traditional orchards, many being sold off to developers. As the orchards disappear, so do local landscapes, histories, customs and knowledge, from tree-grafting to wassailing.

Brown and Green, 3 Shires Garden Centre

Ledbury Road, Newent, Gloucestershire GL18 1DL
01531 828590 • www.brown-and-green.co.uk
Celebrating the distinctive nature of artisan products, husband-and-wife team Euan and Susie Keenan have created a shop that is as enjoyable to look around as the food is to eat. Situated in the heart of the Three Counties (Herefordshire, Gloucestershire and Worcestershire), it has some of the best fresh produce on its doorstep. Come here for local seasonal fruit and vegetables, meats, dairy, breads and ciders.

Farmers' Markets
Stroud Farmers' Market

Cornhill, Stroud, Gloucestershire GL5 2HH
www.fresh-n-local.co.uk • Every Saturday
What can I say? A visit to this market will have you wishing that all food shopping could be this much fun. The market has won every award going and is often cited as one of the best, if not *the* best in the country. Held every Saturday, there are around 50 stalls, with up to seven organic producers, four cooked food stalls as well as seasonal events, cookery demos, entertainment and a great alfresco market cafe.

Gloucester Farmers' Market

The Cross & Southgate Street, Gloucester, Gloucestershire GL1 2NL • www.fresh-n-local.co.uk
Every Friday • There is also a country market every Thursday

BBQ BAKED APPLES

You'll need a lidded barbecue to make this delicious apple dessert. Or it can be cooked in the embers of a campfire.

Serves 4

4 eating apples (try some heritage ones from Stroud market)

1 large knob of butter

2 tbsp light brown sugar

1 tsp ground cinnamon

a handful each of sultanas and chopped nuts

2 tsp demerara sugar

a splash of booze if there's some around (rum, brandy, cider – not beer or wine!)

- Core the apples, leaving the bottom 2cm in if possible. If that's too hard, take the whole core out, cut the bottom 2cm off the core and plug it back into the bottom of the apple. This is to stop all the melted butter flowing out later.

- Score a line around the centre (fattest part) of the apple.

- Put the butter, light brown sugar and cinnamon in a bowl. Mix in the nuts and sultanas. Use your hands if it's easier to blend it all up into a lumpy paste.

- Push some of the mixture into each apple until it's all used up.

- Place each apple on the centre of a large double-thickness square of foil. Sprinkle a little demerara sugar and some rum or brandy (if using) over the top, then wrap each apple up tight in its own square of foil.

- Put the foil parcels on your barbecue away from the direct heat and close the lid. You'll need to rotate the apples occasionally to enable them to cook evenly.

- They will take about 20 minutes to cook and go soft enough to eat (you don't want mushy), but this will depend on the size of apples and your heat source. So keep an eye on them.

- Serve with cream or plain yoghurt.

27

T 'OAT' ALLY DELICIOUS

Food, with all its traditions, customs and regional recipes, has often had a way of bringing people together. So it was especially poignant when the Hole in the Wall, the last surviving 'front room' Staffordshire oatcakes shop, was demolished in 2012 to make way for a regeneration housing project. Another important bit of British food culture had disappeared for good.

For over 100 years, people had been queuing at the window of the small red-bricked terraced house in Hanley to buy their Staffordshire oatcakes, a local delicacy made from a batter of water, milk, oatmeal and yeast, which is poured on a hot griddle to make a circular pancake-like wrap, to be rolled around a variety of fillings.

Once a rural tradition, oatcake baking became an urban industry around the time of the Industrial Revolution, a time when the pottery factories thrived around Stoke-on-Trent. As the ceramics trade grew, people living in the terraces surrounding the pottery factories baked oatcakes and sold them through their open windows to passing factory workers. Although many of the factories have long gone, the desire for oatcakes remains strong.

I visited the Hole in the Wall just weeks before it closed and the bulldozers moved in. All the terraced houses around the little shop lay as rubble on the ground, yet there was still a throng of people outside this one remaining building, loyal customers who continued to travel every Saturday morning to this particular street corner, drawn together by the humble oatcake – and a sense of community.

Inside the tiny kitchen, smaller than that in many modern six-berth caravans, Glenn Fowler and his wife produced over 2,800 oatcake tortillas a day. A large gas hot plate, cooling rack, a big vat of oatcake mixture and the eponymous hole in the wall – a window through which the waiting masses outside are served – were the simple but vital elements of this busy kitchen.

The customers were a mixed crowd. A quick straw poll among them revealed that top fillings were bacon, cheese, sausage and beans, or any combination of the above. Staffordshire oatcakes are recession-busting food; a cheap and basically nutritious meal for a couple of pounds.

I stood on that street corner and scoffed my tasty cheese and bacon oatcake among the friendly locals. It is refreshingly unpretentious food, but more importantly it is a local product that represents a great deal more than the oats and milk it is made from. Selling Staffordshire oatcakes through this window was a piece of social history that had existed for 100 years. As one customer put it: "this place keeps our community alive; without it, we have nothing left to bring us together."

Fortunately there are still around 30 oatcake shops in and around Stoke-on-Trent. None have the history of the Hole in the Wall, but many make extremely good oatcakes. There are a couple of great traditional options to be found in the residential streets of Stoke-on-Trent. There has been an oatcake shop in High Lane for 100 years, and the current owners of **High Lane Oatcakes** have been there over 35 years, making oatcakes to their closely guarded recipe. Or try the **Oatcake Kitchen** that serves them on tin plates.

A little bit further out of Stoke-on-Trent, and on the last stop of the beautiful Churnet Steam Railway, you'll find **Station Kitchen**, run by Chris Bates. Chris was born just 200 yards from the Hole in the Wall, and grew up with the smell and taste of oatcakes inspiring him to open his own shop. He still makes them to the same 85-year-old recipe that was handed down to him.

High Lane Oatcakes
597-599 High Lane, Burslem, Stoke-on-Trent, Staffordshire ST6 7EP
01782 810180

The Oatcake Kitchen
8-10 Carlisle Street, Dresden, Stoke-on-Trent, Staffordshire ST3 4HA

Station Kitchen
Station Road, Endon,
Stoke-on-Trent,
Staffordshire ST9 9DR

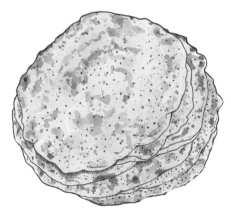

Pitch Up

Castle Camping (CS)

Congleton Road, Mow Cop, Staffordshire ST7 3PL
01782 522604 • www.castlecampingltd.co.uk
Set up in 2014 by the Boote family, themselves
seasoned campers who know what makes a good
camping experience: a great welcome, clean facilities,
electric, plenty of hot water, and somewhere to wash
up. Set on a ridge, the site takes in panoramic views
of the Biddulph Valley, Stoke-on-Trent and the Peak
District. There are great walking opportunities and it's
an easy drive into Stoke. Oh, and you can buy eggs
laid by the free-range hens and ducks.

Leek Camping and Caravanning Club Site

Blackshaw Grange, Blackshaw Moor, Leek,
Staffordshire ST13 8TL • 01538 300285
www.campingandcaravanningclub.co.uk
If you want an easy, carefree camping trip, this highly
organised site has all the comforts you'll need: spotless
facilities, electric at your pitch and helpful hosts. If you
like wild-and-quirky-with-campfires kind of sites, this
is possibly not for you, but it does what it does really
well, and with a smile. You'll never run out of things
to do. Situated in the Staffordshire Moorlands it's
great for exploring the southern Peak District. You can
walk to Tittesworth reservoir with its bird hides and
adventure playground, head into Stoke to explore the
Potteries or visit Leek to sample some oatcakes at the
much-loved Leek Oatcake Shop (see page 218).

Glencote Caravan Park

Station Road, Cheddleton, near Leek, Staffordshire
ST13 7EE • 01538 360745 • www.glencote.co.uk
The Churnet Valley Railway steam trains run straight
past the site; an impressive diversion while you brew
your morning coffee. The Caldon Canal is just a
short walk away so you can enjoy watching the boats,
too. The canal paths mean you are well connected
for cycling to Etruria, the old Wedgewood factory or
perhaps just to the Hollybush pub on the canal. This
is a measured-out-pitches, organised, functional type
of site that is shared with the park's static holiday
homes, but for an easy and comfortable stay in a good
location, this one is a great option.

Eat Local

Walkers Farm Shop and Florist

17-19 Hulton Street, Hanley, Stoke-on-Trent,
Staffordshire ST1 6AU • 01782 274075
www.walkersvegbags.co.uk
This wonderful family business started in the 1920s
selling groceries from a stall in Hanley market. The
produce was brought in by local farmers on their
horse and carts. (Vegetables are still sourced from
the grandson of one of these original suppliers.) By
the 1980s the stall had become a shop, which has
developed over the years into this great 'farm shop in
a city'. They still obtain their stock from local farmers,
bakers and growers – and oatcakes from the award-
winning High Lane Oatcakes.

Staffordshire is known for beer as well as oatcakes, and has a number of successful breweries. The Staffordshire Brewery (www.staffordshirebrewery.co.uk) is a stone's throw from both Glencote and Leek campsites, and the National Brewery Centre, a museum and tourist attraction, can be found in Burton-on-Trent. The Leek Real Ale Trail takes in 13 pubs and bars around the town, along with a selection of shops and markets, showcasing the best local ales and food to go with it.

Cuttleford Farm Shop

Newcastle Road, Astbury, Congleton, Cheshire CW12 4SD • 01260 272499 • www.cuttlefordfarmshop.co.uk
Farming along organic principles, Cuttleford Farm has 40 acres of mouthwatering vegetables and fruit that they sell through the shop. Tomatoes, salad leaves, asparagus, peas and beans, leeks and potatoes – you feel healthy just looking at it all. Bread, eggs and dairy are local, as are the Staffordshire oatcakes. It's just 10 minutes from Castle Camping.

Glebe Farm Shop

Astbury, Congleton, Cheshire CW12 4RQ
01260 273916 • www.glebefarmastbury.co.uk
Set in the beautiful village of Astbury on the outskirts of Congleton and close to Castle Camping, this farm shop has a quality butchers' counter. The pork and lamb is reared locally and the beef, matured for 21 days, comes from Nantwich. Burgers and sausages are home-made and the bacon is home-cured. They also sell barbecue packs of meat. There's a coffee shop and an animal petting corner where you can meet Rashers and Bangers, a pair of Kune pigs.

Brown and Green

Trentham Shopping Village, Stone Road, Trentham, Staffordshire ST4 8AX • 01782 641976
www.brown-and-green.co.uk
One of five Brown and Green shops which combine smart convenience with carefully selected local, ethical and artisan produce.

Leek Oatcake Shop

2 Haywood Street, Leek, Staffordshire ST13 5JX
01538 387556
See history in action as you stand in this traditional Staffordshire oatcake shop. It's so tiny, you'll fit five of you in at the most. This shop has remained completely unchanged since it opened in 1964 and continues to churn out hundreds of oatcakes to waiting customers (and mail-order ones) every day. It opens at 5am and closes at 1pm.

"Once a rural tradition, oatcake baking became an urban industry around the time of the Industrial Revolution..."

Farmers' Markets

Newcastle-under-Lyme Farmers' Market

Guildhall, High Street, Newcastle-under-Lyme,
Staffordshire ST5 1PW • 3rd Friday of the month
This monthly market sells a good range of local
produce including fruit, vegetables, eggs, preserves,
fish, baked goods, wine, meat and cheese – and of
course oatcakes.

On Monday, Wednesday, Friday and Saturday there
is a general market here with around 80 stalls, a few of
which sell local fruit and vegetables.

Leek Farmers' Market

Market Place, Leek, Staffordshire ST13 5HH
3rd Saturday of the month
Held in the 'Fine Food Market', as it is known locally,
this market brings together local and regional specialist
food producers, with cookery demonstrations and
musical entertainment. On Wednesday, Friday and
Saturday you can shop for fresh fish, meat and farm
produce as part of the indoor Butter Market in the
attractive Victorian Indoor Market Hall.

WRAPTASTIC: GOAT'S CHEESE, HONEY AND THYME WEDGES

The following are recipes for what to do with Staffordshire oatcakes, as opposed to how to make them. If you are camping in Staffordshire, you must buy the genuine articles, which are like large pancakes. Normal wraps will do if you aren't in the area.

Wraps, like oatcakes, are the perfect 'vehicle' for camping food. You can wrap your entire meal up in an easy-to-eat parcel and you don't have to wash a plate up. I also like the fact that wraps are a great way of turning simple local food-finds into something a bit special. Buy some oatcakes, a unique local cheese and a jar of pickle from a farm shop, and you'll have the DNA of your surroundings in one easy meal.

Serves 2

- Put an oatcake into a large dry frying pan and begin to heat gently.

- Crumble half the goat's cheese on to the wrap, leaving about 2cm clear of the edges of the wrap. Drizzle a tsp of honey evenly over the cheese. Sprinkle on a couple of pinches of fresh thyme leaves. Season with salt and pepper.

- Now fold the wrap in half and push it down with a spatula. Keep the heat low and keep it there just long enough for the cheese to start to melt.

- Flip the oatcake or wrap over and warm it through on the other side.

- Slide on to a plate and cut into wedges. Keep warm while you repeat with the other oatcake.

2 Staffordshire oatcakes/wraps

125g goat's or sheep's cheese (Whitmore Ewe's Cheese is good, as is Innes Log)

2 tsp runny local honey

a sprig of fresh thyme

salt and pepper

Alternatives and additions

sun-dried tomatoes, rocket leaves, thinly sliced spring onion, walnuts, fresh pear slices

CHICKEN MOJITO WRAPS

A bit of a talking point, these chicken wraps have all the Mojito flavours and are also served looking like a cocktail glass. The perfect thing for impressing your friends and raising a smile. They taste great, too!

You'll need a griddle pan on your gas stove, or a large frying pan for this.

Makes 4 wraps

2 free-range chicken breasts, skinned and cut into 2cm strips

grated zest and juice of 1 lime

1 garlic clove, finely chopped

½ fresh green chilli, deseeded and very finely chopped

½ tsp caster sugar

a handful of mint leaves, chopped

a splash of rum (if you have it!)

To serve

1 lime, cut into 8 wedges

4 soft tortilla wraps

4 tbsp crème fraîche

4 spring onions, shredded lengthways

a few mint leaves

- Mix the lime zest, lime juice, garlic, green chilli, sugar, mint and rum (if using) together in a freezer bag.

- Put the chicken strips into the bag and seal it. Squidge the contents around gently to mix the marinade into the chicken. Pop the bag into the cool-box to marinate for a couple of hours.

- When ready to cook, heat your pan to a medium heat and put your chicken strips on. Put the 8 lime wedges on to heat through at the same time.

- Cook the chicken for about 5 minutes on each side. Timings will depend on the thickness of your slices, so check they are cooked before taking them off.

- Take the lime wedges off the heat when they have started to caramelise and char a little on the edges.

- Take a wrap, fold it in half and spread the side facing you with thick crème fraîche. Fold that on to itself, so the wrap is now quartered and you have got a couple of 'pockets' if you open it at the top.

- Pile the chicken pieces into the front 'pocket' and arrange the shredded spring onions and mint leaves in the back. Pop a hot lime wedge in too. Squeeze the hot lime juice over the chicken just before eating.

28 STINKY CHEESE

Question: When is Stilton not Stilton?
Answer: *When it's made in Stilton.*

The story behind this most famous of British cheeses is perhaps as curious as our love of eating it. Stilton is one of only 12 British cheeses to be protected by PDO status (Protected Designation of Origin), which effectively means it can only be made in a particular area to a prescribed method.

What is really unusual about Stilton is that it appears to be named after the place it was sold, rather than the place it was made. In the early 18th century a favoured coach house, The Bell Inn in Stilton village, Huntingdonshire, developed a roaring trade selling this particularly pungent and moulding cheese to travellers.

The owner of the Bell Inn had reportedly discovered the cheese when visiting a farm in Melton Mowbray and made an arrangement with the maker to have exclusive rights to sell it. Being on the Great North Road, the little town of Stilton was a busy hub and stopover point for travellers, businessmen and drovers travelling back and forth from London. Many of the town's residents made their money selling ales and cheeses to travellers.

Daniel Defoe famously wrote about the cheese in his *A tour thro'the whole island of Great Britain* (1722-26) after he stayed at the pub on his travels. The town Stilton was 'famous for cheese, which is called our English Parmesan, and is brought to the table with mites or maggots around it, so thick that they bring a spoon with them for you to eat the mites with, as you do the cheese.'

So, the Bell Inn had the monopoly on the blue-veined cheese. Locals and travellers passing through went crazy for the stuff. Thus the connection between village and the cheese was made.

No-one really knows who made it first, other than it was created in a farmhouse near Melton Mowbray – a district already known for great cheesemaking in the early 18th century. Food historians think the original 'Stilton' cheese was white, with a tendency to blue. Now Stilton is made by piercing the crust of the cheese with steel needles then letting the air into the core of the cheese and moulding to develop over a period of a couple of months.

Originally Stilton was made using unpasteurised milk, but a listeria outbreak in the 1970s was blamed on unpasteurised cheeses, so many cheese-producers began to use pasteurised, heat-treated milk instead. Great interest in this cheese led to the Stilton Cheesemakers Association forming in the 1930s to prevent inferior copies being made outside the region. They were eventually granted a trademark protection stipulating that to be called 'Stilton' the milk must come from dairy cows from the Melton Mowbray area, within the counties of Leicestershire, Derbyshire and Nottinghamshire. It must be full cream, pasteurised milk, forming its own crust and in a cylindrical shape. The irony being, of course, that any Stilton-type cheese made in the village of Stilton, Cambridgeshire, can't call itself Stilton.

There are currently only six dairies licensed to produce Stilton located in the three counties of Derbyshire, Nottinghamshire and Leicestershire. The smallest, and in my humble opinion the best, is **Websters Dairy** in Saxelbye just outside Melton Mowbray. It's now run by sisters Margaret and Helen. Their Stilton is so sought-after that they regularly send it to customers in Australia and the Himalayas. The only place you can buy it in the UK is either directly from the dairy (at a minimum of 2kg) or in smaller amounts from **Derek Jones Family Butchers** shop in Melton Mowbray (see page 228). If you go to the dairy, you'll get 'cheese matched'. Answer questions about yourself and your preferences in terms of wine or gin, and you'll be matched with the perfect age of Stilton!

The Bell Inn (see page 229), meanwhile, still exists and continues to serve good food to passing travellers – including, of course, the well-loved smelly old blue cheese.

Websters Dairy

Saxelbye, Melton Mowbray, Leicestershire LE14 3PQ • 01664 812223
www.webstersdairy.co.uk

Pitch Up

The Paddock (CS)

Lyndon Road, Manton, Rutland LE15 8RN
07880 721638 • www.thepaddockrutlandwater.co.uk
A top class, award-winning Certificated Site in a very special part of the country offering views over Rutland Water. This is an adults-only site that offers electric but not toilets or showers. A big plus is that the **Horse and Jockey** pub in the nearby village of Manton is within staggering distance.

Wing Hall Camping

Wing Hall Estate, Wing, Oakham, Rutland LE15 8RY (no phone, online booking only) • www.winghall.co.uk
In the grounds of a rather grand-looking country house, this 'real' campsite keeps things basic. It's a peaceful and friendly campsite unencumbered by too many frills. Just a mile from Rutland Water, the campsite has views across the Rutland countryside. Rope swings on oak trees and space to run make this a winner for families. The farm shop is a huge asset – you'll be able to cook up a feast at your pitch with all the lovely local organic meats and produce on offer. In the summer the **Veranda Cafe Bar** is open for weekend breakfast, lunches and sundowners overlooking the garden. Gorgeous.

Belvoir Caravan and Campsite (CS)

Main Road, Redmile, Nottinghamshire NG13 0GQ
01476 870131 • www.belvoircampsite.co.uk
Set in the picturesque Vale of Belvoir, in prime Stilton-making country. The Certificated Site has a modern toilet block with washbasins and electric hook-ups if needed. The hosts are helpful and friendly. **The Windmill** pub is both walkable and wonderful.

Eat Local

The Good Grub Company

Farm Shop at The Grange, The Grange Garden Centre, Asfordby Hill, Leicestershire LE14 3QU
01664 810310
Devoted to the local food movement, Michael and Gemma Wilford have opened three local produce shops in the area. Each of these attractive stores stocks an abundance of fresh produce, home-made cakes, Hambleton Bakery bread, Rutland Charcuterie, olives, quiches, vegetables, fruit, locally sourced meat prepared in their own butchery and a great selection of local cheeses – including Stilton, naturally.

The other two Good Grub Company shops are:

Eastwell, Crossroads Farm

Scalford Road, Eastwell, Leicestershire LE14 4EF
01949 860669

Kinoulton

Grove Farm, Hickling Road, Kinoulton, Nottinghamshire NG12 3ED • 01949 81199

Derek Jones Family Butchers

51 King Street, Melton Mowbray, Leicestershire LE13 1XB • 01664 565328
This fantastic and friendly traditional butchers makes great pies and is the only place you can buy Websters Dairy Stilton.

Wing Hall Estate Farm Shop

Wing Hall, Wing, Oakham, Rutland LE15 8RY
www.winghall.co.uk

'Low on food miles, high on animal welfare' is the
focus for the stock in this farm shop that is also
the village shop. All basics are covered, alongside
'cheese of the week' with free tastings, pâtés, steaks
and sausages and bread from the award-winning
Hambleton Bakery – all from Leicestershire.

Northfield Farm Shop

Whissendine Lane, Cold Overton, Oakham, Rutland
LE15 7JD • 01664 474271 • www.northfieldfarm.com

It's all about quality, taste and good provenance at this
small, but oh so perfectly formed farm shop. Meat is
the farm's own beef, pork, lamb, mutton and goose.
All animals are naturally reared and most are rare and
traditional breeds chosen for their eating qualities
not just their commercial capabilities. Then there are
the thoughtfully sourced treats like honey and jams,
artisan crackers and plentiful cheeses, and how about
some sloe gin or damson whisky made on the farm?

Farmers' Markets
Melton Mowbray Farmers' Market

Scalford Road, Melton Mowbray, Leicestershire LE13
1JY • 01664 562971 • www.meltonmowbraymarket.
co.uk • Every Tuesday and Friday

Being so regular, this market replaces many of the
locals' need to use supermarkets, making it a vibrant
and busy place to be. It's well worth a trip if you are
camping nearby, just to get a glimpse of the volume
of incredible food and drink producers there are
in the area. Naturally pork pies and Stilton are well
represented, but so are fabulous breads, smoked
foods, rare-breed meats and fresh vegetables.

Eating Out
The Bell Inn

Great North Road, Stilton, Peterborough,
Cambridgeshire PE7 3RA • 01733 241066
www.thebellstilton.co.uk

The famous cheese pub still serves Stilton to weary
travellers, as well as offering a mouthwatering menu
of modern and classic dishes. A popular pub, with a
welcoming atmosphere, there's a village bar, a bistro
area as well as a more formal dining experience if you
want it.

MUSHROOM BURGERS
WITH A STILTON STUFFING

Too often we assume that barbecue means sausages and burgers, but being vegetarian doesn't mean that you need to miss out on the joy of alfresco cooking and your clothes smelling of smoke.

This recipe uses big portobello mushrooms that look like burger buns – and I fill them with local cheeses and different flavourings that I find as I travel about the markets. This version uses Stilton, naturally.

Serves 4

8 large portobello mushrooms, wiped not washed

olive oil

4 thick slices stale white bread

2 spring onions, thinly sliced

1 unwaxed lemon

1 garlic clove, finely chopped

a good pinch of fresh thyme leaves

150g Stilton

2 tbsp chutney (a fruit-based one, like pear or apple, would work well)

a handful of chopped walnuts

salt and pepper

- Take the stalks off the mushrooms and put them to one side. Don't peel the skin off the mushroom caps though.

- Use your hands to rub about 2 tbsp olive oil into the mushrooms and then put them upside-down on a plate.

- Get a bowl to make your breadcrumbs. Stale bread is better, because just rubbing the slices together tends to make crumbs, or you can carefully use a grater.

- Add the sliced spring onions to the breadcrumbs. Finely grate the zest of ½ the lemon into the breadcrumb bowl, then add the garlic and fresh thyme leaves (use half the quantity dried if you need to).

- Chop some of the mushroom stalks and add them to the breadcrumbs as well. Add a splash of oil and a squidge of lemon juice to make it just moist enough to mix into a stuffing with your hands.

- Cut your Stilton roughly into 2cm cubes and add it to your mixture with the chutney and walnuts. Season and mix well.

- Divide the mixture between 4 of the mushrooms, then pop the empty mushrooms on top to make a burger effect. Press them together but not so hard that you split them.

- Put the mushroom burgers on an oiled griddle preheated to medium. They will take roughly 8 minutes on each side. Keep an eye on them! The mushrooms will reduce in size, and can be cut into wedges like a small pie. Serve with some salad leaves.

WALES

Never despair at the Welsh rain pitter-pattering on your campervan roof. Instead, console yourself that this is the reason the fertile valley pastures produce such great-tasting Welsh Black cattle steaks, distinctive creamy cheeses and top-quality lamb. The basic ingredients from this wild and rugged landscape's natural larder make even the most economical of dishes taste wonderful. This small country is big on passion when it comes to food, and low on fuss. You'll find dishes that are simply prepared, fresh, and all about the taste. As good food should be.

32 35 29 33 30 34 31

29

BLACK GOLD
FROM THE HILLS

Gazing out of the window as Custard, my campervan, backfired her way through the Welsh valleys, I noticed beautiful black cattle grazing the hillsides. These bovine beauties, appropriately named Welsh Blacks, were once so frequently used in place of currency in Wales that they became known as the 'black gold from the hills'. The breed is one of the oldest in Britain.

The stocky Welsh Blacks are well suited to the Welsh landscape. They are tremendously hardy and as adept at negotiating rugged terrain as they are grazing the fertile lowlands. Their thick, curly coats give them the ability to withstand extremes of temperature and wet weather.

Much of the early infrastructure of Wales was established for taking Welsh Blacks across the border to sell at English markets. The routes became notorious for ambush by bandits who knew the drovers were returning with large amounts of money. One drover, David Jones, formed a bank in 1799 to encourage other drovers to invest their earnings on their way home. It became known as the Black Ox Bank and its bank notes were embellished with pictures of Welsh Blacks.

The Nixon family at Penmincae Farm have a herd of 120 pedigree Welsh Blacks by the banks of the River Wye near Builth Wells. The Nixons pride themselves on using traditional methods of farming and animal husbandry, farming at 'nature's pace'. Herds reared like this are healthy, live long and calf well. For the meat eaters among us, this pays dividends in the quality, flavour and texture of the meat. There are also health benefits associated with eating beef raised on a pure grass diet as opposed to concentrates.

If we only ever choose our meat and milk based on the cheapest price, we encourage intensive farming and artificial feeding practices, and only the highest yielding breeds of cattle are favoured while some of the rarer breeds get lost altogether. Supporting specialist breeders and farmers to maintain their high standards is beneficial to us all.

Many butchers in Wales proudly sell Welsh Black beef. Its dark colour and intense flavours make it worth seeking out.

The Nixons' beef is available at the farm by appointment welshblackbeef@btinternet.com or at Brecon Farmers' Market.

Pitch Up

Priory Mill (CS)

Hay Road, Brecon, Powys LD3 7SR • 01874 611609
www.priorymillfarm.co.uk
Check in at the back door of the stunning mill
conversion and Noel and Susie Gaskell, along with
Moss the Jack Russell, will welcome you warmly.
Choose your pitch alongside the babbling brook and
borrow one of the fancy fire pits and grills. You can
buy locally made charcoal or logs on site.

This is a calm and quiet place, made even more
relaxing by the sound of the river, home to kingfishers,
dippers, salmon and the occasional otter. Watching
the horseshoe bats fly overhead as you sit by the fire
just adds to the magic.

Fforest Fields Caravan and Camping Park

Fforest Farm, Hundred House, Builth Wells, Powys
LD1 5RT • 01982 570406 • www.fforestfields.co.uk
After selling their own herd of Welsh Blacks some
years ago, George and Katie Barstow turned their
farmland over to a fantastic campsite offering plenty
of holiday magic. There's a swimming lake with
pontoons to leap off, inviting pathways taking you
over little wooden bridges, streams and fishing lakes.
This is 'get away from it all' camping. The facilities
block is luxurious and carbon neutral; the water and
underfloor heating are all powered using their own
timber and lit by sun tunnels. Hire fire pits from the
site shop and, while you are there, indulge in the
sausages made by Will, Katie and George's son, using
pork from his own woodland-raised pigs.

Rhandirmwyn Camping and Caravanning Club Site

Llandovery, Carmarthenshire SA20 0NT • 01550
760257 • www.campingandcaravanningclub.co.uk
Nestled in the Welsh hills, with a river running
alongside, this lovely secluded site has 90 touring
pitches and fully equipped holiday lodges for hire or
sale. The invigorating walk into the village rewards you
with two good pubs. **The Towy Bridge Inn** has good
home-cooked food. **The Royal Oak** supports local
producers and brewers and has converted the snooker
room into a produce shop. Half a mile up the road,
a local smallholding sells home-made sausages and
burgers. Ask the site manager for the phone number.

Eat Local

Morgans Family Butchers

103 The Struet, Brecon, Powys LD3 7LT • 01874
623522 • and 12 High Street, Builth Wells, Powys LD2
3DN • 01982 551008 • www.morgansbrecon.co.uk
Deep in the heart of Welsh Black country, Morgans is
a well-respected family butchers specialising in Welsh
Black beef.

Eric Bujok

16 High Street, Builth Wells, Powys LD2 3FE
01982 553681
Get your Welsh Black beef and local lamb butterflied
for barbecues here. Eric provides Fforest Fields
campsite with home-cured and locally smoked bacon.

Mathews Butchers

6 Stone Street, Llandovery, Carmarthenshire SA20 0JR
01550 721277 • www.mathewsbutchers.co.uk
Llandovery was once an important meeting point
for cattle drovers. This wonderful traditional family
butchers sells Welsh Black mince to make your own
burgers with and sources all meat from local farms.

Talgarth Mill

The Square, Talgarth, Powys LD3 0BW
01874 711352 • www.talgarthmill.com
The restored Victorian mill is open for tours and also
has an exquisite artisan bakery and cafe on site.

Just So Scrumptious

Kings Road, Llandovery, Carmarthenshire
SA20 0AW • 01550 720824
Home-made quiches, salads and gorgeous breads are
sold in this deli – they also do great coffee.

Penpont

Brecon, Powys LD3 8EU • 01874 636202
(just off A40 between Brecon and Llandovery)
In an enchanting 17th-century estate on the banks of
the Usk. Organic fruit, vegetables and flowers grown
in the walled gardens.

As you tour around the countryside on your camping travels, a bit of cow-spotting will reveal a vast array of colours, markings, sizes and physiques. Most are named after their county of origin: Herefords, Ayrshires, Sussex, Jerseys and Devon Reds are just a few. Many are bred to suit the weather, vegetation and terrain of the area they originate from. For example, the dense-boned, large-shouldered Sussex was bred as a strong working animal that could plough the heavy clay of the county, while the Ruby Red of North Devon was bred to easily digest the harsh grasses of the area's moorlands.

Vans Good Food Shop

Elmswood, Llandrindod Wells, Powys LD1 5ET
01597 823074 • www.organicfoodpowys.co.uk
There's a vaguely hippyish air to Llandrindod Wells.
This fruit and veg shop still rocks it. It's been selling
great quality organic fruit and veg and wholefoods for
over 36 years.

Farmers' Markets

Brecon Farmers' Market

Market Hall, Brecon, Powys
2nd Saturday of the month

Brecon Country Market

Market Hall, Brecon, Powys • Every Friday

Llandovery Farmers' Market

Market Square, Llandovery, Carmarthenshire
SA20 0AW • Last Saturday of the month

WELSH BLACK BEEF BURGERS

WITH GRIDDLED COURGETTE, CORN AND FARM-SHOP SURPRISE

You'll not find tastier, juicier burgers than this. The Welsh Black beef mince stays super-moist when you cook it.

My 'farm-shop surprise' refers to the delightfully distinct and inventive selections of chutneys and pickles you'll find in any farm shop. I call them 'joy in a jar': the flavours of a field or a hedgerow captured and sealed. What better way to take home a memory of a holiday? Pickles not postcards, that's what I say! So enjoy picking your pickle (or your chutney) to go with your burger. It certainly makes a great talking point.

Serves 4

500g minced Welsh Black beef

1 onion, very finely chopped, or grated if you can bear it

a handful of fresh coriander leaves, chopped

1 tsp Welsh mustard (English will do!)

1 egg yolk

1 tbsp rapeseed oil

salt and pepper

To serve

2 sweetcorn cobs, with husks on

2 courgettes, sliced about 5mm thick

4 soft buns

a farm-shop chutney

- Once your barbecue is hot, put your sweetcorn cobs, in their husks, over the heat. The husks will keep the corn moist. Turn occasionally. They'll take about 20 minutes to cook. While that is happening...

- Put all the burger ingredients in a big bowl, including a decent pinch each of salt and pepper, and stir thoroughly. Form 4 large patties with your hands, making sure all the mixture holds together well.

- Brush the griddle or barbecue with a little oil and cook your burgers until cooked through (around 15 minutes), turning once.

- Once the burgers have been on for about 8 minutes, put your courgette slices on. Turn regularly until they have softened and cooked.

- Remove the husks from the cobs (once they have cooled a little!) and cut each into two.

- Serve your burgers and courgette slices in the soft white buns, topped with chutney, with a hunk of corn on the side.

30 SPRING MEADOW FARM

The most westerly tip of Wales is a wild, exposed and windy place. There are very few trees, but much natural beauty – of the rugged kind. The coastline is a haven for walkers, swimmers and surfers, the sunsets are spectacular and, with very little light pollution, the vast star-filled night skies are awe-inspiring. It is certainly a special place to camp.

Thirteen-acre Spring Meadow Farm is at the heart of the peninsula, in the Pembrokeshire Coast National Park. It is run by Tim Young and Lynne Whittemore who, over the last 20 years, have transformed six 'blank canvas' fields into an impressively productive market garden. The on-site farm shop is an open-sided barn brimming with beautifully displayed baskets of produce. They sell a huge range, from herbs, carrots, beans, leeks, peppers, courgettes and garlic to strawberries, blackcurrants and plums.

Spring Meadow Farm is obviously a labour of love. I watch Tim, a lone figure in the middle of a vast field, toiling the land and tending to his plants. Growing produce in such an exposed part of the country must be tough, but Tim obviously enjoys the challenge. "It's all about trying to outwit the weather," he says with a smile, "and accepting when you can't. I'd love to grow runner beans but I can't grow tall things – it is too windy. They'd just blow down."

Lynne, a ceramicist by trade, now puts most of her creative energy into growing plants and flowers to sell alongside Tim's fruit and vegetables. The abundant and colourful selection in their shop is testament to her hard work and skill at taming the wild and rugged terrain of this area.

The campsite, positioned at the centre of the farmland, is a true haven, hidden behind a natural wall of willow hedge and sycamore. You can hide from the world here, with the sound of birds, bees and the rustling of willow trees providing a calming soundtrack. Each pitch has a campfire hearth and its own picnic table – the perfect invitation to source some fresh ingredients and cook up a feast over the open fire.

Within moments of our arrival, my two children had headed off with Tim to explore the farm, admire the old red tractor parked by the shop and join Lynne picking some herbs for our meal.

Food is often a topic of conversation between Lynne and the campers that stay on her site. "It gave me the idea of putting a recipe board up in the washrooms," says Lynne. "Campers can now exchange notes on things they have cooked over their fires using the produce from the farm."

Tim had been to the area's farmers' market on the morning I visited and bought some local sausages that he offered up for the pot. In the time it took for him to help start the fire while I chopped herbs, sliced onions and diced peppers and courgettes, the Spring Meadow Farm Vegetable and Sausage Stew was born (see recipe on page 245). It was certainly a very relaxed way to cook lunch; sitting in a beautiful sheltered hideaway surrounded by butterflies and rustling trees, watching my children enjoying the space. We chatted, drank wine and took it in turns to poke the fire or stir the bubbling stew in my cast-iron Dutch oven pot.

Lynne appeared with a delicious salad she had made from the leaves and herbs Maisy, my daughter, had just helped her to pick. So there was our feast. As fresh and as local as it is possible to get.

Spring Meadow Farm (CS)

Caerfarchell, Solva, Haverfordwest, Pembrokeshire SA62 6XT • 01437 721800 • www.spring-meadow-farm.co.uk • Spring Meadow Farm shop is open May to September, Wednesday to Sunday 10am–2pm

Fishguard Farmers' Market

Every Saturday in Fishguard Town Hall • It's about 20 minutes' drive from Spring Meadow Farm

"Spring Meadow Farm is so obviously a labour of love.

SPRING MEADOW FARM VEGETABLE AND SAUSAGE STEW

As this rustic dish is cooked over a fire, heat and cooking times will vary. The best advice is to keep checking the stew. The times used in this recipe would suit a gas stove, too.

The vegetables and herbs can be swapped or supplemented, according to preference/what is available. For example butternut squash, red peppers and celery would also work well.

- Heat the oil in your pot or heavy-based saucepan and brown the sausages for about 10 minutes. Then remove from the pot and set to one side.

- Back in the pot, soften the onion for a few minutes, then add the bacon pieces and cook for about 3 minutes. Add the finely chopped garlic and the sliced leek. Stir all the time to make sure nothing burns.

- Cook this for a couple of minutes, and then add the chopped carrots, diced courgette, and the pepper (or other seasonal vegetables). Cook for a further 5 minutes until the vegetables begin to soften.

- Add the vegetable stock and a decent glug of red wine if you have it. Then add the chopped tomatoes to the pot and give it all a big stir. Leave to cook for 10 minutes, stirring occasionally, adding a bit of extra wine or stock if it needs more liquid. Add the basil (and other herbs to suit your taste, such as parsley or thyme) and stir well.

- Pop the sausages back on the top, season with some salt and pepper, then let everything simmer for another 10 minutes until the sausages are piping hot again. Serve with some fresh bread and salad leaves.

- Invite some friends over to your pitch, pour some good wine and enjoy.

Serves 4

1 tbsp vegetable oil

8 locally bought pork sausages

1 onion, finely chopped

3 rashers of smoked bacon, cut into 2cm pieces

2 garlic cloves, finely chopped

1 leek, sliced and washed

3 carrots, peeled and chopped

2 courgettes, trimmed and diced

1 green pepper, deseeded and diced

350ml vegetable stock (a stock cube is fine)

red wine (optional)

8 tomatoes, chopped

a handful of basil leaves, roughly chopped

salt and pepper

SUNNY
SUMMER VEG
FRITTATA

Eggs are a campsite staple, not least because many of the independent and smaller campsites are located on farms, and a supply of fresh eggs is on the doorstep. Also, the summer camping season brings with it an abundance of fresh produce. It's the time when fruit and vegetables take centre stage and flaunt their natural goodness wherever you turn. Farm shops and markets come into their own as a wealth of courgettes, aubergines, broad beans, peas, lettuce and tomatoes fill our baskets for pennies not pounds, and excess allotment veg can be picked up for 'donation' prices via honesty boxes perched on gates.

Serves 4 generously

300g summer veg: broad beans, courgettes, asparagus, peas – your choice – chopped as/if appropriate

½ large red onion, finely chopped

6 spring onions, sliced

olive oil

3 rashers smoked bacon, cut into small pieces

300g cooked new potatoes, sliced

a handful of fresh parsley leaves, chopped

6 large fresh eggs

salt and pepper

grated hard cheese like Cheddar (optional)

a good handful of salad leaves to serve

- Put your chopped summer veg in a pan of boiling water. Bring back to the boil then reduce the heat and simmer for 3–4 minutes. Drain.

- In a large frying pan, sweat the red onion and spring onion in a splash of olive oil for about 3 minutes.

- Add the bacon and let it fry for a couple of minutes then add the drained vegetables, the potatoes and parsley. Toss it all together and turn the heat down low.

- Beat the eggs together in a bowl with some salt and pepper and pour over the vegetables. Cook gently on a low heat and don't stir.

- When the egg is nearly set (you can sprinkle a cheese of your choice on now if you want), put the pan under the grill for about 5 minutes until it has completely set.

- If you haven't got access to a grill, cook the frittata until the top has almost set completely. Cut down the middle with the spatula and slide one half out of the pan and put on a plate. Flip the remaining half over in the pan, and let it cook for about a minute. Then do the same again with the other half.

- Slice the frittata into wedges and serve with some salad leaves.

31 A FLOCK IN THE FOG

It's no surprise that the Gower was the first part of Britain to be designated as an Area of Outstanding Natural Beauty. It has it all: empty stretches of fine sandy beaches, graceful crescent coves, untouched dunes, limestone cliffs and rolling surf.

If you are camping in the Gower, head for the lesser-visited northern shores that consist of about 4,000 acres of saltmarsh. On the day I visited there was a low mist in the air, hanging close to the shoreline. I could just about make out the sheep dotted among the marshes. To add to the slightly eerie setting, I came across a haunting-looking castle ruin on the hillside. Two signs on a gate, 'Gower Salt Marsh Lamb' and 'Weobley Castle', directed us up the driveway.

Fourteenth-century Weobley Castle is on Rowland Pritchard's farm. You can buy tickets to visit the castle from the small farm shop. At the same time you can buy some of his Gower saltmarsh lamb – a much sought-after product. In 2004 Rowland paired up with neighbouring sheep farmers Colin and Vicky Williams to form the Gower Salt Marsh Lamb Company. Within a few years they had won the National Trust's Fine Farm Produce Award and several Great Taste awards.

All the lambs are slaughtered less than five miles away and butchered locally, then a range of cuts is sold from their on-site shop. The flavour of the meat is truly exquisite. Grazing on Llanrhidian Marsh with its saltmarsh grasses, marsh mallow, samphire, sorrel and sea lavender is what gives it a distinctly sweet yet rich flavour. If you want a truly local product, this is it. In it you'll taste the uniqueness of this place and also be supporting local farmers who look after that landscape you have just enjoyed.

The season for buying saltmarsh lamb runs from mid-June to Christmas, so just right for the summer and autumn camping season. It you want to stay local too, then the farm also has a small campsite.

Gower Salt Marsh Lamb
Weobley Castle Farm, Llanrhidian, Gower, Swansea SA3 1HB
01792 390012 • www.gowersaltmarshlamb.co.uk

Pitch Up

Bank Farm (CS)
Llangennith, Gower, Swansea SA3 1JB • 01792 386223
www.campingandcaravanningclub.co.uk
Beware – there are four sites called Bank Farm on the Gower. This one is towards the western edge of the peninsula, making it a top spot for peace and quiet and a great base for walks, even if it is just to the **Kings Head** pub – a great village hostelry. **Gower Salt Marsh Lamb farm shop** is just 10 minutes away and a pleasant drive around the country lanes will bring you to local farms selling produce by the roadside.

Oxwich Camping Park
Gower, Swansea SA3 1LS • 01792 390777
sites.google.com/site/oxwichcampingpark
A cracking location, set over three large fields surrounded by trees and hedges – the top field has sea views. The heated swimming pool adds to the fun and the beach is a 15-minute walk away. It's worth noting that there isn't a shop on site (though a butcher's van does the rounds in the mornings) and you have to bring your own loo roll!

Phillistone Farm
Llanmadoc, Gower, Swansea SA3 1DE • 07967 820990
www.phillistonegower.co.uk
This is a caravan and motorhome-only site as they don't have their own facilities, although every pitch has electric hook-up. What you get is a well-run, exclusive site with gorgeous views over Broughton Bay (pronounced 'Bruffton'), no light pollution so you can admire the starry nights, and the occasional bleating of sheep. Bliss.

Eat Local

Llanmadoc Community Shop
Llanmadoc, Gower, Swansea SA3 1DE
This is a great example of a community shop, run by volunteers. It's stocked with local produce, meats, fish, saltmarsh lamb, cockles, laverbread, home-made cakes and chutneys. Stop for a cuppa and a slab of cake made by one of the ladies from the village.

Murton Farm Shop
34 Mansfield Road, Murton, Bishopston, Gower, Swansea SA3 3AR • 01792 232732
Open on Friday and Saturday, this gem of a place sells a huge variety of seasonal fruit and vegetables, all grown on the farm.

Nicholaston Farm
Penmaen, Gower, Swansea SA3 2HL • 01792 371209
www.nicholastonfarm.co.uk
A small farm shop selling home-grown seasonal fruit and veg. Even better, you can make a morning of it and pick it yourself. There is also a great campsite here.

Farmers' Markets and Community Markets

Penclawdd Community Market

3rd Saturday of the month

Penclawdd is a village on the north coast famous for its cockle-picking industry. This monthly market has plenty of tempting produce, including saltmarsh lamb, cockles and laverbread.

Mumbles Farmers' Market

Seafront Car Park, Newton Road, Mumbles, Swansea SA3 4AY • 2nd Saturday of the month

Swansea Market

Oxford Street, Swansea SA1 3PQ • 01792 654296 Monday to Saturday

If you are heading into Swansea, do visit the famous indoor market, the largest in Wales. There are over 100 stalls of fresh, local produce and traditional Welsh fayre, including specialist butchers and fishmongers, many of whom have been serving the people of Swansea for generations.

There are also a couple of great monthly street markets in Swansea:

Uplands Market

Gwydr Square, Uplands, Swansea SA2 0HD • www. uplandsmarket.com • last Saturday of the month

Marina Market

Dylan Thomas Square, Swansea SA1 1TT 2nd Sunday of the month

Eating Out

The Bay Bistro

Rhossili, Swansea SA3 1PL • 01792 390519 www.thebaybistro.co.uk

Filled with local arts and crafts, this stylish little place boasts panoramic vistas across Rhossili Bay. The food is an exciting mix of vegetarian and exotic flavours (with a few options for meat eaters). Booking recommended.

BUTTERFLIED LAMB

Serves 4

If you have a barbecue with a lid, this is a real treat. It's super easy yet feels special. I serve my lamb with a summer salad (see page 255), which I make while the lamb's cooking.

'Butterflied' leg of lamb means the bone is taken out so you can open it up. The thinner meat cooks quicker, so is perfect for the barbecue. You can buy ready-butterflied lamb at Gower Salt Marsh Lamb farm shop.

I love Moroccan marinades like cumin and coriander, but this summer one with lemon, garden herbs and garlic is fantastic, too.

boned leg of lamb, around 1.5kg when butterflied

grated zest of ½ lemon

a few sprigs of mixed fresh herbs (thyme, rosemary, parsley, bay or whatever you can get hold of), finely snipped

4 garlic cloves, crushed and chopped

2 big glugs (or 2 tbsp) olive oil

- Lay the lamb out on a meat chopping board, boned side up. Flatten it out with your hands by giving it a good smack. Sprinkle on the lemon zest and the snipped-up herbs.

- Sprinkle on the chopped garlic cloves and evenly pour the olive oil over the meat. Massage it in. Don't be afraid to get your hands oily.

- Put the lamb in a freezer bag or dish to marinate in your cool-box for at least 2 hours. Take it out 20 minutes before cooking.

- If cooking with gas, get the barbecue hot, then reduce the heat to medium-high. Lay the lamb on the barbecue and cook for about 8-10 minutes. Turn the lamb over, and cook for another 8 minutes. Then reduce the heat to medium-low. Put the lid on the barbecue and cook for another 15 minutes for medium, or until cooked to your liking.

- If cooking over coals, wait until the coals are glowing very hot. Put the lamb on the cooking grid, directly over the hot coals, and cook for around 8 minutes on each side. Carefully remove the grid and the lamb. Using a heatproof spatula move the coals to one side, put the grid and the lamb back, and cover with the lid. Allow the lamb to cook for a further 15 minutes over the indirect heat.

- When the lamb is cooked to your liking, remove it, cover with foil and leave to rest for about 10 minutes. Slice the lamb across the grain to serve. Serve with Summer Salad (see page 255).

SUMMER SALAD

Serves 4

Rather than just shoving a few leaves on a plate, it's worth experimenting with all the fabulous summer veg that are usually having a bit of a glut at this time of year. You are likely to come across gardeners leaving out courgettes for donations at the end of their driveways. If you are lucky you'll find some vibrant yellow ones, too. Raw courgettes are a great salad ingredient, and they make a really meaty dish like lamb feel a bit lighter and more summery...

- Use a very sharp knife — or a veg peeler — to slice your courgettes lengthways. Make sure the slices are very thin.

- Now make your dressing. Squeeze the juice of the lemon into a glass, add in double the amount of olive oil, then mix in the sugar, lemon zest and some salt and pepper. Mix it all together well.

- Pour this dressing over your courgettes and leave them to 'cook' for about 5 minutes. They will soften over this time.

- Crumble up your goat's cheese, and toss this, with the mint leaves and some more pepper, into the courgettes just before serving.

4 large courgettes

salt and pepper

about 50g crumbly goat's cheese

a handful of mint leaves, roughly shredded

For the dressing

juice and grated zest of 1 lemon

olive oil

½ tsp caster sugar

32 ANGLESEY
MENAI MOULES

Mussels are nature's convenience food. Quick and easy to cook, healthy and cheap, they even come with their own disposable cutlery. Pick the first fleshy morsel out then use the empty shell as pincers to grab the rest.

Surprisingly, the Menai Strait, that narrow, melancholic stretch of water separating Anglesey from mainland Wales, is one of the most prolific mussel production areas in the UK. Around 12,000 tonnes are harvested here each year, making it one of the richest areas of farmland in Wales. The fast-flowing tidal system (the tide flows in from both west and east) and the sheltered nature of the straits has created a eco-system so unique that the School of Ocean Sciences, part of the University of Bangor, was set up here.

Local lad Shaun Krijnen used his Masters degree in Shellfish Biology from Bangor to set up his Menai Oysters company in the early 1990s. As oysters are extremely slow growing, he added mussels to his repertoire and they've now become the main part of his business. Shaun's mussel and oyster beds are in a peaceful spot overlooked by Caernarfon Castle.

In a kind of half-farming, half-fishing set-up, the mussel seeds are collected from further afield and brought into the local beds along the shoreline. They are cultivated on ropes suspended from rafts floating in the waters, where they hang around consuming the nutrient-rich plankton and filtering out the bad stuff. As part of the process they are UV-filtered, which purifies them and makes them safe to eat. Most of the mussels we buy in shops and restaurants are farmed mussels like these. They are a brilliantly eco-friendly and sustainable 'crop', as they don't need any feeding.

Menai Oysters
Tal-y-Bont Bach, Dwyran, Llanfairpwll, Anglesey LL61 6UU
01248 430878 • www.menaioysters.co.uk

Pitch Up

Ty Croes Farm

Dwyran, Llanfairpwll, Anglesey LL61 6RP
07784 092836 • www.vineyardcamping.com
A campsite in a vineyard on the southwest side of
the island, close to lovely beaches and the pretty
village of Newborough. Friendly and spotless, the
site has huge pitches with electric hook-ups suitable
for caravans, motorhomes, campervans and tents.
The views of Snowdonia across the Menai Strait are
very special indeed. And, just to add to the magic,
campfires are permitted.

Head to the **Marram Grass** (see right) for good
food and drink; the local farm shop is **Hooton's
Homegrown** and it's a 15-minute walk to the mussel
man. The grapes on the vines are made into wine near
Caenarfon (www.pantdu.co.uk).

Dafarn Rhos Caravan and Camping Site

Lligwy Beach, Moelfre, Anglesey LL72 8NN
01248 410607 • www.angleseycamping.co.uk
You'll get the all the best bits of Anglesey's
natural beauty here without even moving from
your pitch. Hear the sea, gaze across the stunning
Lligwy beach and coastline backed by unspoilt
countryside. This is a site for peace-lovers, and so the
rules for quiet and no driving on-site after 10pm are
enforced. But who wants headlights in their tent in
the middle of the night?

Bodewran Bach (CS)

Tyn Lon, Holyhead, Anglesey LL65 3LZ • 01407
721244 • www.campingandcaravanningclub.co.uk
Aside from the gorgeous views and sunsets, this
small campsite has a charming little bar called the
Pig Inn set among old pig pens tucked away at the
bottom of the site. With six hard standings and 10 tent
pitches, Bodewran Bach is in a peaceful setting in the
middle of the island.

Eat Local

Menai Oysters

Tal-y-Bont Bach, Dwyran, Llanfairpwll, Anglesey
LL61 6UU • 01248 430878 • www.menaioysters.co.uk
You can buy mussels and oysters directly from Shaun
Krijnen at Menai Oysters on Wednesday and Sunday.

Holy Island Seafood

Llainysbylldir, Beach Road, Rhoscolyn, Anglesey
LL65 2NJ • 01407 861699 • www.holyislandseafood.
co.uk
Look out for a sign propped up against a garden wall
in a single-track lane heading to the beach. Follow the
arrows and you'll be in the back garden of Richard
and Tracy. He heads out in the bay every day to
catch lobsters and crabs, she prepares and dresses
them in her specially designed catering shed, and we
the customers can buy the freshest, most delicious
seafood imaginable.

> **We** started out just selling some strawberries at the end of the drive ... then people began coming to the back door for the asparagus ... followed by more produce. By 1998 we gave in and built the farm shop ... then the cafe. **"**

Hooton's Homegrown

Hooton's Homegrown

Gwydryn hir, Brynsiencyn, Anglesey LL61 6HQ
01248 430644 • www.hootonshomegrown.com
This place is so no-frills it is constructed out of shipping containers joined together. All the pork, Welsh Black beef, lamb and chicken are raised and finished on the farm. All your food and fresh produce for the camping week is available here, or you can pick your own in the right seasons. There are picnic tables out front with views of Snowdonia.

Valley Butchers

The Old Court House, Station Road, Y Fali, Ynys Mon, Anglesey LL65 3EB • 01407 742391
www.valleybutchers.co.uk
Dripping in awards and national recognition, customers are happy to travel across the island to this great craft butchers on the northwest of Anglesey. Using only the best-quality local meats they favour traditional breeds, including grass-fed Welsh Black beef from the island. The lamb is from Anglesey and they are proud of their home-cured bacon.

Farmers' Markets
Anglesey Farmers' Market

David Hughes Secondary School • Menai Bridge
www.angleseyfarmersmarket.co.uk • 3rd Saturday of the month

Conwy Farmers' Market

Conwy RSPB Reserve, Llandudno Junction
www.conwyfarmersmarket.co.uk • Last Wednesday of the month

Eating Out
The Marram Grass

White Lodge, Penlon, Newborough, Anglesey LL61 6RS • 01248 440077
www.themarramgrass.com
This stylish neighbourhood hub cafe serves local beers and creatively prepared, locally sourced food.

The Lobster Pot

Church Bay, Anglesey LL65 4EU • 01407 730241
www.thelobsterpotrestaurant.co.uk
Start with complimentary winkles picked from the bay, then enjoy the freshest lobster, crab, mussels, oysters and scallops. If you are a seafood lover this is the place to be on Anglesey.

MENAI MOULES

WITH LEEKS AND WELSH CIDER

Apart from the mussels, all the ingredients here can be bought in Hooton's Homegrown farm shop in Anglesey. You will need a gas ring stove and an aluminium tray or roasting tray and foil. And lots of lovely rustic crusty bread for mopping-up purposes is vital.

Serves 4

1kg Menai mussels, debearded and scrubbed clean

olive oil

6 rashers smoked streaky bacon, sliced into 1cm pieces

1 large leek, halved lengthways, washed and finely sliced

150ml good-quality Welsh cider

1 garlic clove, finely sliced

2 tbsp double cream

1 small bunch of fresh flat-leaf parsley, leaves roughly chopped

salt and pepper

- Make sure your mussels are really clean. Wash them in cool water. Check for any open ones. If they don't close when tapped, chuck them.

- Depending on what barbecue or stove you have, put a big saucepan, roasting tray or even a disposable aluminium tray (if you are using a campfire) over the heat. Add some oil.

- Snip your smoky, streaky bacon into it and let it fry. Try and keep the heat down so it doesn't burn. As it starts to colour, add in your leeks and fry until they go soft, about 6 minutes.

- Using a slotted spoon, take out the leeks and bacon and put to one side.

- Put the mussels in the pan, with the measured quantity of cider. (Feel free to drink the leftovers.) Add the garlic then cover with a lid or with sheets of foil tucked over the edges. (Use gloves!)

- Leave the mussels to steam for about about 4 minutes, giving an occasional shake to the pan.

- Now check that they have all opened. Those that haven't also get chucked. Using that slotted spoon put the mussels into a big serving bowl.

- Put the bacon and leeks back into the pan or tray. Add the cream and let it come to the boil and bubble for a little while. Keep stirring. Add half the chopped parsley and lots of salt and pepper, and stir again.

- Then pour this sauce over the mussels. Sprinkle the remaining parsley on the top, and serve with bread. Let everyone tuck in and drink more cider.

33 TEIFI CHEESE

The River Teifi, considered the most beautiful river in Wales, flows through the Cambrian Mountains and out to the sea at Cardigan. The lush valley that meets the sea is home to the Teifi Valley Cheese Producers, five of the most outstanding artisan cheesemakers in Wales – Carmarthenshire Cheese Company, Caws Cenarth, Hafod Welsh Organic Cheddar, Sanclêr Organic and Caws Teifi Cheese.

The mild climate and abundant rainfall create lush green grazing pastures for the Friesians and Ayrshires that provide the milk for the cheeses. The result is an exciting range of cheeses from gooey blues, Caerphilly, Dutch Gouda styles and hard cheeses to suit every palate.

Caws Teifi Cheese

Glynhynod Farm, Llandysul, Ceredigion SA44 5JY • 01239 851528
www.teificheese.co.uk
Founded in 1982 by Dutch cheesemakers who moved to Llandysul from the Netherlands, the cheeses are a wonderful combination of Welsh milk and Dutch expertise. Their award-winning 'Teifi' is a Dutch-style Gouda with a smooth, creamy texture. They also produce a Gouda-style cheese with seaweed. After stocking up on cheese, pop across the farmyard to the Dà Mhile Distillery to sample their exquisite botanical gins.

Caws Cenarth Cheese

Glyneithinog, Lancych, Carmarthenshire SA37 0LH • 01239 710432
www.cawscenarth.co.uk
This family-run business draws on six generations of cheesemaking to produce a gorgeous creamy Caerffili. Started by Gwynfor and Thelma Adams in 1987 at their farm, Glyneithinog; their son Carwyn runs the business and indulges his passion for creating new cheeses such as the Brie-like Perl Wen and the Golden Cenarth, an oozy washed-rind cheese.

Hafod Welsh Organic Cheddar

Holden Farm Dairy, Bwlchwernen Fawr, Llangybi, Lampeter, Ceredigion SA48 8PS • 01570 493283 • www.hafodcheese.co.uk
Sam and Rachel Holden make a small batch of cheese every day, piping raw, unpasteurised milk from their 65 Ayrshire cows directly into their dairy. They credit their traditional techniques and creamy Ayrshire milk with giving Hafod its buttery, rich and nutty flavour.

Pitch Up

Cardigan Bay Camping and Caravanning Club Site

Llwynhelyg, Cross Inn, Llandysul,
Ceredigion SA44 6LW • 01545 560029
www.campingandcaravanningclub.co.uk
A lovely rural campsite within striking distance of
beautiful coves and secluded beaches. There's easy
access to great walks and the Ceredigion Coastal Path,
and dolphins and seals are often spotted basking in
the local waters. Most pitches are sloping so levellers
and chocks are required.

Teifi Meadows Caravan and Camping Park (CS)

Fach Ddu, Llanfair Clydogau, Lampeter, Ceredigion
SA48 8LE • 01570 493220 • www.teifimeadows.com
A small, unspoilt campsite close to the River Teifi.
Hidden away and family-friendly, it's a great base
from which to explore the countryside. Campfires are
allowed and you can buy logs, kindling and firelighters
on site. There's also a daily dog-boarding facility.
And for the romantics there's a bothy for two, hidden
away in a tranquil garden setting. The local village of
Llanfair Clydogau is about a mile away and has a well
stocked, licensed shop.

Cwrt Hen Campsite (CS)

Cwrt Hen Farm, Beulah, Newcastle Emlyn,
Carmarthenshire SA38 9QS • 01239 811393
www.cwrthen.co.uk
A small, pretty and very relaxed site ringed by ponds,
meadows and woodlands that are home to a wealth
of local wildlife. Touring caravans, motorhomes,
campervans and tents are all welcome and campfires
are permitted. Best of all, Cwrt Hen is also a market
garden so there's an abundance of lovely fresh fruit,
vegetables and free-range eggs for sale.

Eat Local

Llwynhelyg Farm Shop

Sarnau, Ceredigion SA44 6QU • 01239 811079
www.llwynhelygfarmshop.co.uk
Open for over 30 years, Llwynhelyg has won a
bucketful of awards. They deal directly with around
130 small-scale producers, most within 40 miles. Their
prizewinning *folia fragrantia* (fragrant leaves) are well
known around Ceredigion and fresh herbs are picked
'while-u-wait' from the herb patch. The place is full of
great produce and a fantastic range of over 80 Welsh
cheeses (the Teifi Valley cheeses included).

The Organic Fresh Food Company

Unit 23, Lampeter Industrial Estate, Tregaron Road,
Lampeter, Ceredigion SA48 8LT • 01570 423099
www.organicfreshfoodcompany.co.uk
Don't be put off by the address! This fruit and veg
box delivery company also has a great on-site shop.
They sell a huge range of locally grown produce,
many from the nearby award-winning small family
farm at Blaencamel.

Rhydlewis Trout Farm & Smokery

Rhydlewis, Llandysul, Ceredigion SA44 5QS
01239 851224
A traditional smokery that uses wooden chambers to
slowly smoke products over the finest oak sawdust.
Brian and Rose smoke a great range of local offerings:
salmon, trout, cheeses, bacon, ham, garlic and
chocolate, and their shop stocks other local produce
alongside the smoked delicacies. The Rhydlewis
Fishery has a beautiful 3-acre lake stocked with
Rainbow and Brown trout for fly fishing (day tickets
available at the local post office). And if you land a
trout, pop back into the smokery; they will be more
than happy to smoke it for you.

Wild Pickings

01239 654021 • www.wildpickings.co.uk
Jade Mellor runs a small rural foraging business collecting wild food from the hedgerows, woodlands and coast of West Wales. She sells her seasonal wild foods at farmers' markets, food festivals and restaurants and does guided wild food walks throughout the year as well as hosting practical workshops from her woodland site.

Farmers' Markets

Aberystwyth Farmers' Market

North Parade, Aberystwyth, Ceredigion SY23 2JW
www.aberystwythfarmersmarket.co.uk • 1st and 3rd Saturday of the month
Though Aberystwyth is beyond the Teifi Valley, it warrants a mention as it was judged Britain's top Farmers' Market in the BBC Food and Farming Awards. With up to 30 stalls, it is one of the biggest in the area.

Aberaeron Farmers' Market

Inner Harbour, Aberaeron, Ceredigion SA46 0AJ
1st Saturday of the month (May-September)

Aberaeron Country Market

Alban Square, Aberaeron, Ceredigion SA46 0AD
Every Tuesday

Lampeter Farmers' Market

Market Street, Lampeter, Ceredigion SA48 7DR
Every other Friday

New Quay Country Market

Memorial Hall, Towyn Road, New Quay, Ceredigion SA45 9QQ • Every Friday except in January

> The lush valley that meets the sea is home to the Teifi Valley Cheese Producers, five of the most outstanding artisan cheesemakers in Wales...

Eating Out

Cartws Café

Penbryn Beach, Sarnau, Ceredigion SA44 6QL
01239 810218 • www.cartws.co.uk
This family-run gem overlooking the very special cove at Penbryn sells delicious home-made cakes, smoothies, fresh local crab, king prawns, spicy curries and noodles, all lovingly prepared and served within ancient whitewashed stone walls.

Harbourmaster

2 Quay Parade, Aberaeron, Ceredigion SA46 0BT
01545 570755 • www.harbour-master.com
In a fantastic harbourfront location, Cardigan Bay lobster, fresh sea bream and hake, smoked haddock and leek crumble and Cefn Gwyn wild duck all feature on the menu, depending on the time of year.

Y Talbot

The Square, Tregaron, Ceredigion SY25 6JL
01974 298208 • www.ytalbot.com
This inviting old stone inn offers fresh fish from Cardigan Bay, Cambrian mountain lamb, rare roast Tregaron beef, home-made cawl and Teifi Valley Per Las soufflé.

HOT AND CIDER DIP CHEESE

A camper's snack for the barbecue that's so simple, so gooey and so good. For the cheese, I used Golden Cenarth from Caws Cenarth (and you could also try their Perl Wen) or any Teifi Valley-produced washed-rind cheese with a Camembert consistency. For the cider, try Toloja Orchards Guinevere, a medium-dry cider, made with Welsh varieties of cider apple. Contact them at www.tolojaorchards196.vpweb.co.uk.

Serves 2 as a snack

1 x Teifi Valley rinded cheese, about 250g

1 bottle of local cider

a handful of fresh herbs (rosemary or thyme)

1 loaf of fresh crusty bread (or some cooked new potatoes, if preferred)

- Get 4 appropriately sized sheets of thick aluminium foil, and lay them on top of each other. Lay the cheese (out of its box) in the middle on top. Cut a big cross in the cheese, but not all the way through, and pour a little bit of cider into this. Put a small bunch of fresh herbs on the top and enclose the cheese completely in the foil.

- Place the foil parcel over warm coals or a low-heat barbecue for around 15-20 minutes until warm and really gooey. (If you have an oven in your caravan you can keep the cheese in its wooden box, if it has one, rather than use foil. Cook it at 180ºC/350ºF/gas mark 4 for about 25 minutes.)

- Unwrap the foil, check the cheese has melted, and dip small chunks of crusty bread (or new potatoes) into it. Enjoy with a glass of cider. It's amazing.

34

WELSHMAN'S CAVIAR

While modern culinary tastes have embraced seaweed in sushi or crisped to a cinder in a Chinese restaurant, most of us still haven't got to grips with laver, an edible seaweed that the Welsh have made part of their national cuisine.

To make laver okay to eat, it is repeatedly washed to remove the sand and then boiled until it becomes a stiff green mush. To make laverbread, the seaweed is boiled again for several hours, then minced or puréed, coated with oatmeal and fried. It's traditionally served with bacon and cockles, and has a 'seaside' flavour: not as salty as you might expect, but a whack of sea air and a slightly metallic taste – it's packed with iodine and iron.

If there is one man responsible for bringing laverbread to the masses it's Jonathan Williams from the Pembrokeshire Beach Food Company. In 2010, after chucking in his office job in Swindon, Jonathan set up a small stall outside a Fishguard farm shop selling seaweed flatbreads with seafood fillings. He took his inspiration from food he'd tasted on world travels and blended it with traditional Welsh ingredients. The positive feedback led to him selling seaweed and seafood wraps with crab and lobster rolls from a beach shack. A year later, he won the award for Best British Street Food.

The flagship beach shack sets up home for the summer at Freshwater West in Pembrokeshire. "I still come down here to harvest my own laver, but it was once the centre of a cottage industry that kept the whole Freshwater community in business," explained Jonathan. Just one thatch-roofed seaweed-drying hut remains on the cliff-top on the south side of the beach, near the car park. At one time there were 20 along the beach: the seaweed would be thrown over the top of the huts to dry then taken by horse and cart to Swansea.

Today, this stunning beach is a mecca for surfers and hosts Welsh surfing championships each year. Jonathan's beach shack is up in the car park, not far from the old seaweed drying hut, where he serves up laverbread flatbreads with bacon and cockles to a new generation.

Pembrokeshire Beach Food Company
www.beachfood.co.uk • 01646 278101

Pitch Up

St Davids Camping and Caravanning Club Site

Dwr Cwmwdig Berea, St Davids, Haverfordwest, Pembrokeshire SA62 6DW • 01348 831376
www.campingandcaravanningclub.co.uk
A simple and friendly little site. Peaceful, out of the way and with views and sunsets you'll never want to leave, unless it's to catch the bus just outside the site to the city of St Davids.

Mill Haven Place

Middle Broadmoor, Talbenny, Haverfordwest, Pembrokeshire SA62 3XD • 01437 781633
www.millhavenplace.co.uk
When each pitch has its own picnic bench and fire pit you know you are staying somewhere special. Mill Haven is suitable for caravans, motorhomes and tents, but there are also four fully equipped luxury yurts available. You can have lessons on bushcraft, how to prepare and cook fish or even sea kayaking from Matt, who runs the place. A short walk takes you to Mill Haven beach, perfect for picnics.

> **Most of us still haven't got to grips with laver, an edible seaweed that the Welsh have made part of their national cuisine.**

Windmill Farm (CS)

Dale, Haverfordwest, Pembrokeshire SA62 3QX
01646 636428 • www.campingandcaravanningclub.co.uk
A truly lovely spot with beautiful views across Milford Haven. Up on a hill (the one with the windmill) there are hard standings, a camping field and a spotless facilities block in a converted outhouse on this working dairy farm. A 10-minute stroll takes you into the village of Dale.

Eat Local

Nash Farm Shop and Corn Mill Café

Pembroke Dock, Pembrokeshire SA72 4SU
01646 682445 • www.lowernashfarm.co.uk
Just off the A477 between Pembroke Dock and Milton this family farm produces lamb, beef and pork (including spicy chorizo sausages) for the shop and sells seasonal veg and fruit. They also sell Welshman's Caviar.

Yerbeston Gate Farm Shop

Cresselly, Pembrokeshire SA68 0NS • 01834 891637
www.farmshopfood.co.uk
Great selection of home-raised beef, lamb and pork as well as fresh produce, Welsh cheeses and deli goods. They'll make welcome hampers ready for your arrival at your campsite.

St Davids Food and Wine

High Street, St Davids, Pembrokeshire SA62 6SB
01437 721948 • www.stdavidsfoodandwine.co.uk
This is the kind of delicatessen that makes you want to work your way through everything on the shelves. At one end is a takeaway sandwich bar where your choice is made-to-order from a menu of mouthwatering rolls, baguettes and doorsteps. I never made it as far as the beach to scoff mine.

Claws Shellfish at St Davids Market

www.clawsshellfish.com • Find them here every Thursday and at Haverfordwest every Friday
Whole and dressed crab, lobster, scallops, cockles and mussels, wet fish, mackerel pâtés and fishcakes.

Solva Seafoods

Solva Farm, Panteg Road, Solva, Haverfordwest, Pembrokeshire SA62 6TN • contact Jono Voyce, 01437 729169 • www.solvaseafoods.co.uk
Cooked and live shellfish plus some wet fish, all own-caught.

The Fish Plaice

Milford Fish Docks • 01646 692331
The Fish Plaice has a large wet-fish counter of locally landed and other wet fish.

Farmers' Markets

Haverfordwest Farmers' Market

Riverside Shopping Centre, Haverfordwest, Pembrokeshire SA61 2LJ • Every Friday
One of the best. Fifty stallholders come from up to 40 miles away to sell fine Welsh cheeses, whole cooked lobsters and crab from local waters, prizewinning sausages, wild boar meat and local honey.

St Davids Country Market

Cross Square, St Davids, Pembrokeshire SA62 6SE
Every Thursday.

Fishguard Farmers' Market

Town Hall, Fishguard, Pembrokeshire
Every Saturday

Eating Out
The Griffin Inn

Dale, Haverfordwest, Pembrokeshire SA62 3RB
01646 636227 • www.griffininndale.co.uk
Local seafood caught from their boat *Griffin Girl*.

Pembrokeshire Fish Week is one of Wales' biggest festivals. It takes place at the end of June (see www.pembrokeshirefishweek.co.uk) based around Milford Haven docks. With other events around the county, it's a vibrant week of food demos, tastings, music and celebration.

Quayside

Lawrenny Quay, Pembrokeshire SA68 0PR
01646 651574 • www.quaysidelawrenny.co.uk
Fabulous fresh crab lunches. It's also worth checking out their sister cafe Wavecrest Cafe.

Wavecrest Cafe

West Angle Bay, Pembrokeshire SA71 5BE
01646 641457 • www.wavecrestangle.co.uk

The Shed

Porthgain, Haverfordwest, Pembrokeshire SA62 5BN
01348 831518 • www.theshedporthgain.co.uk
This quayside 'fish and chip bistro' is the kind of place you'll tell your friends about. Watch the fishing boats come in while you eat. The fish on your plate was in the sea just a couple of hours ago.

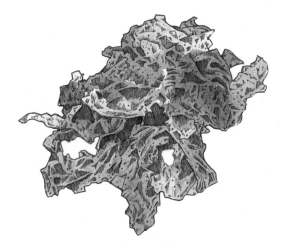

SCALLOP, CHORIZO
AND WELSHMAN'S CAVIAR BUTTY

Serves 1

This recipe is courtesy of Jonathan Williams at the Pembrokeshire Beach Food Company. It's the king of butties and uses his 'Welshman's Caviar' – dried laver seaweed – that you can buy from the beach cafe at Freshwater or at local delis (or online from the above company).

- Heat up a non-stick frying pan and add a touch of olive oil. Once the oil is warm, add the sliced chorizo and start cooking over a medium heat. Keep turning the chorizo over to make sure both sides are cooking.

- When the chorizo starts crisping up, add the Welshman's Caviar. While this is sizzling away check out your scallops. If they have come in the half shell take them out and if you've got any big fat ones cut them in half and place them on a bit of kitchen roll. The scallops you buy have been prepared so you can eat the whole thing, including the coral (the orange bit on the side).

- Now turn the heat up to high and add all the scallops to the pan. Scallops don't need cooking for that long, around 2 minutes depending on the thickness. As soon as they are warm to the touch in the middle, they are ready.

- When the scallops are cooked, take the pan off the heat and add a pinch of salt and pepper and a squeeze of lemon and orange juice and give it all a mix in the pan.

- Slice your crusty roll in two, fill with all the goodness from the pan, and enjoy one of the finest butties in the land!

olive oil

5 slices chorizo sausage

1 tbsp Welshman's Caviar

3 scallops (hand-dived, the sustainable choice)

salt and white pepper

a wedge each of lemon and orange

1 crusty white roll (or tortilla wrap)

35 SNOWDONIA
FFANTASTIC FARM SHOPS
A FUTURE FOR TRADITION

The landscape dictates life in a place like North Wales, especially in Snowdonia. Mountains dominate, people fit in around them. Small villages, once busy mining communities, are linked by slow, snaking roads that feel their way around the crags and boulder-strewn slopes.

It's walking boots not mining boots that tread the mountain paths now, and they come in their thousands each year. But, while lovers of Gore-Tex® are well-served in shops in the centres of Betws-Y-Coed and Capel Curig, what about the food?

On recent trips here, I have discovered an embarrassment of riches in this relatively small area when it comes to artisan food and drink. I've found brewers of beer and cider, cheesemakers, pickle and preserve producers, specialist mushroom growers, bakers and creators of charcuterie, many of whom are working from remote rural communities. Small batch, hand-made and wonderfully crafted regional foods are all here, sold from a handful of extraordinarily good farm shops and 'food centres'. As well as offering produce from their own farms, they are passionate about providing an outlet for other local, smaller suppliers. I can't recommend the following places highly enough. This is definitely where to get supplies on the way to your Snowdonia camping adventure.

Bodnant Welsh Food Centre

Furnace Farm, Tal-y-Cafn, Conwy LL28 5RP • 01492 651100
www.bodnant-welshfood.co.uk
Furnace Farm, part of the Bodnant Estate, is a collection of 16th-century granite buildings housing an extensive selection of Welsh produce.
The butchers work in full view of the customers and a board details the provenance of the meat. The central bakery has an array of artisan breads piled high on shelves; the smell is wonderful. If you fancy honey on your speciality bread, the National Beekeeping Centre of Wales is based here, too. The deli has an abundance of pies including Welsh Oggies (a pasty) and a huge range of cheeses made in the on-site dairy, which you can watch being made. The rest of the shop is a treasure box of small artisanal products.

Rhug Estate

Corwen, Denbighshire LL21 0EH • 01490 413000 • www.rhug.co.uk

Hearing there was a burger bar in front of the farm shop made me think of a mobile unit frequented by the usual big-bellied burger barflies of the sort found in DIY car parks. How wrong I was. It's actually a stylish wood and glass building off the chic main shop and restaurant. But hey, why shouldn't farm shops be chi-chi? The Rhug Estate has been farmed by the same family since 1637 and the current Lord Newborough has pushed it to the forefront of large-scale ethical food production, converting 6,500 of the estate's 12,500 acres into organic status.

The butcher's counter plays the starring role in this shop. As well as bison meat, there are cuts from the estate's Aberdeen Angus cattle. And unlike most chicken suppliers, who slaughter their birds at 4–6 weeks old, Rhug chickens roam in clover-rich pastures until 11–16 weeks. The texture and flavour are superb.

The shop is packed with a bewildering selection of locally made sauces, relishes, marinades and rubs plus local beers and ciders. Fresh eggs and just-cooked bakes make it a food-shopping fantasy.

> *Please support the farm shops when you visit Snowdonia. You'll be supporting all those passionate remote and rural artisan producers who are keeping local skills alive.*

Pitch Up

Cefn Cae Camping Site (CS)

Rowen, Conwy LL32 8YT • 01492 650011
www.campinginnorthwales.co.uk
With panoramic views of the surrounding mountains, Cefn Cae is set on a 300-acre farm in the picturesque village of Rowen, within the boundaries of the Snowdonia National Park. The grassy pitches are big and the facilities are great. A barn has been converted into a kitchen, with fridge, freezer and microwave for all to use. There are a couple of pre-pitched bell tents for hire too.

The local pub **Ty Gwyn** is only a 200-yard walk away – it has great food, local ales and the occasional singsong. The local shop and post office are just a few steps further. The site is five minutes' drive from **Bodnant Welsh Food Centre**.

The local butcher in Bala makes a fabulous pork pie with a black-pudding bottom, a pork filling in the middle and a quail's egg on top.

Bala Camping and Caravanning Club Site

Crynierth Caravan Park, Cefn Ddwysarn, Bala, Gwynedd LL23 7LN • 01678 530324
www.campingandcaravanningclub.co.uk
Expect a super-friendly welcome and a clean and tidy site. Small by Club standards and surrounded by trees, this secluded spot is perfect for star-gazing, as light pollution is so low. This site is close to Lake Bala, the largest natural lake in Wales, with plenty of opportunities for fishing and sailing. The village of Bala is full of independent shops and cafes and the village butcher, **T J Roberts**, is heartily recommended by locals. The nearby **Bryntirion Inn** offers decent pub food and a great selection of local ales. **Rhug Estate farm shop** is 10-minutes drive away.

Bryn Awel (CS)

Llanuwchllyn, Bala, Gwynedd LL23 7DD • 07805 122771 • www.campingandcaravanningclub.co.uk
Joan and Roy who run this simple little site are great hosts. Their site, on top of a hill, has the most astounding views of the valley and Lake Bala; I could have stared at it all day. A 20-minute walk takes you to a wonderful old stone village pub, **The Eagles Inn** (www.yr-eagles.co.uk) serving home-cooked meals.

WELSH LAMB, SWEET POTATO
AND CHICKPEA SALAD

This was made for me on a campsite by my friend and wonderful campsite cook, Helen Jenkins. She is married to a Welshman, and champions Welsh produce at every opportunity.

Serves about 4

3 lamb steaks

2 medium sweet potatoes, peeled and halved

salt and pepper

1 tsp Welsh honey

olive oil

1 x 400g tin of chickpeas or cannellini beans, drained and rinsed

150g baby plum or cherry tomatoes, halved

4 spring onions, sliced

a few handfuls of greenery like lamb's lettuce or rocket

For the marinade

1 tbsp dried mint

1 tsp harissa (or look for another exciting chilli-based paste in the farm shops)

2 tbsp lemon juice

2 tbsp olive oil

For the dressing

½ tsp Welsh honey

1 tbsp lemon juice

3 tbsp extra virgin olive oil

- Start by marinating the meat. Rub the dried mint and harissa on the steaks and place them in a freezer bag. Then add the lemon juice and olive oil, squidge to mix, and leave to rest for an hour or two.

- Boil the sweet potatoes in salted water for about 15 minutes. Drain and leave to cool.

- When the potatoes have cooled, cut them into slices no more than 1cm thick. Put these in a bowl, then add the honey, a glug of olive oil and a pinch of salt. Gently mix to coat the potato.

- Put both lamb and potato on the barbecue — both will need about 3 or 4 minutes on each side.

- Prepare the salad while it cooks. Put the rinsed chickpeas or beans in a bowl, and add the tomatoes and spring onions.

- Mix all of the dressing ingredients together in a jug or cup, and then pour into the bowl of chickpeas and tomatoes.

- Once the lamb is cooked to your liking, cover in foil and leave it to rest for 5 minutes or so. Then cut the lamb into bite-sized cubes and halve the slices of sweet potato.

- Mix the lamb and sweet potatoes into the bowl with the chickpeas and dressing.

- Divide your green leaves between 4 plates and pile the lamb, potato and chickpea mixture on top.

- If you have it, a sheep's or goat's cheese crumbled over the top would finish this off beautifully.

NORTHERN ENGLAND

From the scenic splendour of the Lakes to the beautiful bleakness of the Yorkshire moors and rugged Northumberland's endless horizons, this is a landscape for hardy breeds. And I'm not just talking about the animals. The forced rhubarb of Yorkshire traditionally provided fresh produce in the winter months. Smoking herring into Craster kippers prolonged the 'shelf' life of fish for leaner times. It's not just cultural pride that keeps these foods with us – they taste fantastic, too.

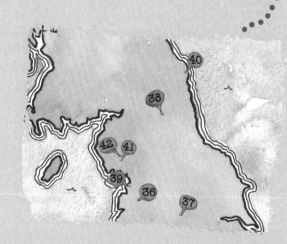

36 SAY CHEESE!

The craft of traditional cheesemaking is centuries old in Britain. Before mass production, the process took place in farmhouse kitchens; the result was a truly local cheese made to a unique family recipe handed down through generations.

Cheeses made in different parts of the country were easily recognisable and genuine regional varieties such as Wensleydale, Cheddar and Cheshire thrived. But improvements in road networks led to milk from herds hundreds of miles apart being combined for large-scale cheesemaking in factories, and the subtle distinctions in flavour were lost.

The introduction of milk quotas in the early 1980s kick-started the revival of small-scale cheesemaking on British farms. Farmers needed ways of using excess milk; some made ice-cream or butter, others cheese. There are now over 700 named British cheeses being produced. It is the return to the traditional methods and recipes using milk from single herds grazed in a particular area that makes seeking out these cheeses exciting. Wherever you go camping this season, sample the local cheeses and you will truly be tasting the landscape around you.

One area where artisan cheesemakers are thriving again is in the north of England. I visited Mrs Kirkham's Cheese in the village of Goosnargh, near Preston, where fourth-generation cheesemaker Graham Kirkham uses his great-grandmother's recipe to make delectable Lancashire cheese from his single herd of Friesians.

Graham explained that the technique of blending fresh curds with those from previous milkings derives from a time when farmers only had a few cows and there wasn't enough milk to make cheese every day. Curd would be stored until there was enough to mix together to make a wheel of cheese. It is then milled, moulded and pressed in traditional hand presses to extract all the moisture.

A day later they are lovingly wrapped in cotton cloth, painted with melted butter and put away to store. Like wine, the length of storage affects the flavour. Graham gave me a piece of one-month-old cheese, then a more complex-flavoured three-month-old cheese to try. Both were delicious. Although only made in small batches, theirs is a highly sought-after product, sold to the likes of Harrods. But good cheese should be available to everyone, and as if to prove this point a local policeman pops his head around the dairy door to swap a box of his best chicken eggs for a large chunk.

Because all of the milk comes from their own cows, the Kirkhams don't need to pasteurise. As Graham sees it, "Raw cheese has more interesting and complex flavours and that makes the character of our cheese." Factors such as the weather, the season and the flowers in the fields all influence the flavour. This is truly a food 'of the land', as witnessed by the large round stones in fields close to many farms. These are cheese-stones once used to press the cheeses.

Forget trainspotting or stamp-collecting, cheese-tasting is where it's at. Sampling local cheeses on your travels and finding out about where they were made can turn into a rewarding hobby.

Mrs Kirkham's Cheese

Beesley Farm, Mill Lane, Goosnargh, Preston, Lancashire PR3 2LF
www.mrskirkhams.com

Pitch Up

Crawshaw Farm Caravan and Camping Site (CS)

Back Lane, Newton-in-Bowland, Clitheroe, Lancashire BB7 3EE • 01220 446638
www.campingandcaravanningclub.co.uk
One field – a bit uneven, a loo in a lean-to, two cold taps (spring-fed), drystone walls and blissful isolation pretty much sums up Crawshaw Farm. If you like camping that leaves modern life behind and fills your soul with the freedom of the natural world, this is the campsite for you.

Brickhouse Touring Caravan Site

Swinglehurst Lane, Chipping, Lancashire PR3 2QW
01995 61747 • www.brickhouseccs.co.uk
Within the boundaries of Bowland Forest, this 45-pitch family-run site is aimed at 'mature campers and quiet families'. If you fit the bill then you'll enjoy great facilities including underfloor heating in the shower block. The attractive village of Chipping, with good cafes and a pub, is 400 yards away.

Clitheroe Camping and Caravanning Club Site

Edisford Road, Clitheroe, Lancashire BB7 3LA
01200 425294 • www.campingandcaravanningclub.co.uk
Set in Lancashire's glorious Ribble Valley, this traditional touring site in a parkland setting is an oasis of calm close to the River Ribble – a popular spot for swimming, canoeing and fishing. A little over a mile away, the market town of Clitheroe is becoming a foodie haven, with a lively Food Festival every August. Most campers head for Cowmans Famous Sausage Shop to choose from over 75 flavours of sausage. **Roy Porter Butchers** sells organic meats from heritage breeds and **Bashall Barn** is a fabulous farm shop.

Eat Local

Dewlay Cheesemakers

Garstang Bypass Road, Garstang, Preston, Lancashire PR3 0PR • 01995 602335 • www.dewlay.com
Nick and Richard Kenyon follow the Lancashire cheesemaking methods used by their father and grandfather before them, using milk sourced less than 6 miles away. They have an on-site cheese shop, complete with viewing platform, and a cheese museum.

Cheesie Tchaikovsky

The Ground Floor, Lee Carter House, Castle Street, Clitheroe, Lancashire BB7 2BX • 01200 428366
My idea of heaven. A specialist cheese shop, delicatessen and cafe, the shop stocks great cheese from Rungis market in Paris and other continental suppliers, but Jan the owner is careful to always showcase the best local cheese, including Greenfields Tasty, Blacksticks Blue and Mrs Kirkham's. Can't choose? Just order the cheese platter in the cafe and scoff the lot.

Booths

Berry Lane, Longridge, Preston, Lancashire PR3 3NH
Cherestanc Square, Park Hill Rd, Garstang, Preston, Lancashire PR3 1EF
This classy northwest supermarket chain features local produce and sells Mrs Kirkham's cheese.

Little Town Farm Shop

Chipping Road, Thornley, Preston, Lancashire PR3
2TB • 01772 786198 • www.littletownfarmshop.co.uk
A little farm shop on the edge of the Forest of
Bowland selling home-reared Aberdeen Angus Beef,
Gloucester Old Spot Pork and Bowland Lamb. Get
the full range of products from their **Little Town
Dairy** too – yoghurts, crème fraîche and ice-cream
as well as some fabulous home-made ready meals.

The Lancashire Tourist Board has
devised three wonderful 'cheese-
walking trails' that take you around
many of the artisan dairies.
www.visitlancashire.com

Eating Out
Bashall Barn

Bashall Town, Clitheroe, Lancashire BB7 3LQ
01200 428964 • www.bashallbarn.co.uk
Even the magnificent view of the Ribble Valley from
the restaurant might struggle to distract you from the
delights on your plate. Order the Bashall Herdsman's
Platter with home-cooked ham, liver pâté, pig pie
and Lancashire cheese or perhaps the Steamed Rag
Pudding (minced beef and onions in suet pastry).
Just make sure you leave enough room for ice-cream
from the on-site parlour. The Farm Shop is just as
good; it specialises in its own range of home-made
ready meals and cakes.

GRIDDLED SUMMER VEGETABLES WITH LANCASHIRE CHEESE

Head off to a local market in the summer months, and it will offer up a hugely varied, colourful, flavour-packed glut of veggies, costing next to nothing. This dish lets those flavours sing out. Barbecuing helps to release all the sugars in the vegetables, and gives them that lovely caramelised flavour. Top it with a rich, tongue-tingling, Lancashire cheese.

Serves 2 as a main, 4 as a side

1 aubergine, sliced lengthways

2 courgettes, sliced lengthways

1 fennel bulb, sliced lengthways

1 red pepper, sliced lengthways into 1cm strips

2 garlic cloves, finely chopped

olive oil

1 tbsp balsamic vinegar

grated zest and juice of ½ lemon

fresh herbs of choice: try 1 tbsp each of mint, basil and thyme leaves, chopped

salt and pepper

150g Mrs Kirkham's or other Lancashire Cheese (tasty or crumbly)

50g walnut halves

- Put the prepared aubergine, courgette, fennel and pepper, half the chopped garlic and a glug of olive oil in a big bowl. Mix gently with your hands, making sure the oil covers all the veg.

- Lay the veg on the preheated grill, griddle or hotplate. You may have to do this in batches. Keep a close eye and turn them occasionally until they have softened, caramelised and have those lovely char-grilled marks on them.

- While they are cooking, get your dressing ready. Put 3 tbsp olive oil, the balsamic vinegar, the remaining garlic, lemon zest and juice, the chopped fresh herbs and a big pinch of salt and plenty of black pepper into a large serving bowl. Give it a really good mix.

- When the vegetables are all nicely cooked, put them in the bowl and gently but thoroughly mix them with the dressing.

- Crumble your choice of cheese and the walnuts over the top and serve.

- (For a more substantial meal you can serve this mixed through couscous.)

37

RHUBARB, RHUBARB, RHUBARB

I am standing in a large, dark shed in Yorkshire. It's snowing outside, but in here it's hot and humid. All around me, lit only by candlelight, are hundreds of sticks of bright crimson rhubarb standing to attention, while clicks, creaks and squeals fill the air. These eerie sounds are the buds splitting as the rhubarb forces itself up to look for light.

Forcing rhubarb is a technique used since the early 1800s. It prolongs the growing season of the plant, which otherwise harvests outside from April to October. A forced crop yields from January to the end of March and is sought after because of its superior flavour.

It is a long and labour-intensive technique which starts two years before the plants even get into the sheds. New plants are left to grow naturally in outdoor fields for two years without the stalks being harvested and this allows plenty of energy to build up in the roots. A ground frost is then required for the roots to start releasing that carbohydrate energy and it's at this point the roots are dug up and carefully packed together in the forcing sheds. By leaving them in the dark and providing heat and moisture, all the energy that has been stored in the root will force the pink stalk upright, creating a wonderfully flavoured stick of rhubarb.

The lady showing me around is Janet Oldroyd Hulme, known in the trade as the High Priestess of rhubarb. Her family's 800-acre farm is based in the area known as the Rhubarb Triangle, between Leeds, Wakefield and Bradford. As the plant derives from Southern Siberia I am curious to know why it grows so well in this part of Yorkshire. Janet explains that rhubarb likes the cold and plenty of water. Being in the shadow of the Pennines creates a great frost pocket and provides plenty of rain. The soil is just right too; it's 'loamy', which retains water. So it's not quite Siberia – but it works just as well.

At its peak, there were over 200 producers in the Triangle; now there are just 12. Their long, low, forcing sheds are a feature of the landscape. Determined to secure a future for the remaining producers, Janet has worked hard to achieve the coveted Protected Designation of Origin (PDO) status, a mark of quality and assurance that traditional skills have been used to produce the crop. This is particularly important in an area that has lost its other two main industries – coal mining and the wool industry, both of which once supported the growing of rhubarb. The coal heated the forcing sheds and the waste wool, known as 'shoddy', was used to fertilise the soil.

Every year during the forcing season, people come from all over the world to visit the sheds, especially during the Wakefield Rhubarb Festival in February. And they never leave without buying a stash of these glorious pink sticks.

www.yorkshirerhubarb.co.uk

Pitch Up

Crowden Camping and Caravanning Club Site

Woodhead Road, Crowden, Glossop,
Derbyshire SK13 1HZ • 01457 866057
www.campingandcaravanningclub.co.uk
Although certainly not in the heart of the Rhubarb
Triangle, this site offers a beautiful back-to-nature
experience after a day in the culture-rich cities of
Leeds and Bradford or nearby Manchester. At the
northern tip of the Peak District National Park, it is
a walker's paradise too.

Harrogate Caravan Park

Great Yorkshire Showground, Harrogate,
North Yorkshire HG2 8NZ • 01423 546145
www.harrogatecaravanpark.co.uk
What to mention first? The fancy pink units in the loo
block? Those glorious views across the Crimple Valley?
The fact you are so close to the joys of Harrogate? Or
that there is *the* most fantastic farm shop and cafe,
Fodder, in the Yorkshire Showground next door?
You choose.

Wintersett Lakes Caravan and Camping Park

Haw Park Lane, Wintersett, Wakefield, West Yorkshire
WF4 2EB • 07901 880095 • www.wintersettlakes.co.uk
Right next door to Wintersett Lakes and a Country
Park, but also close to the cities and the rhubarb sheds
– so best of all worlds. Super-friendly owners make
for a welcoming stay that is great value for money.
It's worth pointing out that this site is better for self-
sufficient tourers or 'soap dodgers', as there are no
showers here, but the loos are spotless.

Eat Local

Blacker Hall Farm Shop

Branch Road, Wakefield, West Yorkshire WF4 3DN
01924 267202 • blackerhallfarmshop.co.uk
The fact that this place has been named Best Farm
Shop in the UK gives a clue to what you can expect.
Over 80 per cent of the stock comes from their own
farm; the rest is the best of the small, local producers
from Yorkshire and elsewhere in the UK.

The Rhubarb Triangle Farm Shop

Green End Farm, Carlton, Wakefield,
West Yorkshire WF3 3QR • 0113 288 7034
www.therhubarbtrianglefarmshop.co.uk
These fabulous folk are fiercely proud of their
rhubarb. Get yourself over to the butchers' counter,
where Calvin will delight you with his inventive
selection of meat and rhubarb combinations:
chicken breasts stuffed with rhubarb and a ginger
preserve glaze, rhubarb and chilli sausages, and
pork, mushroom and rhubarb kebabs, to name but a
few. Yorkshire pride is evident in their other produce
too, mostly from local fields, bakeries and brewers.

Fodder

Great Yorkshire Showground, Harrogate,
North Yorkshire HG2 8NZ • 01423 546111
www.fodder.co.uk
Technically it's not a farm shop because it's on the
Yorkshire Showground, but the shop and cafe are
supplied by over 300 local farmers, bakers, makers
and brewers. This is a happy, well-run place that
stocks everything you'll need for a holiday's worth
of tasty fresh food. If you don't want to cook, their
cafe is a real treat, too.

For details of tours around the forced
rhubarb sheds from January to
March: www.yorkshirerhubarb.co.uk.
Wakefield's annual Rhubarb Festival,
including tours and cooking demos,
takes place every February. See www.
wakefield.gov.uk for more details.

Avid Farm Shop

Lee Lane, Millhouse Green, Sheffield, South Yorkshire
S36 9NN • 01226 764800 • www.avidfarmshop.co.uk
"We evolved from a passion for the good life,"
explains owner Karen Close. To keep miles low,
food is seasonal and local, the meat is from their own
farm, the baker delivers on a bike. The cafe alone is
worth making a detour for. Try the vegetable soup
with dumplings or the hot pulled pork sandwiches
followed by bread and butter pudding.

RHUBARB
CRUMBLE CAMPING STYLE

Okay, so this is a bit of a cheat's version, but it still gives you the tongue-tingling taste of glorious rhubarb with a exciting zing of ginger. Use fresh rhubarb; it doesn't have to be the forced variety.

Serves 2

- Lay 2 pieces of aluminium foil, about A4 size, on top of each other to make a double thickness rectangle. Repeat so you have 2 double rectangles.

- Turn the foil pieces so they are portrait, not vertical, in front of you. Lay a piece of baking parchment, around A5 size, in the middle of each foil rectangle.

- Cut each piece of rhubarb into 2cm pieces and divide these pieces between the 2 foil/parchment rectangles. Pile the rhubarb up in the centre, rather than out to the edges.

- Now sprinkle the fresh ginger evenly between them. And then add 2 tsp of brown sugar to each.

- Now make your parcels. Fold the foil as if you are folding a piece of A4 to fit in a long envelope. Bring the left side across the rhubarb mixure, then the right side over that. Fold the shorter edges over and over a few times to seal it.

- Place your packages on the heated barbecue, hotplate or large dry frying pan or even over some glowing embers.

- Leave to heat, cook and soften for about 6-7 minutes. It may take longer or less time according to heat strength. The only way to be sure is to check by opening one of the parcels.

- Once the rhubarb has softened, remove the parcels and put each one on a plate. Open them up and fold the sides down to create a little rectangular foil dish.

- Crumble 3 ginger biscuits over the rhubarb in each parcel, then add a generous blob of thick crème fraîche or clotted cream on the top.

2 sticks of rhubarb, about 30cm long

2 tbsp grated fresh root ginger

4 tsp soft brown sugar

To serve

6 ginger biscuits

2 tbsp crème fraîche or clotted cream

38 GAME ON

The joy of camping is that we reconnect with the seasons and the weather (good and bad!), and we have more time to take in the landscape and to notice what is growing and living in the fields, orchards and hedgerows. For me, it seems the perfect opportunity to choose food that is 'of the place' too.

Knowing the problems associated with intensively farmed animals, wild meat seems like a good alternative. These animals and birds live in their natural habitat, foraging the fields and hedgerows. Their meat is organic, free-range, nutritious, lean and free from medicines and antibiotics. In many cases it's cheaper too.

In Northumberland, pheasant and grouse are in abundance. Every mile or so we had to slow down to watch the trademark strut of the jewel-coloured cock pheasant crossing in front of us, or the rudderless run of his dowdier friends, grouse and woodcock. The vast moorlands are the perfect habitat for these birds, which provide a great source of local food.

I met David Ridley, owner of **Ridley's Fish and Game,** at his stall in Hexham Farmers' Market (see page 297). One side of his stall displayed fresh fish, the other was dedicated to a wide range of game: rabbit, pheasant, grouse, quail and venison. "It's all from local shoots," he said.

"I remind customers that shoots are great for the local economy as well as providing food," explained David. "Local lads and lasses help out on the moors, and the meat is supplied to butchers in the area. Game is a way of life around here."

It's an old-fashioned idea that eating game is for posh folk. A glance at the prices on the stall showed me that pheasant breast can be cheaper than chicken. David beckoned over a fresh-faced chap in overalls. William Stonehouse lives in nearby Allendale and most weekends he and his friends catch rabbits to supply the local butchers, something they have done since they were lads. I ask if he eats much game. He laughs, "Loads! I had a rabbit stir-fry last night. It was great." David continued, "A new generation are buying it. Young mothers are starting to feed rabbit meat to their children; it's cheaper than chicken and has a good flavour."

Inspired, I picked up a pack. "You know, grey squirrel is becoming quite popular ..." mused David. "I'll stick with the rabbit this time," I smiled. But never say never.

www.ridleysfishandgame.co.uk

Pitch Up

Herding Hill Farm

Shield Hill, Haltwhistle, Northumberland NE49 9NW
01434 320175 • www.herdinghillfarm.co.uk

Just a mile from Hadrian's Wall, the owners strive
to have the best site in Northumberland. As well as
the hard standing and touring pitches you can hire
wigwams, lodges or stay in the bunkhouse. There's
underfloor heating, a sauna and a petting farm with
donkeys and alpacas. Breakfast rolls and pizzas can
be delivered to your pitch and there's also a great shop
... but none of this detracts from the truly wild beauty
surrounding you.

Bellingham Camping and Caravanning Club Site

Bellingham, Hexham, Northumberland NE48 2JY
01434 220175 • www.campingandcaravanningclub.
co.uk

If it's tranquillity that you are after, this site has it in
spades. Situated on the edge of Northumberland's
National Park, you can camp in utter peace (bar the
owls at night and birdsong in the morning). The
campsite shop is really well stocked, although the
walk into Bellingham village is an easy one.

Rye Hill Farm (CS)

Slaley, Near Hexham, Northumberland NE47 0AH
01434 673259 • www.ryehillfarm.co.uk

This great little campsite is on a 300-year-old working
sheep farm, so you'll be surrounded by free-range
hens, sheep and ponies. Children will love the nearby
wood with its car-tyre constructions and dens; there
is also a play barn for rainy days. Well located for the
beautiful Roman town of Corbridge and the market
town of Hexham.

Eat Local

Vallum Farm

Military Road, East Wallhouses, Matfen,
Northumberland NE18 0LL • 01434 672406
www.vallumfarm.co.uk

A group of food artisans operating from one stylish
courtyard near Hadrian's Wall. More than 90 per cent
of the produce sold or cooked on site is produced at
Vallum or within a very few miles. You can watch the
chefs pick their ingredients from the kitchen garden
while you enjoy your lunch in the tea room. The
wooden play park is a draw for the younger crowd, as
is the ice cream parlour, with ices made from the rich
and creamy milk of the farm's Brown Swiss cattle. The
separate 'higher-end' restaurant in the complex serves
contemporary English food and tapas.

Brocksbushes Farm Shop

Brocksbushes Farm, Corbridge, Northumberland
NE43 7UB • 01434 633100 • www.brocksbushes.co.uk

Brocksbushes has grown from being a tiny shed on
an acre of fruit farm to a busy, popular shopping
destination. You can still pick your own in the summer
months, or do your weekly shop of fresh produce,
home-cooked hams, meats, cheeses and freshly
baked bread.

North Acomb Farm Shop

Bywell, Stocksfield, Northumberland NE43 7UF
01661 843181 • www.northacomb.co.uk
You can buy seasonal game here, alongside home-farmed free-range poultry, spring lamb and pork. The farm shop started in 1978 selling surplus free-range eggs from the back door and has grown over the years in response to demand. Now you can buy the best of the produce you see in the fields around the shop. The peacocks aren't for sale though.

Robert Grant's Butchers Shop

Vallum Farm, Military Road, East Wallhouses, Matfen, Northumberland NE18 0LL • 01434 672652 www.grantsbutchers.co.uk
A great selection of game, plus the famous 100-strong selection of sausages. Lamb and Thai Green Curry sausage anyone? Less local is their stock of frozen python, crocodile and emu meat!

Billy Bell

Market Place, Haltwhistle, Northumberland
NE49 0BQ • 01434 320253
Close to Herding Hill campsite, this butchers sells all you need for a true Northumbrian feast.

Farmers' Markets

North East England Farmers' Markets (NEEFM) is an umbrella organisation for farmers' market operators in the region and their website gives you all the info you need on what's happening where: **www.neefm.org.uk**

Hexham Farmers' Market

Market Place, Hexham, Northumberland NE46 1XQ www.hexhamfarmersmarket.co.uk • 2nd and 4th Saturday of the month
A well-established market in the shadows of beautiful Hexham Abbey. All producers come from within a 50-mile radius. Ridley's Fish and Game Stall is a highlight, as are the local breads.

Hadrian's Wall Farmers' Market

Greenhead Village Hall, Greenhead, Northumberland CA8 7HE • 01697 747448 • 2nd Sunday of the month
Known as 'the friendly village market'. A chance to meet local food producers and perhaps even learn new recipes.

RUSTIC RABBIT STEW
WITH DUMPLINGS

High on flavour and low on cost, this comforting stew can be made in one pot on the stove or over a fire, so is very campsite friendly. Obviously the dumplings are optional and can be replaced by hunks of bread to serve. However, they are simple to make, and add an extra comfort food 'hug'.

Serves 4

500g diced rabbit meat (Ridley's Fish and Game sell this: see page 234)

4 heaped tbsp plain flour

1 tsp each of English mustard powder, paprika and dried oregano

salt and pepper

2 tbsp olive oil

8 shallots, whole, or 1 large onion, cut into 8 segments

2 garlic cloves, chopped

4 carrots, peeled and diced

425ml dry white wine

700ml chicken stock (a cube is fine)

For the dumplings

100g self-raising flour

50g suet

a handful of fresh parsley leaves, chopped

- Mix the flour, mustard powder, paprika, oregano and some salt and pepper together in a large freezer bag. Put the rabbit meat in and give it a shake to coat the meat.

- Heat the oil in a large saucepan with a lid, and add the rabbit pieces. Fry for around 5 minutes until browned all over.

- Add the shallots or onion, garlic and carrots and fry for another 5 minutes.

- Add the wine and stock and stir well to get all the flavours off the bottom of the pan. Bring to the boil, then turn the heat down to a gentle simmer and put the lid on. Allow it to simmer for 25 minutes.

- To make the dumplings, in a bowl mix the flour, suet and parsley with a large pinch each of salt and pepper. Add enough cold water to make a stiff dough with your hands. Form into 8 balls.

- Put the dumplings on top of the stew, put the lid back on, and cook for a further 20 minutes.

- Serve the stew in bowls, with 2 dumplings per person.

39 A POTTED HISTORY

Beyond the faded grandeur of the buildings and arcades of Morecambe Bay there is a natural beauty to be enjoyed. The Bay also has a wonderful natural asset. Its shifting sands and expansive mudflats are rich in seafood, particularly shrimps – small, brown and absurdly tasty.

Morecambe's native shrimps are the basis for the centuries-old regional delicacy, potted shrimp – cooked shrimps packed into a little pot and preserved under a layer of spice-infused butter. Like many regional dishes, it started as a practical preserving technique, but the sheer gastronomic genius of combining these simple flavours and textures meant that potted shrimp became a favourite far beyond the county borders.

The industry once provided employment for many Morecambe families but now only a handful of shrimpers remain. One is Ray Edmondson, who has been shrimping in Morecambe Bay for over 50 years. With his wife Pat, he owns Edmondson's fish shop on Yorkshire Street, where they sell their own potted shrimps as well as fresh fish.

When conditions are right, Ray heads out into the bay before dawn in his home-made boat. He sieves through each haul of shrimps, taking only the biggest ones, then plunges them into boiling water to kill any bacteria and cook them while they are as fresh as possible.

Back at the shop they are hand peeled before being piled into pots and sealed with that delectable spicy butter. Peeling large numbers of shrimps this small requires dexterity, concentration and patience. But, doing it by hand remains the preferred method among the remaining potted shrimp businesses around the bay – including **Baxters** (see page 303), the largest in the area. Baxters, based in Grange-over-Sands on the northern side of the bay, has been in the shrimp business since 1799 and holds a Royal Warrant on its product.

Royal approval or not, potted shrimps are a delicious national treasure. So let's do our bit to ensure the shrimp-fishing industry survives.

Edmondson's

32a Yorkshire Street, Morecambe, Lancashire LA3 1QE • 01524 412828

Pitch Up

Red Bank Farm and Campsite

The Shore, Bolton le Sands, Carnforth, Lancashire
LA5 8JR • 01524 823196 • www.redbankfarm.co.uk
Red Bank Farm Campsite is a small, family-run site
on a working farm, on the shores of Morecambe Bay.
Chickens wander free range across the campsite, so
make sure you zip up your tent as they do like a warm
sleeping bag. You can buy their eggs from the lovely
on-site **Archers Cafe**. Run by the family, it offers
hearty home-cooked bakes made with the farm's eggs,
saltmarsh lamb burgers from the farm's own flock and
Morecambe Bay potted shrimps. There is a wood-
burner inside for cosy autumnal days, and decking for
enjoying the views in the summer.

For centuries Morecambe Bay shrimps
were caught by people wading out into the
bay with hand nets on the end of a pole. It
was dangerous work; the undercurrents
and quick sands on the bay are notorious.
Horse-drawn carts with nets attached
replaced the hand nets, enabling bigger
hauls in deeper water. By the 1960s
tractors had replaced the horses.

Hollins Farm

Far Arnside, near Carnforth, Lancashire LA5 0SL
01524 701508 • www.holgates.co.uk
A gorgeous little site with top-notch facilities and a
very relaxed vibe, helped by the resident goats, ponies
and chickens. This tourer's site is a 5-minute walk
from its sister, Silverdale Holiday Park, where Hollins
Farm campers have access to the swimming pool,
bar and restaurant. The site shop sells local eggs and
dairy from a nearby farm. It's a 20-minute walk into
Carnforth village, where the local fishmonger brings
his van every Wednesday.

Gibraltar Farm Campsite

Jenny Browns Point, Silverdale, Lancashire LA5 0UA
01524 701736 • www.gibfarm.weebly.com
This working farm has given several fields over
to campers. Ancient woodland, caves and
limestone outcrops provide the perfect setting for
adventurous young spirits, while for nature lovers
and ornithologists, it's paradise. Caravans and
motorhomes are welcome and the tent pitches are
down by the shore. A true gem.

Eat Local

Edmondson's
32a Yorkshire Street, Morecambe,
Lancashire LA3 1QE • 01524 412828
Freshly potted shrimp, brown shrimps and fresh wet
fish straight from the bay.

Baxters
Thornton Road, Morecambe, Lancashire
LA4 5PB (behind the Spar shop) • 01524 410910
www.baxterspottedshrimps.co.uk
Sells fresh and frozen potted shrimps, smoked
salmon, crab, lobster and scallops.

Port of Lancaster Smokehouse
West Quay, Glasson Dock, Lancaster, Lancashire
LA2 0DB • 01524 751493 (about 20 minutes
south of Red Bank Campsite)
Watch the fishermen land their daily catch right
outside this shop on Glasson Dock, then head inside
for potted shrimps as well as a huge selection of
smoked fish and game.

Greenlands Farm Village
Tewitfield, Carnforth, Lancashire LA6 1JH
01524 784184 • www.greenlandsfarmvillage.co.uk
This place is great for a morning's outing for families.
You can groom donkeys, handle chicks and feed
lambs. There are tractors to climb on, go-karts to race
and a soft play area. The cafe uses Lancashire cheeses
and local sausages. Finish off with a mooch around
the artisan craft village and load up on supplies in
the farm shop, which has a butchers counter and
Lancashire cheese counter.

Farmers' Markets
Lancaster University Farmers' Market
Alexandra Square, Lancaster University, Bailrigg,
Lancaster, Lancashire LA1 4YW • Every Thursday
(during term time)
A suitably vibrant market, packed with Lancashire's
best eats at great prices.

Lancaster Charter Market
Market Square, off Market Street, Lancaster,
Lancashire LA1 1JQ • www.lancaster.gov.uk/
chartermarket • Every Wednesday and Saturday
It's not a certified farmers' market, but still has a
decent amount of regional produce, including freshly
cooked food.

Milnthorpe Farmers' Market
Market Square, Milnthorpe, Cumbria LA7 7PN
(15 minutes from Hollins Farm and Gibraltar
Farm Campsites) • Every 2nd Friday
Just over the border in Cumbria, this pretty
little market town comes to life on the fortnightly
market day.

SPAGHETTI SHRIMP SUPPER

Serves 4

- Heat the butter with a little splash of oil in a large frying pan. Add the courgette and asparagus (if using), and fry until they start to go golden brown. Remove them from the pan and put to one side.

- Meanwhile, start cooking the spaghetti in a saucepan of boiling salted water according to the instructions on the packet.

- Turn the heat down under the vegetable pan, add the garlic and heat for a minute, being careful not to let it burn. Now add the white wine, turn the heat up, and let it bubble for a couple of minutes.

- Turn the heat down again, and add the shrimps, along with the courgette and asparagus.

- When the pasta is just tender, drain it well, saving a little of the cooking water. Add this along with the tomato purée to the frying pan of shrimps and courgette and stir.

- Toss the drained spaghetti with the shrimp and courgette sauce over a very low heat for a minute, then stir in the lemon zest and juice, some of the parsley and generous black pepper. Serve with the remaining parsley on the top.

If you have never had potted shrimps before, then eat them spread thickly on hot toast for some unadulterated joy. If (like me) you start to buy them so frequently that you feel you need to do something else with them, stir spoonfuls through steaming hot pasta. Just as joyful.

In this recipe I am using brown shrimps (un-potted) for a light, zesty and summery dish that shows how good these little shrimps taste even without all that spicy butter.

300g spaghetti

salt and pepper

For the sauce

50g butter

olive oil

2 courgettes, halved and cut into eighths lengthways

8 asparagus stalks, halved (if available)

2 garlic cloves, crushed

50ml white wine

100g brown shrimps

2 tbsp tomato purée

grated zest and juice of 1 lemon

a handful of parsley leaves, finely chopped

40 CRASTER KIPPERS

If there is one area of the UK that is synonymous with the kipper it's Craster on the Northumberland coast. The stone-built fishermen's cottages in the tiny harbour stand shoulder-to-shoulder, bravely facing the mighty power of the North Sea that thunders onto the harbour wall in front of them.

The seas here were once swarming with silver shoals of herring, bringing great prosperity to the fishing and smoking communities. Scotswomen, skilled in high-speed splitting, gutting and cleaning the fish, would travel down the coast, following the fleets. They become known as the 'fish wives' or 'herring lassies'.

In 1843, John Woodger from Seahouses, just north of Craster, tried giving the humble herring the smoked salmon treatment – that is, splitting it down the back before curing and smoking it – 'kippering'. Until then, as far back as the Middle Ages, the fish had been prepared whole as 'red herrings', involving curing them in super-strength brine for a week then cold-smoking them for a month, which gave the fish their red colour and strong smell.

Kippering raised the cheap and salty status of the herring into something more palatable. The technique caught on and, during its heyday, kippering smokehouses could be found all along this area of coast. But the popularity of the herring was also its downfall. Stocks became depleted, resulting in bans on herring fishing in the 1970s. When they were eventually lifted in 1983, many of the smokehouses had shut down.

Only one remains in Craster now. L Robson & Sons is a family business specialising in the traditional method of oak-smoking kippers, salmon and other fish. They have been smoking herring here for 130 years, and still use the same smokehouse. Their Craster kippers remain a sought-after delicacy. The technique and skills remain the same, except herring lassies have now been replaced with a machine capable of splitting 500kg herring per hour.

You can try the kippers in **The Craster Seafood Restaurant** (see page 309). On my visit, just before lunch, I watched a little blue boat surf into the harbour on a huge wave. A white van appeared on the quayside, three boxes of fish were offloaded ... and five minutes later the same van appeared in the smokehouse yard.

I find that kind of simple, local exchange between fisherman, fishmonger or chef really satisfying, maybe because I know that the loss of the fishing industries from our waters is changing the lives of the communities that have lived by the sea. Seeing it continue gives us a glimmer of hope for the future.

L. Robson & Sons Ltd
Craster, Northumberland NE66 3TR • 01665 576223 • www.kipper.co.uk

Red herrings
Ever wonder where the term 'red herring' comes from? Red herrings were once used to train hunting hounds. The pungent aroma of the fish was used to lay a false trail in an attempt to stop the hounds from getting distracted from the more subtle scent of the fox. So, when someone is deliberately distracted from their path, we call it a 'red herring'.

Pitch Up

Dunstan Hill Camping and Caravanning Club Site

Dunstan Hill, Dunstan, Alnwick,
Northumberland NE66 3TQ • 01665 576310
www.campingandcaravanningclub.co.uk

A large, well-organised site close to the 'castle coast'. Split over two grassy fields, it has plenty of hard standings and the comforts of electric, laundry and play area. Despite the Northumberland coast's renowned 'sea breezes', this site is just far enough (about a mile) from the coastline and sheltered by trees. However, you can walk to the sandy dunes for a face-full of sea air, then head south for a mile to Craster for lunch.

Longbank Farm (CS)

Alnwick, Northumberland NE66 3AP • 01665 577243

A perfect base for exploring the coastline and the lovely town of Alnwick. It's a very friendly, well looked after site with basic but clean facilities. It's probably better suited to caravans and motorhomes as there are no showers and the exposure to the wind might be rather challenging for tents. The wandering geese and friendly horses in the neighbouring field just add to the charm.

Proctors Stead Caravan and Camping Park

Craster, Alnwick, Northumberland NE66 3TF
01665 576613 • www.proctorsstead.co.uk

A small, quiet site on a working farm. You can see ruined Dunstanburgh Castle from here, maintaining its majestic presence on the shoreline. The force of the waves can be heard when the wind is in the right direction, and the night skies are vast.

Eat Local

L. Robson & Sons

Craster, Northumberland NE66 3TR • 01665 576223
www.kipper.co.uk
You can buy the world-renowned Craster Kippers from the shop, as well as smoked salmon. Or, if you want someone else to prepare your lunch, their highly recommended restaurant is next door.

Swallow Fish of Seahouses

Fisherman's Kitchen, 2 South Street, Seahouses, Northumberland NE68 7RB • 01665 721052
www.swallowfish.co.uk
They claim that this is where the 'kipper' was invented, and they are still smoking kippers in the traditional way, in the original smokehouses that have operated since 1843.

Sunnyhills Farm Shop

South Road, Belford, Northumberland NE70 7DP
01668 219662 • www.sunnyhillsfarmshop.co.uk
Owners Robert and Brenda are staunchly proud of Northumbrian produce, not just their own from their 1,000-acre arable farm and their 56,000-plus free-range chickens but also of all the local small-scale livestock farmers and dairy producers. You can get your entire holiday food shop here; milk, bread, vegetables and meat. The light and airy cafe does great lunches, with a Young Farmers' menu for the under-12s.

Alnmouth Country Store

15-16 Northumberland Street, Alnmouth, Alnwick, Northumberland NE66 2RS • 01665 830997
An outstanding village store in attractive Alnmouth. You will find everything you need for your regular shop, but the dedicated owners make sure that most of it is sourced from local farms and bakers while remaining great value for money. Pick up regional cheeses, wonderful ice-creams, locally caught fish, local meat, cakes, beers and wine. Or just come for a freshly ground coffee and a takeaway pie and wander down to the beach to enjoy them.

Farmers' Markets

Alnwick Farmers' Market

Market Place, Alnwick, Northumberland
NE6 1HS • www.alnwickmarkets.co.uk
Last Friday of the month.
A bustling affair in the heart of Alnwick town centre. Additionally, a traditional market is held in Alnwick market place every Saturday, and on Thursdays too from April to December.

Morpeth Farmers' Market

Market Place, Morpeth, Northumberland NE61 1LZ
0845 600 6400 • www.neefm.org.uk • 1st Saturday of the month.
The town got its market licence in 1199 and by the mid-18th century it was the most important cattle market in the country.

Eating Out

The Craster Seafood Restaurant

Craster, Northumberland NE66 3TR • 01665 576223
www.kipper.co.uk
Next door to the smokehouse and serving their smoked wares and other food in a traditional setting.

CAMPERS'
KIPPER KEDGEREE

Serves 2

Kippers taste especially good cooked on a barbecue out in the open air, and the added bonus is that the distinct aroma is carried away on the breeze. Alternatively this campers' kipper kedgeree makes an occasion out of them, and provides a more substantial meal. The cream is optional; it just depends how indulgent you are feeling.

To enjoy kippers as they should be, you need to 'jug' them. Fill a large jug with boiling water, and simply put the kipper in head first, keeping the tail just above the surface of the water. Leave it for 6 minutes, no more, no less, and you'll have the perfect kipper.

2 medium-sized kippers

50g butter
(⅕ of a block), plus an extra knob to serve

1 onion, finely chopped

1 level tsp medium curry powder

salt and pepper

150g long-grain white rice

2 eggs, hard-boiled, peeled and quartered

juice of ½ lemon

a handful of fresh parsley leaves, finely chopped

2 tbsp double cream (optional, but makes the dish much richer)

• Jug the kipper, as above, in a jug of boiling water. Reserve 150ml of the water, and drain the fish well.

• Flake the fish flesh into bite-sized pieces and throw away the head, skin and bones. Put the flaked fish to one side.

• Melt the 50g butter in a saucepan and fry the onion for about 5-6 minutes until it has softened.

• Add the curry powder and a pinch of salt, and stir well. Now add the rice, and stir again so that the rice is fully coated with the butter and curry powder. Let it fry for about 1 minute, no more.

• Add the reserved kipper water, and bring the pan up to a simmer. Pop the lid on and let it cook gently for about 12 minutes, until all the liquid has been absorbed and the rice is tender to the bite. Remove from the heat.

• If you haven't already, boil the eggs for 8 minutes, let them cool then peel and quarter them lengthways.

• Now add the flaked fish, lemon juice and most of the chopped parsley to the rice. If using, you can add the double cream at this point. Fork everything together carefully, trying not to break up the fish. Taste and season with salt and pepper as required.

• Serve in a warmed dish, with the egg quarters dotted across the top, garnished with parsley and the extra knob of butter.

Damson Gumbo
70% fruit! Delicious with cheese and meat

Crosthwaite Damson
Jam
50% Damsons from our orchard
and 40% sugar
Mind the stones!
LA8 8HX MH 360G

Damson C
A Slice with cheese will ple

41

DAMSONS IN DISTRESS

The flowering of the Westmorland damson tree is such a rare and beautiful spectacle, it is worthy of an early season camping trip just to experience it. "It's like a chain of starlight moving across the valley every April," smiles Mary Harkness, known locally as 'the damson lady', as she describes the frothy white blossom around Cumbria's Lyth Valley.

Mary, a founder member of the Westmorland Damson Association (WDA) and prolific jam-maker, explains, "The Lyth Valley is ideal for damsons because of its damp conditions and the fact that the soil sits on a layer of limestone, which a damson tree loves." The Westmorland damson is small with an intense flavour, which makes it particularly good for jam-making, but Mary also uses it to make damson cheese – a solid preserve that you cut into slices and serve with cold meats.

According to the WDA, damsons were first grown for their purple colour, not their flavour. Nearby Kendal was a textile town and damsons were used to dye cloth before being noticed for their eating qualities. This tiny delicacy became hugely important to local life, with the orchards and jam factories bringing much-needed employment to the area. Sadly, sugar rationing and relocation of manpower during the war meant that the factories were forced to close down and damsons were all but ignored.

It's a familiar scenario, but the knock-on effect goes way beyond the shopping basket. No market for home-grown fruit means no need for orchards. This means no spirit-lifting blossom in the spring and a distinctive feature of the landscape is lost forever.

Luckily, the WDA supports growers and encourages appreciation of the damson. It holds an annual Damson Day to celebrate the spring blossom and if you are camping here during September harvest time you can't miss the roadside stalls selling this local fruit.

Mary Harkness is the only commercial jam maker still in the Lyth Valley. She grows damsons in her own orchard and makes 3,000 jars of jam every year from her farmhouse kitchen in Crosthwaite. What better way of taking home a taste of this place? All that Lyth Valley uniqueness captured in a jar.

www.lythdamsons.org.uk

Pitch Up

Windermere Camping and Caravanning Club Site

Ashes Lane, Staveley, Cumbria LA8 9JS • 01539 821119 • www.campingandcaravanningclub.co.uk
A great family-friendly site between Bowness-on-Windermere and the market town of Kendal. Lots of facilities: separate tent, backpacker and family areas, electric hook-up, washing machines, children's play area and a pub and restaurant, **The Whistling Pig**. This isn't a lakeside location, but there are lots of lovely walks from the campsite and the village of Staveley is a foodie hotspot.

Park Cliffe

Birks Road, Windermere, Cumbria LA23 3PG
01539 531344 • www.parkcliffe.co.uk
Great for home comforts after a strenuous day on the fells. It's large and efficiently run, there are shower blocks with underfloor heating, family bathrooms and even private ones that you can rent. There is a great play park for children as well as a stream to muck about in and the setting is parkland with mountain views.

> For such a tiny delicacy, the damson was hugely important to local life and economy.

Sykeside Camping Park

Brotherswater, Patterdale, Cumbria CA11 0NZ
01768 482239 • www.sykeside.co.uk
Nestled in the Dovedale valley, Sykeside offers that steeped-in-nature vibe, but with welcome facilities. The shop is really well stocked and there is even a cool on-site bar on Friday and Saturday evenings in summer.

Borderside Farm (CS)

Crosthwaite, Kendal, Cumbria LA8 8JQ
01539 531783
A site in a lovely, peaceful location in a farmer's field in the heart of damson country. There are only basic facilities – a cold water tap and a disposal area for chemical loos. The field is not level but you can pitch anywhere. It's a great escape from the busy tourist attractions of the Lakes. There are two pubs a short walk across the field.

Eat Local

Low Sizergh Barn Farmshop & Tearoom

Low Sizergh Farm, Sizergh, Kendal, Cumbria LA8 8AE • 01539 560426 • www.lowsizerghbarn.co.uk
This attractive shop on a working farm has received national recognition for its 'shop local' commitment. Indulge in the impressive range of specialities and seasonal foods sourced directly from Lake District farmers, growers, makers and producers, including Mary Harkness' Crosthwaite Preserves.

Plumgarths Farm Shop

Crook Road, Kendal, Cumbria LA8 8QJ
01539 736300 • www.plumgarths.co.uk
Packed with the flavour of the Lake District, the shop stocks a great range of locally sourced vegetables, preserves, chutneys, ales, cakes and pies. Their lamb comes from Kendal and they sell varieties of the local damson jams.

Eating Out
Hawkshead Brewery and Beer Hall

Mill Yard, Staveley, Cumbria LA8 9LR • Brewery:
01539 822644 • www.hawksheadbrewery.co.uk
Cumbria's largest independent brewery, serving great local food of the hearty classic variety.

The Punch Bowl Inn

Crosthwaite, Lyth Valley, Cumbria LA8 8HR
01539 568237 • www.the-punchbowl.co.uk
An idyllic location in the heart of the Lyth Valley, this is the place for a lunch with a touch of class. The pub constantly wins good food awards.

Greens Cafe and Bistro

College Street, Grasmere, Cumbria LA22 9SZ
01539 435790 • www.greensgrasmere.com
Greens are big on local seasonal produce and comfort food. All diets are catered for, including vegan, and they stock Mary's preserves.

Food historians believe the damson was introduced here from Damascus by returning Crusaders – hence the name. It has certainly grown in British soil for a long time. Stones from the fruit were excavated at the Coppergate dig, where York's Jorvik Viking Centre now stands.

LAMB
CHOPS WITH A DAMSON SAUCE

With lamb from the fields and damsons from the hedgerows, you'll be tasting the best of the Lakes' landscape with this recipe. Serve it with heaps of mashed potato and a side of seasonal greens.

Serves 2

- Put the rosemary, garlic, 1 tbsp oil and the red wine into a freezer bag and then add the lamb chops. Squidge it all about gently so the ingredients mingle and the lamb is covered in the liquid, herbs and garlic. Put in a cool-box or fridge for a couple of hours.

- Take the bag out 10 minutes before cooking, remove the chops and season them with a little salt and pepper. Keep the marinade.

- Heat up a little more olive oil in a large frying pan to a medium heat (or griddle if using) and cook the chops, turning occasionally. Depending on how you like your meat, it should take about 4 minutes on each side.

- When cooked, remove the chops from the pan and put to one side to keep warm.

- Put the pan back on the heat, and deglaze it by pouring in the red wine marinade from the bag, as well as the 100ml red wine, and stirring to get all the lamb flavours off the bottom of the pan.

- Now add the damson jam, Worcestershire sauce and balsamic vinegar. Stir and let it bubble away and reduce into a thicker sauce, for about 4 minutes.

- Put a lamb chop on each plate and pour the sauce over the top.

2 large lamb chops

1 sprig of fresh rosemary, finely chopped

1 garlic clove, finely chopped

olive oil

2 tbsp red wine

salt and pepper

For the sauce

100ml red wine

2 tbsp damson jam

a slosh of Worcestershire sauce if you have it to hand

1 tbsp balsamic vinegar

42 HARDY HERDWICKS

There few relationships between an animal and its landscape more symbiotic than that of the Herdwick sheep and the fells of the Lake District. Their ability to graze the most inaccessible areas of the fells, and thus control the vegetation, means the magnificent natural environment is maintained.

The Herdwick is certainly top of the 'hardy sheep' chart. They have been grazing the central and western dales of the Lake District (with some fells at 3,000 feet) for over 1,000 years. Their appearance demonstrates how well designed the breed is for adapting to bad weather: small ears, fleecy faces and legs, and a thick coat of waxy wool.

But their suitability to this landscape isn't just physical. The flocks remain in 'heaved' or 'hefted' areas, meaning they live in their own part of the mountain and respect virtual boundaries, rarely straying beyond this. Even after being brought into the lower fells for dipping, shearing or lambing, Herdwicks return to their own part of the fells afterwards. It's a natural homing instinct.

Their propensity to graze widely and instinctively across the fells enables the sheep to mature slowly and is at the heart of farmer Jon Watson's approach to his 1,000-strong flock of Herdwicks. He is the tenant on the National Trust-owned 700-acre Yew Tree Farm in Coniston, once owned by Beatrix Potter, who loved Herdwicks and did a great deal to protect the breed and champion traditional farming methods. "This farmland habitat is a nationally treasured wildlife haven," explains Jon. "So I farm it in a way that protects the landscape and produces tasty and succulent meat, very distinct from other breeds".

You can buy Yew Tree Farm's Herdwick lamb direct from the farm. "Give me a call on my mobile beforehand," says Jon, "just to check I am not out on the fells. We sell all kinds of cuts from roasting joints to chops and racks for holidaymakers and campers."

Buying Herdwick meat for your supper goes way beyond planning your next meal. You are doing your bit to enable the deeply rooted heritage of this place to continue, and that can only be a good thing.

Yew Tree Farm
Coniston, Cumbria LA21 8DP • 07798 517392 • www.heritagemeats.co.uk

Pitch Up

Eskdale Camping and Caravanning Club Site

Boot, Holmrook, Cumbria CA19 1TH • 01946 723253
www.campingandcaravanningclub.co.uk

This is a five-star site in a five-star setting. It's got all the mod cons needed after a day out on the hills: heated facilities include a drying room, showers, and family bathrooms, washing machine and a small but well-stocked shop – you can even make toast, porridge and hot drinks to take out. You can get plentiful supplies for your supper here – Herdwick lamb steaks, Cumberland Curl sausages and bacon for your breakfast. There are two fabulous pubs, visible from the site, perfect for a stumble back to your pitch in the evening. Check out the **Brook House Inn** for great food and a good range of local ales. The campsite also has 10 camping pods and a camping barn sleeping up to eight if you fancy glamping or want to camp as a group, although it can't take caravans.

Shepherds View (CS)

Torver, near Coniston, Cumbria LA21 8BQ
01539 441239 • www.browsideconiston.co.uk

It's motorhomes and caravans only here, as there aren't facilities for tent campers. So the lucky few get to enjoy all the pleasures of this small and low-key site

where the views of the fells, sprinkled with sheep, speak for themselves. A short walk into Torver village takes you to **The Wilson Arms** country inn. There's an impressive menu inspired by produce from the fells and the lakes, and a small but perfectly formed deli next door.

Keswick Camping and Caravanning Club Site

Crow Park Road, Keswick, Cumbria CA12 5EP
01768 772392 • www.campingandcaravanningclub.co.uk

In a stunning location on the shores of Derwentwater with breathtaking views over the lake to the hills beyond. Sleep to the sounds of the lake lapping the shore. Great for lakeside and hillside walking: you can conquer Skiddaw mountain from the site and engage in no end of water-based activities right outside your tent on Derwentwater. Good facilities: showers, toilets, washing-up area, a laundry and a new backpacker room, particularly useful for those arriving on foot or by bike. Keswick town is within walking distance.

Great Langdale Campsite

Great Langdale, Ambleside, Cumbria LA22 9JU
01539 437668 • www.nationaltrust.org.uk

A National Trust gem. Set in glorious countryside away from the bustle of the Lakes themselves, the scenery, with a backdrop of the Langdale Pikes, is stunning. There's great walking for all abilities direct from the site up into the Pikes. Laid out over several small grassy camping areas, the campsite caters for tents, trailers, campervans and organised groups, but caravans and large parties are not allowed. (Cars are also not allowed in the camping areas.) There are two good separate shower blocks and laundry facilities, a well stocked on-site shop, a children's play area and a bouldering wall to practise climbing on.

...Eat Local

If staying in Eskdale

The Club Site shop is well supplied with local meats from **Wilson's** (29 Main Street, Egremont, CA22 2DR), a great traditional butcher from Egremont who is dedicated to sourcing all of his meat from the fells. The site shop also sells supplies of veg, fruit and dairy.

Eskdale Stores

Eskdale Green, Holmbrook, Cumbria CA19 1TX
01946 723229 • www.eskdalestores.co.uk
In the picturesque village of Eskdale Green, you'll find the week's essentials, a selection of Cumbrian products, outdoor clothing and equipment.

Yew Tree Farm

Coniston, Cumbria LA21 8DP • 01539 441433
www.heritagemeats.co.uk
All cuts of Herdwick mutton and lamb can be bought directly from the butchery at Yew Tree Farm. Call Jon before you go so he has time to come in from the fells.

Coniston Brewing Company

Coniston, Cumbria LA21 8DU • 01539 441335 or 01539 441668 • www.conistonbrewery.com
The award-winning beers, including Bluebird Bitter, are made from the pure waters of the Coniston hills, challenger hops and wonderfully roasted pale and crystal malts. You can buy bottles to take away from the pub out front, **The Black Bull**.

If staying in Torver
The Torver Deli

The Wilson Arms, Torver, Coniston, Cumbria LA21 8BB • www.thewilsonsarms.co.uk

Beatrix Potter was a huge fan of Herdwicks, so much so that when she died she stated in her will that her farms had to be stocked with pure Herdwick breed sheep. By doing this she saved the breed, enabled the hefted areas to remain, and ensured the fells were evenly grazed.

This village pub has opened a wonderful little deli, literally 'on the side', packed with local delights: cheeses, meats, cakes, as well as a supply of vegetables.

If staying in Keswick
Yew Tree Farm

Rosthwaite, Borrowdale, Cumbria CA12 5XB
017687 77675 • www. borrowdaleyewtreefarm.co.uk
This isn't the same Yew Tree Farm as my featured one in Coniston, but it is closer to the Keswick site and sells fabulous Herdwick meats from the on-site cafe.

Keswick Brewing Company

Brewery Lane, Keswick, Cumbria CA12 5BY
017687 80700 • www.keswickbrewery.co.uk
Set up in 2006 on the site of the town's Victorian brewhouse, this small independent craft brewery produces the Thirst range of beers comprising Indian Pale Ales, Golden Ales and Bitters. Tours of the brewery are offered spring to October.

Farmers' Markets
Keswick Farmers' Market

Market Square, Keswick, Cumbria CA12 5JR
Every Thursday

Egremont Farmers' Market

Market Place, Egremont, Cumbria CA22 2DF
3rd Friday of the month

HERDWICK LAMB
CURRY IN A HURRY

Lamb curry washed down with a decent beer is hard to beat. Camping in the Lake District means you are in one of the best areas of the country for both lamb and beer. So here is a camping-friendly lamb recipe that is packed with curry flavours but doesn't need cooking for hours, and can be done all in one pot. Choose a good beer from one of the breweries listed to go with it.

Serves 4

500g lamb leg steak, cut into bite-sized cubes

vegetable oil

2 tsp each of ground turmeric and garam masala

1 tsp each of ground cumin, ground coriander and chilli powder

a small handful of green beans (about 8), trimmed and cut in half

a bunch of spring onions, sliced, including the green bits

350g basmati rice

1 x 400ml tin coconut milk

100ml vegetable stock (made with a cube)

a small bunch of fresh coriander (mint will also work nicely), chopped

salt and pepper

a big knob of butter

- Heat a glug of oil in a large saucepan with a lid, and stir in the spices for a minute.

- Add the lamb, beans and spring onions, and jostle them about in the pan so that the lamb browns, about 2 minutes.

- Now add the rice to the pan, stir well, and then add the coconut milk and the stock. Bring up to the boil, then turn the heat down to a simmer, put the lid on and leave for 10 minutes.

- After 10 minutes check that the rice has cooked, but don't stir it. If it's not done, let it cook for another couple of minutes.

- When ready, stir in the fresh coriander (or mint), keeping a little back to garnish at the end. Season with salt and pepper then add the butter and gently stir through.

- Serve with the remaining herbs sprinkled on top, accompanied by a good local ale.

LAMB
KOFTA PITTAS

We can all buy cheap processed burgers, but with these lamb kofta burgers you know exactly what's in them, and they taste amazing. They are so quick and simple to make – all in one bowl.

Makes 8 good-sized burger-shaped koftas

- Tip the mince into a big bowl, with all the other burger ingredients. Season with salt and pepper. Get your hands in there and mix and squelch all the ingredients together.

- When you are satisfied that it is all mixed well together, mould the mixture into 8 separate patties or mini-burger shapes. If you have the time, put them on a plate and into a cool box or fridge.

- When you are ready to cook, brush/rub your barbecue grid or griddle with a little oil, then lay your burgers over a medium heat. They will need about 5-6 minutes on each side until browned and cooked though.

- Briefly warm the pittas on the barbecue, pile a couple of burgers into each, then add tomato, onion (if using) and leaves. Serve with a little drizzle of yoghurt on the top. Enjoy.

100g lamb mince

1 medium onion, grated

2 garlic cloves, crushed

2 tbsp garam masala

a small handful of fresh coriander leaves (optional)

2 tbsp sweet chilli sauce or ½ teaspoon chilli flakes

salt and pepper

To serve

4 soft white pittas

2 large tomatoes, sliced

½ red onion, sliced (optional)

a handful of salad leaves

1 x 125g pot plain yoghurt

SCOTLAND

It's not all neeps, tatties, whisky and haggis. Rustic comfort food sits alongside stylish cuisine in Scotland – home cooks and professional chefs alike are blessed with their country's bountiful larder. The unspoilt habitats and varied weather of this splendid wilderness provide perfect conditions for naturally grazed meats, game and wonderful seafood. Fish plays a big part in Scottish cuisine. Try the eponymous Cullen Skink – a simple haddock broth from the tiny fishing village on the northeast coast – and other specialities including whisky-soaked cranachan or venison steaks from the Rothiemurchus estate.

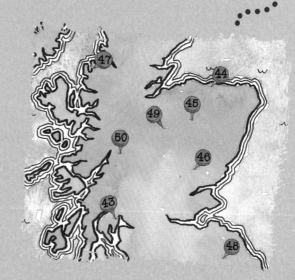

43

WINSTON CHURCHILL IS A DEER STALKER

Eating deer seems to challenge a lot more people than eating cows does: Bambi still looms large in the psyche. But wild deer is actually one of the most sustainable, environmentally friendly and healthy meats to choose – not to mention tasty, versatile and great for campsite cooking.

I am sitting at the kitchen table of Anne and Winston Churchill (his real name) in their home high up in the Argyll Forest. The view is of densely forested mountains: it's beautiful and, as it turns out, extremely bountiful if you are an expert deer stalker like Winston. The couple have a huge customer base for their venison: Winston and his team stalk the deer in the surrounding forests, then prepare the meat in a purpose-built butchery, refrigeration and kitchen unit behind the house.

"I'd give anything for a piece of beef. Chicken is an absolute luxury," laughs Anne. "We eat venison most of the time. Venison stews, venison steaks, venison burgers, venison sausages and venison chilli, so occasionally the thought of a bit of chicken gets me excited."

"I think what she means is venison is a versatile meat," adds Winston. Certainly, as you travel around this area, you'll find that venison is a staple on many menus in the roadside cafes and restaurants. It comes in pies, stews and as steaks, and most of the delis offer venison charcuterie. (The best is made by Great Glen Charcuterie.)

Handled by proper butchers and professional stalkers like Winston, you'll enjoy a tender, tasty meat, similar to a rich, good-quality beef steak. This is an animal that is lean from being a far-roamer and a wild forager, feeding on natural grasses, nuts and berries. You can't get a more natural meat than that.

Winston Churchill Venison

Balagowan, Glen Lean, Sandbank, Argyll & Bute, Dunoon PA23 8RD
01369 705319 • www.winstonchurchillvenison.com

Pitch Up

Sallochy Woodland Camping

Sallochy Bay, Rowardennan, Loch Lomond, Stirling
G63 0AW • www.lochlomond-trossachs.org/visiting/
sallochy-campsite.html

When you get the opportunity to be close to nature
and undisturbed by the tribulations of everyday life
you should take it. On Loch Lomond's east coast, this
virtually wild camping site has discreetly designated
pitches along the water's edge, giving you your own
private view of the loch: a refreshing dip beats a
shower in the morning!

Luss Camping and Caravanning Club Site

Loch Lomond, Luss, Argyll & Bute G83 8NT
01436 860658 • www.campingandcaravanningclub.
co.uk

There are spirit-lifting views of the loch and Ben
Lomond from most of the 90 pitches, some with
their own little bit of lochside 'beach'. Licensing
restrictions mean that caravan and motorhome
owners need to be Club members, but tent pitches
are available to everyone.

Cashel Camping in the Forest Site

Rowardennan, Stirling G63 0AW • 01360 870234
www.campingintheforest.co.uk

Lochside pitches, picnic tables at the water's edge and
the option to launch your boat straight from the site
or hire a boat nearby. This is a water-lover's haven, a
walker's wonder and a nature-buff's delight. There's
even a shower exclusively for dogs.

Eat Local

Ardardan Farm Shop

Ardardan Estate, Cardross, Argyll & Bute G82 5HD
01389 849188 • www.ardardan.co.uk

May Montgomerie and her two daughters run one
of the friendliest, tastiest set-ups I have come across.
Ardardan is a large, bright and modern farm shop
with deli counter, baked goods, oatcakes, fresh fruit,
vegetables and glorious eggs – (they started out as egg
farmers) – and Winston Churchill's venison. It is a
hub for the local community, especially the cafe
where everything is baked fresh each morning. I even
met a man named Gillespie, in his mid 70s, who
travels 56 miles every Sunday to eat here "as the food
and the folk are so fantastic."

Auchentullich Farm Shop

Arden, Alexandria, Argyll & Bute G83 8RF
01389 850240

Auchentullich is a labour of love: an old pigsty renovated into a stylish and homely farm shop. Take the weight off your feet and let owner Ishbel Colquhoun make you a great coffee or venison salami sandwich with onion chutney, all made from produce sold in the shop. There's proper fresh veg and fruit too, with meat from the top-class Aberfoyle butcher.

Edenmill Farm Shop

Edenmill Farm, Blanefield, Glasgow G63 9AX
01360 771707 • www.edenmill.co.uk

Open from Wednesday to Sunday only, this excellent farm shop sells pork, Aberdeen Angus beef, lamb, venison and game from its own land as well as home-smoked goods.

Aberfoyle Butcher

206 Main Street, Aberfoyle, Stirling FK8 3UQ
01877 382473 • www.aberfoylebutcher.co.uk

In the heart of the Trossachs, this butcher is known for exceptional quality and for his good selection of seasonal game: traditional butchery at its best.

Farmers' Market
Loch Lomond Shores Farmers' Market

Loch Lomond Shores, Balloch, G83 8QL
1st and 3rd Sunday of the month

Eating Out
The Oak Tree Inn

Balmaha, Stirling G63 0JQ • 01360 870357
www.theoaktreeinn.co.uk

Opposite the Loch Lomond Visitor Centre, the walls of this inn drip with grandfather clocks and stuffed fish. The menu is full of local tastes and dishes; get venison here, Atlantic char, haggis and Cullen Skink along with a great selection of Scottish ales.

> "Venison is tender, tasty meat, similar to a rich, good-quality beef steak."

The Village Rest

Pier Road, Luss Village, Loch Lomond, Argyll & Bute G83 8NY • 01436 860220

A great little bistro with reasonably priced, impressive food. Find venison dishes, haggis, neaps and tatties, paninis and home-made soups. All served with a smile.

Loch Fyne Restaurant and Oyster Bar

Clachan, Cairndow, Argyll & Bute PA26 8BL
01499 600264

A treat worth driving for. It's world renowned, and not silly expensive. Savour oysters from the clear waters of the loch in front of you or enjoy delicately smoked salmon or hand-dived scallops with black pudding.

VENISON AND JUNIPER CHILLI CHOCOLATE

Chilli is a camper's staple. Make it with venison and a hint of chocolate as here, and you'll raise it to gourmet status.

Serves 4

a glug of olive oil

1 medium onion, finely chopped

3 garlic cloves, finely chopped

1 large red pepper, cut into 2cm chunks

350g minced venison

1 tbsp each of ground cinnamon, paprika and cumin

1 tbsp juniper berries, crushed

2 x 400g tins tomatoes

1 heaped tsp cocoa powder

1 tbsp tomato purée or ketchup

1 tsp granulated sugar

1 fresh red chilli, finely chopped, or a tsp dried chilli/powder (according to your personal chilli tastes!)

1 x 400g tin kidney beans, drained and rinsed

To serve (all optional)

crème fraîche, grated cheese, fresh coriander, lime wedges

- Place a heavy pot over a medium heat (gas or a fire), and add a splash of olive oil. Cook the onion, garlic and red pepper over a medium-low heat until they begin to soften and start to colour.

- Turn up the heat and stir in the venison. As it starts to brown, break up the mince with a wooden spoon, then stir in the ground spices and the juniper (not the chilli), and cook for 2 minutes.

- Tip in the tinned tomatoes. Let the mixture bubble up and reduce a bit till the sauce starts to thicken. Stir in the cocoa powder, tomato purée and sugar then add the chilli. Go as hot as you dare.

- Finally, tip in the drained and rinsed kidney beans. Turn the heat right down and simmer for 30 minutes to let the flavours get friendly.

- Serve the chilli with a big blob of crème fraîche if you have it, or grated cheese. For extra fanciness top with some fresh coriander and a squeeze of lime. It's delicious with rice or jacket potatoes.

44 CULLEN SKINK

Cullen has a special place in my family's heart. It is here that generations of my husband's ancestors, the McBeaths, lived and worked as fishermen in the 18th and 19th centuries. Life as a fisherman at this time was tough and money was scarce, so a basic yet nutritious dish like Cullen Skink, a tasty smoked fish soup, would have been a staple of their diet. The recipe required few ingredients, all of which were locally available: fish in the form of haddock was in abundant supply, potatoes grew in local fields and the cows in the fertile pastures that surround the town provided the milk.

The name apparently comes from the Gaelic word 'essence'. This is particularly apt as, in my opinion, a bowl of Cullen Skink captures the very essence of this pretty town. I'd recommend a walk around the narrow streets of the Seatown area, where the fishing community once lived in a cluster of small, basic houses close to the harbour, many built from stones gathered from the beach. Despite only having one or two rooms, they often housed more than one family. If that wasn't bad enough, the smell might have finished you off: the houses were used for smoking the fish.

As I wandered around the little harbour I thought about my husband's great-grandmother Mary standing at this sea wall day after day, gutting fish, mending nets and gossiping with all the other wives, waiting for the men to return with the next catch. A bracing blast of North Sea wind in my face was enough to get me scuttling off to find a steaming bowl of Cullen Skink to warm my hands around. No doubt many a cold, tired fisherman returning home to Cullen's Seatown did the same.

> "A bowl of Cullen Skink captures the very essence of this pretty town."

Pitch Up

Sandend Caravan Park

Sandend, Portsoy, Aberdeenshire AB45 2UA
01261 842660 • www.sandendcaravanpark.co.uk
Jane and Bernard have proudly run this secluded and beautiful site for the last 25 years and their friendly welcome is a huge draw for a frequently returning clientele. Add this to the fact that the pitches are within feet of a wide, family-friendly sandy beach and you have struck gold. The hint of woodsmoke in the air comes from the smokehouse just over the road, where there's also a fabulous wet fish shop where you can get your smoked haddock. For local potatoes head to the ice-cream shop in Portsoy. Yes, really.

Blackpotts Cottages (CS)

Whitehills, Banff, Aberdeenshire AB45 2JN
01261 861396 • www.campingandcaravanningclub.co.uk
A small, basic but peaceful and grassy caravans-and-motorhomes-only site (because there isn't a facilities block). What you do get though is a great spot for watching dolphins and whales, as just a small wall separates the site from the sea. **Downies** fish shop is a very short walk away.

Findochty Caravan Park

Jubilee Terrace, Findochty, Moray AB56 4QA
01542 835303 • www.findochtycaravanpark.co.uk
Again, lots of statics on this one, but it does mean tent campers and tourers don't ever have to queue for the showers. It's a well-loved and looked after little site right on the shoreline with stunning views across the Moray Firth. In just a few steps you can be on a great sandy beach.

Eat Local

Cullen Corner Shop

14–18 The Square, Cullen, Moray AB56 4RF
01542 841022 • www.cullencornershop.co.uk
A trip to Cullen isn't complete without sampling a bowl of Cullen Skink. Here they sell it in plastic tubs to take away and will heat it for you if you want to eat it there and then – perfect to enjoy from one of the campsites overlooking the bay. The shop also has local butchery and bakery produce as well as supplies of fruit and veg.

Downies of Whitehills

40 Low Shore, Whitehills, Banff, Aberdeenshire AB45 2NN • 01261 861204 • www.downiefish.co.uk
Family-run Downies of Whitehills has over 100 years experience in the fishing industry, buying, processing and selling the pick of the local catch. Whitehills is now more about yachts than fishing vessels but Downies proudly continues the link with the village's fishing heritage. Try their Cullen Skink pies or Smoked Haddock Bridies, or buy the fresh, locally caught wet fish for your barbecue.

J Smith Fish Merchants
Sandend, near Portsoy, Aberdeenshire AB45 2UA
01261 842419
Just across the road from Sandend Caravan Park, this fine smokery and wet fish shop is hugely popular with campers.

Allarburn Farm Shop
Edgar Road, Elgin, Moray IV30 6XQ • 01343 546484
www.allarburn.co.uk
A great one-stop shop for your camping dinner supplies. Buy own-grown neeps, tatties and carrots, plus cheeses, oatcakes and local meat. The cafe is well priced and loved by the locals.

Bogside Farm Shop
King Edward, Banff, Aberdeenshire AB45 3LX
01261 821244 • www.bogsidefarmshop.co.uk
A top-class butchers selling their own Highland beef, home-cured bacon and pork as well as lamb. They also make sausages, burgers and pies.

Farmers' Markets
Banff Farmers' Market
St Mary's Car Park, Low Street, Banff, Aberdeenshire AB45 1AU • 2nd Saturday of the month
Local bakery, butchers, fish and dairy. All the ingredients need for Cullen Skink in one place!

Macduff Farmers' Market
In the Fish Market on the quayside • last Saturday of the month.
Fruit, veg, Highland beef, jams and home bakes.

Huntly Farmers' Market
The Square, Huntly, Aberdeenshire • 1st Saturday of the month
A great range of local producers sell their wares in this lovely little town. Rare breeds meats and much more.

Eating Out
Rockpool Cafe
10 The Square, Cullen, Moray AB56 4RR
01542 841397 • www.rockpool-cullen.co.uk
A lovely modern and airy cafe in Cullen Square. Cullen Skink is served daily, along with a fabulous selection of 'specials' that could include local dressed crab, sole in a roll, smoked fish platters or a barbecued pork bun.

Boyndie Trust
Old School Visitor Centre, Boyndie, Aberdeenshire AB45 2JT • 01261 843249
www.boyndievisitorcentre.co.uk
The Boyndie Trust was established in 1999 to help the regeneration of the area and provide employment for people with special needs. The coffee shop next to the garden centre is a popular spot for great lunches of Cullen Skink, doorstep sandwiches and pancakes.

CULLEN SKINK

These days Cullen Skink has gone from being a poor man's supper to one that is hugely popular in respected restaurants. Some cooks add modern refinements such as double cream instead of milk, or fancy extras such as parsley, even wine. This family recipe keeps things simple and that's the way I like it. Here is Great Auntie Bay's simple recipe for Cullen Skink, passed down through the generations.

Serves 2 generously

2 skinless smoked haddock fillets (about 250–300g)

500g potatoes, peeled and roughly diced

500ml milk

1 dsp cornflour, mixed with a little milk

50g butter

salt and pepper

- Cut the haddock fillets into 2.5–5cm pieces.

- In a large saucepan, boil the diced potatoes in just enough water to cover them. Don't let them go too soft. Drain them.

- Turn the heat down then add the milk to the potatoes, along with the fish, and simmer for 3–5 minutes. Don't overheat, to prevent the fish falling to bits.

- Add the cornflour mixture to the pan, and stir to thicken. Add the butter and stir for a couple more minutes. Season well.

- Serve with some crusty bread.

45 THE WATER OF LIFE

Don't drink whisky without water, don't drink water without whisky.
So says the sign on the wall of The Glenlivet distillery in Speyside.

While its exact origins are unknown, the link between malt whisky and this part of the Highlands is most likely due to the locals finding a use for the surplus barley grown in the area, and delighting in the fact it could be distilled at home into a drink that heated you from the inside out. A useful discovery in a cold climate.

For years, Scottish folk enjoyed unrestricted home whisky production. Despite government attempts to tax them, there were still over 200 illicit distilleries in the Glenlivet valley in the early 19th century: the remote and inhospitable landscape meant the excise men kept away, which allowed the whisky to have time to mature into a smooth, drinkable spirit.

It was this quality that caught the attention of King George IV who demanded, after tasting it, that he should now only drink whisky from the Glenlivet area. The result was legislation to make distilling of small amounts an attractive option. Local farmer George Smith became one of the first licensed distillers in November 1824. He was granted a pair of pistols to protect himself and his whisky from disgruntled smugglers – pistols that are still proudly displayed at the entrance of the distillery. He protected it well: today, the distillery produces around 11 million litres a year.

Producing the good stuff is a highly skilled job, as I witnessed on my tour of The Glenlivet Distillery. It's a simple process, using few ingredients: spring water, malted barley and yeast. I learned that some whisky tastes 'peaty' because the malting barley is dried over burning peat, whereas here in The Glenlivet they just use hot air.

"Every distillery has its own water source, making the flavours of each whisky distinct from one another," explained our tour guide. Looking out of the immense glass windows we could see 'Josie's Well', a white picket-fenced area on the hillside no bigger than a barn door that is the source of all the water for The Glenlivet's whisky.

Likewise each distillery has its own uniquely shaped copper stills. "We think that 20 per cent of the flavour is affected by the copper and the shape of the still," continued our guide. "When we need to replace one, if the old one has a dent in it, then the new one will have a dent put in exactly the same place."

For me, the true poetry of whisky is that it is so intrinsically linked to the landscape. As you taste the complimentary dram at the end of your tour, look around you. The taste of the whisky in your glass is a result of all of those natural elements. It may have grown to become a global enterprise worth billions, but this 'water of life' still manages to retain the spirit of its fiery past and purity of its surroundings with every mouthful.

The Glenlivet Distillery
Ballindalloch, Banffshire AB37 9DB • www.theglenlivet.com

Pitch Up

Speyside by Craigellachie Camping and Caravanning Club Site

Archiestown, Aberlour, Moray AB38 9SL • 01340 810414 • www.campingandcaravanningclub.co.uk
A few miles out of the rather lovely town of Aberlour, this site is a bit of a hidden gem. The fruit trees, flowers around the facilities block, bird feeders and a touch of humour give it a homely feel. I like the water tap that protrudes from a whisky barrel with a 'single malt water' sign. The perfect place for peace and contemplation after a day on the whisky trail.

Aberlour Gardens Caravan and Camping Park

Aberlour on Spey, Aberlour, Moray AB38 9LD
01340 871586 • www.aberlourgardens.co.uk
Sitting within a Victorian walled garden, this is a cosy, sheltered and immaculately kept site with pitches among the trees and flowers. You can even buy a licence from the local post office and go salmon fishing on the nearby River Spey.

Wild Camping on the Glenlivet Estate

www.glenlivetestate.co.uk
The Glenlivet Estate covers over 58,000 acres within the Cairngorms National Park. There is a small, un-serviced, secluded wild camping area for backpackers close to the Glenlivet Estate Information Centre at the southern end of the village of Tomintoul. Pop into the Estate Office if you want to camp (if it's not open, you can still camp): it's free and is for small tents only for a maximum of two nights. Campfires by prior arrangement only.

Eat Local

Spey Larder

96-98 High Street, Aberlour, Moray AB38 9QA
01340 871243

One of my all-time favourite food shops can be found in Aberlour. Like an old library, wooden shelves stretch up to the ceiling, straining under a treasure trove of foodstuffs (there are at least 10 varieties of oatcakes to choose from, for example). The jams, meats, whisky, sweets, chocolates, cakes, fruit and vegetables hail from the length and breadth of the country, while the deli counter offers a tour of Scotland through cheese.

Just Deli...cious

22 High Street, Grantown-on-Spey, Highland
PH25 3EH • www.justdeliciousgrantown.co.uk
Cold meats, pies and sandwiches. Local, organic and Fair Trade food with a smile.

David Brown Butchers

63 High Street, Aberlour, Moray AB38 9QB
01340 871216

Mr Brown is the go-to butcher for the locals; he specialises in organic meats and supports local farms.

Walkers Shortbread

99 Hight Street, Aberlour, Moray AB38 9PD
01340 871555 • www.walkersshortbread.com
The largest independent biscuit maker in the UK started baking in Aberlour in 1898 and now produces 60 per cent of all shortbread exported from Scotland. There are no factory tours but there is a shop selling tartan-clad shortbread in every shape, size and quantity imaginable.

Farmers' Market

Huntly Farmers' Market

The Square, Huntly, Aberdeenshire
1st Saturday of the month

Distilleries

Let's face it, you are here for the whisky. There are over 50 distilleries in the Speyside region which amounts to over half of all distilleries in Scotland. There are 15 open to the public, but some are seasonal so check before you go (www.morayspeyside.com/tourist-information).

Eating Out

Aberlour Station Tea Rooms

Just behind the church
Aberlour's old station deals with tea not trains these days. It's a simple but pleasant spot to stop for a cuppa and look out onto the River Spey. On Wednesdays fruit and local veg is sold from here from 10.30am–12noon as part of a local community scheme.

CRANACHAN

Serves 4

Mixing whisky with water gets some purists a little agitated, so using it in a recipe could seem like sacrilege. However, there is a traditional Scottish pudding that is so 'of the place' that I couldn't leave it out: in addition to whisky, this northeastern area of Scotland is renowned for growing raspberries and that staple of Scottish crops, oats. They are all combined here.

- Lightly toast your oatmeal in a dry frying pan. Don't let it go too dark, just enough to crisp it up. Let it cool.

- Bash the raspberries about in a bowl to crush them slightly and begin to get the juice squidging out. Add a little sprinkle of sugar to sweeten if you think they need it.

- Whisk your cream in a bowl until it just begins to set. Stir in the honey and whisky.

- Add in the oatmeal and whisk a little more until the mix is getting firmer.

- Now alternate layers of cream with raspberries in 4 bowls. If possible put in the cool box or fridge to set for an hour.

- Enjoy, with the rest of the whisky.

Everything for this pudding can be purchased in Spey Larder.

2 tbsp medium oatmeal

300g fresh Scottish raspberries

a little caster sugar

350ml double cream
(I used Jersey double cream)

2 tbsp heather honey

2-3 tbsp whisky, to taste

46 OFFALY GOOD

"Every Scottish butcher is rated on the quality of their pudding and haggis," Kenny Allan tells me as we stand in his butchers' shop in the Perthshire town of Blairgowrie. "The proof really is in the pudding." And while black pudding has its place in other parts of the UK, white pudding and haggis remain very much a Scottish product.

In an age before food wastage, when you killed your cow or pig you used every single scrap of the animal. The heart, lungs, liver, kidneys of a beast don't keep as well as the rest of the carcass, so, in the case of haggis, these parts were minced and put back into the animal's own stomach and boiled. Black pudding also uses up the blood and by-products of an animal with other readily available, cheap ingredients such as Scottish oatmeal, chopped onions and beef suet. White pudding, also known as mealie pud, is the same but without the blood. Add some raisins to the mixture and call it fruit pudding.

"We've got more gold than Chris Hoy," chuckles Kenny. I glance up at the wall of certificates and awards for puddings and haggis above the counter as he leads me through the labyrinth of prep rooms behind the shop to meet Stephen Stewart, black pudding and haggis maker extraordinaire, who's been here for 36 years. 'Budgie', the sausage maker, has been here for 42. In fact there has been a butchers' shop on this site since 1922.

While you will find fabulous black, white and haggis pudding makers all over Scotland, the flavours vary widely between butchers. I've tasted spicy hot ones, others rich with cinnamon or extremely peppery flavours. I'll stick my neck out and say the best black puddings are here at Kenny's shop in Blairgowrie: a richly spiced, dense, coppery flavoured sausage that's fabulous when fried and the edges caramelise.

As I was leaving I spotted a tray of battered black puddings in the corner of the display cabinet, tucked behind the haggis. "You must be joking, surely no-one eats that!" I shriek. Kenny nods sagely, "I saw battered puds in a local chip shop and they seemed to be doing a good trade in them, so just out of curiosity I made six. They sold straightaway. So I made 12. Same again. Now I make 200 a month." I think I'll stick to having it for breakfast.

H W Irvine
17 Perth Street, Blairgowrie, Perth & Kinross PH10 6DQ

Pitch Up

Scone Camping and Caravanning Club Site

Scone Palace Caravan Park, Scone, Perth & Kinross PH2 6BB • 01738 552323 www.campingandcaravanningclub.co.uk
Scone Palace is a sumptuous and historically significant pile two miles outside of Perth. Kings Robert the Bruce and Macbeth were crowned here. The campsite is well placed right next to the palace grounds and also the city of Perth. Pitches are set among the trees, so it's a veritable woodland wildlife haven. I slept to the sound of owls above my campervan. The shop is well stocked and sells fresh morning rolls and strawberries in season.

Five Roads Caravan Park

Alyth, Blairgowrie, Perth & Kinross PH11 8NB
01828 632255
Beautifully kept, quiet, multi-unit site. Twenty minutes drive from Blairgowrie but walkable to the pleasant village of Alyth where you'll find a good butchers (M J Dorward in Commerical Street) and a deli.

Invermill Farm Caravan Site

Inver, Dunkeld, Perth & Kinross PH8 0JR • 01350 727477 • www.campingandcaravanningclub.co.uk
In a woodland setting beside the River Tay. Caravans and campervans are well catered for, tents are on a first come, first served basis. Pitches are all grass and it's worth noting that the site doesn't take cards, so come with cash. The historic town of Dunkeld is just a short woodland walk away and has a number of good options for eating out. Try **Howies Bistro** or the **Inn@ The Atholl** for simple but decent food and good local ales in the latter.

Burnhead Fruit Farm (CS)

Blairgowrie, Perth & Kinross PH10 6SZ • 01250 872521 • www.campingandcaravanningclub.co.uk
A small Certificated Site for Club members (you can join on site) that takes five vans and has extra pitches for tents. A pleasant walk down a country lane will bring you to Blairgowrie and its ample options for food.

Eat Local

The Blairgowrie Farm Shop

14-16 Reform Street, Blairgowrie, Perth & Kinross PH10 6BD • www.blairgowriefarmshop.co.uk
Just off the high street, this cosy shop stocks the best produce from Perthshire fields while supporting all the small, local food producers. A blackboard inside lists the farmers and provenance of all the stock. Also check out the **Cornerstone Deli**, 23 High Street, Blairgowrie, Perth & Kinross PH10 6DA.

The Strawberry Shop

Set in the berry fields on the A93 between Perth and Blairgowrie, this is a brilliant stop-off for just-picked berries. You will find the tastier heritage varieties here too, the kinds that don't appear in the supermarkets.

Blairgowrie is a pretty town 20 minutes drive north of Perth. Fields of polytunnels are testament that this part of Perth & Kinross is the centre of raspberry growing in Scotland, while the home of the eponymous Arbroath Smokie is an hour away on the coast.

Arbroath Smokies
£8.00 Kg

H W Irvine

17 Perth Street, Blairgowrie, Perth & Kinross
PH10 6DQ
Black puddings and haggis made with love the
traditional way, amazing selection of pies cooked
on site and seasonal game. Unbeatable service.

Arbroath Smokies

Within striking distance of the Scone campsite, the
charming coastal town of Arbroath, with its blue
and pink fishermen's cottages, is worth a visit. It is of
course home to the Arbroath Smokie – hot smoked
whole haddock (minus their heads). There are many
smokehouses still operating around the harbour. Visit
M M Spinks at 10 Marketgate. The Spinks name is
synonymous with the Arbroath Smokie. They secured
the Arbroath Smokie PGI status along with the likes
of Champagne and Stilton.

Alternatively visit **Iain Spinks shop** at 3 Perth
Street, Blairgowrie for Arbroath Smokies and a great
selection of locally caught wet fish.

Simon Howie

Findony Farm, Muckhart Road, Dunning,
Perth & Kinross PH2 0RA • 01764 684332
Closest to the Scone site, this smart modern butchers
can offer you an astonishing range of prepared cuts,
pies and puddings and recipe cards. A meat-loving
camper's delight.

The Scottish Deli

1 Atholl Street, Dunkeld, Perth & Kinross PH8 0AR
www.scottish-deli.com
If you are staying at the site near Dunkeld, try this
great deli. They make their own soups, ready meals
and bakes and have a smallholding that produces
vegetables for use in their kitchen along with meat
from their pigs and sheep.

Farmers' Market
Perth Farmers' Market

King Edward Street, Perth • 1st Saturday of the month
This vibrant 45-stall market draws local foodies
every month.

> I'll stick my neck out
> and say the best black
> puddings are at Kenny's
> shop in Blairgowrie.

BLACK PUDDING BREAKFAST RÖSTI

This camper's twist on a Scottish breakfast will set you up for the day.

Serves 2

500g floury potatoes, like Maris Piper

salt and pepper

4 slices black pudding, about 7.5cm in diameter

rapeseed oil, for frying

4 small eggs

- Peel the potatoes and, depending on size, cut them in half, or just keep whole. You are aiming for even sizes, roughly that of a tangerine.

- Bring them to the boil in salted water, then simmer for 7 minutes until they are just underdone. Drain and let them cool completely.

- While the potatoes are cooling, fry your black pudding in a little oil in a frying pan until cooked and crisp on the outside. Remove from the pan.

- Grate the cool potatoes into a bowl and season well with salt and pepper.

- Using your hands, form 8 flat rösti shapes about the size of the bottom of a mug. Make them about 5mm thick.

- Heat some more oil in the frying pan. Put 4 potato rösti into the oil, place the slices of black pudding on top, and then cover with the remaining 4 röstis. Push down on each to seal the black pudding in. Fry without moving for 5 minutes. It should form a lovely golden crust underneath.

- Crack your eggs into a saucepan of boiling water to poach, a few minutes only.

- Flip the röstis over and cook for another 5 minutes. Drain the excess oil on kitchen roll.

- Put two röstis on each plate and pop an egg on top of each.

47 HOLY SMOKE

There is a certain romance about smoking food. Maybe it's because the technique, involving just food and fire, has a seductive simplicity. Or maybe it's just because it tastes so good.

Very little about the process of smoking meat and fish has changed over the centuries. Its popularity in Scotland is ascribed by some to the Vikings bringing over their methods in the 9th century, with the taste for smoke enduring. Another practical reason is that settlements can be remote and far between in the Highlands. Smoking was a necessary method of preserving food long before fridges did it for us.

Alistair Gordon is one of the best smokers I've found. He runs the Isle of Ewe Smokehouse in Aultbea on the edge of Loch Ewe, where he lives with his wife Paula, their two children, and Crusoe the Border Terrier. The approach to their smokehouse is via rollercoaster roads that reveal evermore heart-lifting views of lochs and sea with each twist and turn.

As I get out of the car, an inviting smell of woodsmoke greets me. The Gordons' small deli and shop is joined to a prep kitchen and smoking room, so customers can watch if they want: the techniques may be traditional, but the wrapping is definitely modern and fresh.

I watch as Alistair inspects sides of salmon curing for six hours in trays of brown sugar, sea salt and a 'special' rum. He won't tell what the 'special' bit is, but he does reveal that he leaves the salmon hanging for a couple of days after smoking, which gets rid of the oiliness. The flavour of the fish is enhanced by smoking it using wood chips made from old whisky barrels from Speyside.

Salmon is the main focus of the business, with Alistair using Freedom Food-approved Scottish salmon. Kippers, trout, haddock, hake and cheese also get the smoke treatment here, but there was one product that blew my mind: the hot smoked scallops. Tender, delicate, sweet and smoky, they were absolutely exquisite.

While I'm there a steady stream of customers flows through the door. Paula chats to them all, giving recipe tips and preparing picnic bags. The Gordons may run a new generation of smokehouse, but the personal touch, the methods and the close relationship between the food and its surroundings keep all that is best about tradition.

Isle of Ewe Smokehouse
Ormiscaig, Aultbea, Highland IV22 2JJ • www.smokedbyewe.com

Pitch Up

Inverewe Gardens Camping and Caravanning Club Site

Poolewe, Achnasheen, Highland IV22 2LF • 01445 781249 • www.campingandcaravanningclub.co.uk
With just a small road between the site and the edge of Loch Ewe, nearly every pitch has a view of the water. This immaculate site is loved by the site managers as if it were their home. There are beautiful flowerbeds with sweet peas and roses and framed landscape photography in the loos. The inclusive mix of tent pitches among the hard standings makes for a really welcoming vibe.

The shoreline is abundant with mussels – check with reception for advice on when it is safe to forage and cook them. Look out too for the resident otter that appears each day to delight the campers. Oh, and the sunsets are sublime.

Sands Caravan and Camping Site

Gairloch, Highland IV21 2DL • 01445 712152
www.sandscaravanandcamping.co.uk
Combines the best of wild camping with full amenities. An impressively well stocked site shop, hard standing pitches, some static caravans and a truly great on-site cafe and restaurant do not detract from the sheer natural beauty of this place. Pitch your tent among the grassy sand dunes and huddle down between the hillocks before running onto the near-deserted beach with turquoise waters.

Gruinard Bay Caravan Park

Laide, Highland IV22 2ND • 01445 731225
www.gruinardbay.co.uk
It's quiet and basic and yes, there are static caravans
on site, but the position is unbeatable: you will be
camping virtually on the beach. Getting up to watch
the sun rise over the mountains is a must.

···Eat Local

Kenneth Morrison Butchers

Strath, Gairloch, Highland IV21 2BZ
01445 712485
Fabulous butcher in Gairloch with a huge selection
of local meats. He sells from his van to campers at
Inverewe Gardens campsite twice a week.

Strath Village Stores

Strath, Gairloch, Highland IV21 2BZ
01445 712499 • www.strathstores.com
The heart and hub of the community of Gairloch.
It has a fabulous deli, a great range of produce and
a finger on the pulse of all the local news.

Shellfish Safaris

Dry Island, Badachro, Gairloch, Highland IV21 2AB
01445 741263 • www.shellfishsafaris.co.uk
Watch your dinner of langoustines, crabs and lobsters
being caught by joining skipper Ian McWhinney on
his traditional creel-fishing boat in the beautiful setting
of Badachro Bay. Ian's partner Jess sells their shellfish
from Gairloch Pier (harbour) and in Poolewe Village
Hall market on Tuesdays.

> **One product in particular blew my mind: the hot smoked scallops.**

Farmers' Market
Poolewe Farmers' Market

Poolewe Village Hall, Poolewe, Achnasheen,
Highland Every Tuesday
You'll find local cheesemakers, an artisan bakery, a
shellfish stall and, if you get there early, a table where
people donate their excess vegetables.

Eating Out
The Steading

Gairloch, Highland IV23 2BP • 01445 712382
This bistro is relatively new to the area and has
already established itself as a favourite with the locals.
Try the hot smoked salmon salad infused with ginger,
chilli and lime marmalade.

HOT-SMOKED SCALLOP RISOTTO

A simple, silky smooth risotto that lets the smoky flavours sing out. The scallops can be replaced by smoked salmon or any other smoked fish.

Serves 2

6 smoked streaky bacon rashers, chopped into 2.5cm pieces

2 tbsp olive oil

1 large onion, finely chopped

30g butter

200g risotto rice, such as arborio

150ml white wine

1.5 litres vegetable stock, warm

6 large hot-smoked scallops, sliced (or 150g smoked salmon, roughly sliced)

75g Parmesan, grated (optional)

1 tbsp chopped parsley

a little lemon juice

- Fry the bacon in a frying pan with a smidge of the olive oil until crisp. Remove from the pan and put to one side.

- Gently fry the onion in the rest of the oil and a knob of the butter in the same pan for about 5 minutes until soft.

- Add the rice, coat it in the oil, then turn the heat up and fry for a minute, stirring.

- Pour in the wine and stir until it has evaporated.

- Add a quarter of the stock. Turn the heat down and stir until the liquid has nearly been absorbed. Add another quarter of the stock and repeat. Do this until all of the liquid has been absorbed and the rice has softened. This should take about 20 minutes tops.

- Add the remaining butter, plus about 50g of the cheese, if using, and mix in vigorously.

- Add the bacon and sliced scallops and gently stir in. Serve topped with the rest of the grated Parmesan, again if using, and the parsley and a cheeky squidge of lemon juice.

48 GET YOUR OATS...

When Robert Burns referred to southern Scotland as a 'land o' cakes' he didn't mean the sweet sort. He meant oatcakes. Used throughout Scottish cuisine, this 'grain of choice' is grown all over Scotland, but especially down its eastern coast and across the southern borderlands.

Oats are synonymous with Scotland, probably because the conditions are perfect for this hardy crop. The lengthy summer days along with cooler temperatures and higher rainfall are just right for slow ripening and natural swelling to a plump oat that is suitable for milling. It is also a grain that can thrive in less than perfect soil.

A belly full of oats has long been the perfect start to a chilly Scottish day. I've read many historical accounts of families having a 'porridge drawer': a tin-lined drawer in the dresser into which big pots of porridge were poured. Once it had cooled and turned solid, slices of it were cut and taken out in the fields as sustenance for a hard day's labour. Modern dieticians explain that oats deliver slow-release energy and are packed with zinc, vitamin B6, iron, folic acid, calcium and magnesium. Farm labourers just knew that oats filled them up.

On the workers' return, they'd cut off a few more slices and fry them up with a piece of fish or some eggs. Certainly, across Scotland oats are about a lot more than just breakfast: they are used in black pudding and haggis, they make a deliciously crunchy topping for fish but are probably eaten more frequently as oatcakes – a staple found in every Scottish larder.

One of the largest and most celebrated mills in the Borders is John Hogarth, which uses oats from crops in the River Tweed flood plain – the Merse – providing perfectly fertile alluvial soil for oats. If you are salmon fishing in the area, it will be these golden crops you'll be gazing at as you wait for that all-important bite.

John Hogarth Ltd
Kelso Mills, Mill Wynd, Kelso, Scottish Borders TD5 7HP
01573 224224

Pitch Up

Ruberslaw Wild Woods Camping

Spital Tower, Nr Denholm, Hawick, Scottish Borders
TD9 8TB • 01450 870092 • www.ruberslaw.co.uk
Set in 500 acres of unspoilt upland, this unique
campsite has isolated, wild pitches where you can
camp on the slopes of Ruberslaw Hill or deep in the
woods – a fire bowl and logs are supplied. Or you
can pitch your tent in the Edwardian walled garden
and enjoy facilities such as The Barn, a large covered
area for socialising and eating and a well-equipped
kitchen area.

Lauder Camping and Caravanning Club Site

Carfraemill, Oxton, Lauder, Scottish Borders
TD2 6RA • 01578 750697
www.campingandcaravanningclub.co.uk
A peaceful and relaxing campsite with 60 mainly level
pitches and modern facilities. There's great walking
and cycling from this rural site. A burn runs alongside,
perfect for children and dogs to paddle in and home
to a wealth of local wildlife.

Jedburgh Camping and Caravanning Club Site

Elliot Park, Jedburgh, Scottish Borders TD8 6EF
01835 863393 • www.campingandcaravanningclub.
co.uk
A small, rural site catering for all types of campers.
Tents have their own separate tree-lined level area and
there's a recreational field and a lovely gentle riverside
walk into Jedburgh.

Eat Local

John Hogarth Ltd

Kelso Mills, Mill Wynd, Kelso, Scottish Borders
TD5 7HP • 01573 224224
John Hogarth has been manufacturing oats in
Kelso for over 100 years. Though the mill isn't open
to the public, you can buy delicious oat flakes,
medium oatmeal and pinhead oatmeal from their
shop at reception.

Teviot Game Fare & Smokery

Kirkbank House, Eckford, Kelso,
Scottish Borders TD5 8LE • 01835 850253
www.teviotgamefaresmokery.co.uk
This family-run smokery uses time-honoured
methods to bring out the best of Border fish and game.
Salmon, trout, eel, duck and cheese are smoked over
smouldering oak chips. The shop is packed with local
and Scottish produce including eggs from the local
farm, oatcakes, jams, chutneys, wild boar pâté and
cheeses. There's also a cafe open all day where you
can sample the smokery delicacies.

> **A belly full of oats has long been the perfect start to a chilly Scottish day.**

Border Berries

Rutherford Farm, Kelso, Scottish Borders TD5 8NP
01835 823763 • www.borderberries.co.uk
A delightful pick-your-own fruit farm with an on-site cafe, **Tutti Frutti**. This is one of Scotland's oldest family-run fruit farms, growing strawberries, raspberries, red and blackcurrants, tayberries and gooseberries. All the fruit is grown outside and ripens naturally. Their season runs from the start of July until late August.

Julian's Veg at Mayfield Garden Centre

Glebe Lane, Kelso, Scottish Borders TD5 7AU
07596 704783 • www.juliansveg.co.uk
Julian has a fantastic range of seasonal vegetables, fruit and herbs, as well as milk and local eggs and fresh bread from the **Running Fox Bakery** in Felton. You can also pick up Julian's fantastic fresh veggies at local farmers' markets, including Kelso.

Farmers' Markets

Kelso Farmers' Market

Kelso town square • 4th Saturday of the month
Sir Walter Scott called Kelso 'the most beautiful, if not the most romantic town in Scotland'. The farmers' market here includes Angus beef, venison, wild game, fresh and smoked fish.

Hawick Farmers' Market

Civic Space • 3rd Saturday of the month

Jedburgh Farmers' Market

Market Place • 1st Friday of the month

Haddington Farmers' Market

Court Street • last Saturday of the month

Peebles Farmers' Market

Eastgate Car Park • 2nd Saturday of the month

OATMEAL PANCAKES
SMOKED SALMON AND SCRAMBLED EGGS

A typical Borders breakfast would include oats grown on the fertile river plain of the Tweed. However, the Tweed is also one of the most famous salmon-fishing rivers in the country, so it would almost be rude not to combine those oats with salmon.

Serves 4

- You need to soak the oatmeal in the milk for at least 2 hours. I suggest doing this in a jug the night before and leaving in the fridge/cool box.

- About 30 minutes before cooking, put the salmon pieces (for the scrambled eggs) in a bowl with the cream and put to one side. Take the oat mixture out of the fridge (it will look like goo but don't worry).

- When you are ready to cook, mix your oat mixture vigorously with a fork, then beat in the salt, baking powder and egg.

- Heat a large frying pan — not too hot — and melt some butter to grease it. Drop 4 large spoonfuls of the oat mixture into the pan — you are aiming for roughly the diameter of a crumpet, about 8cm, and about 3mm thick. Spread out the oatmeal element of the mixture evenly as it hits the pan.

- Turn the pancakes over when they are set around the edges, when some bubbles come up and they start to brown a little. Mine took about 2 minutes on each side, but this depends on your pan, and how hot it is. Keep the first batch warm in a cloth while making more. This mixture easily makes 2 pancakes each, 8 in all.

- To make the scrambled egg, melt the butter in a saucepan on a medium heat, and swirl around to coat the sides.

- Beat the eggs lightly and season with salt and pepper. Pour the eggs into the butter in the pan, and stir continuously, making sure it doesn't stick to the sides.

- As soon as the eggs start to stiffen (about 1 minute - there should be about half solid, half liquid left in the pan), add the salmon and cream. Stir for about 15 seconds more, then take off the heat. Keep stirring until it is a gorgeous mass of creamy egg.

- Put the scrambled egg on your oat pancakes to serve.

100g medium oatmeal

250ml milk

1 tsp salt

1 tsp baking powder

1 egg, beaten

butter, for greasing

For the scrambled eggs

200g smoked salmon trimmings, snipped into small pieces

8 tbsp single cream or milk

20g butter

8 eggs

salt and pepper

49 LIFE ON THE ESTATE

Philippa Grant, along with her husband Johnnie, the Laird of Rothiemurchus, owns and manages over 20,000 acres of highland, pink granite mountains, river, lowland and lochs in the heart of the Cairngorms National Park. The privately owned estate has been in the Grant family for nearly 500 years. That's 17 generations.

I am in awe. Not just because of the natural and impressive beauty that I've seen out of the window as we raced around the estate's wild tracks in Philippa's knackered old 4x4, but also because of her.

First impressions are of a feisty Laird's wife. Beyond that you realise that the 'feist' is pure passion for every single aspect of this place; every animal, tree, bird, head of cattle and deer and every person that works here. She clearly has devotion and a deep sense of responsibility for making this estate function as a workable environment for local people and an attractive place to visit for tourists, while simultaneously protecting and regenerating its unique environment. It's a bit more than your average work/life juggle.

"We are the custodians of the natural heritage of this place," Philippa says, as we wend our way past clumps of juniper bushes and Scottish heather to meet a fold of Highland cattle. Taking hairpin bends in the track at speed, Philippa explains her conservation plans to protect their resident capercaillies, a near extinct species of black grouse that exist on the estate. This is one of the few places left in Scotland to have them. "We also get plenty of ospreys here too. I'm proud of that ..." She moves swiftly on to telling me about their forestry management policies, showing me parts of woodland that have remained unchanged and uninterrupted for centuries and how they work to keep the delicate balance of diverse species that live in it.

While I'm busy photographing the Highland cows, Philippa explains the estate's farming activities. Husband Johnnie oversees the farming side of things. As well as raising livestock they grow barley, which they use as feed, but also sell on to the local whisky distilleries. Along with the mixed cattle they maintain a population of wild deer in their woodlands and farm deer too, so they can keep up with demand for the meat.

Producing the highest quality Highland beef and venison is a key focus for Philippa. She put herself on a butchery course so that she understands the intricacies of her product and how she should sell it through her estate farm shop. The meat is butchered on-site, sold here and also used in the exceptionally good Druie Cafe on the estate. I can vouch for its excellence, having devoured the enormous Highland beef burger there.

Continuing on through the estate, we pass a large work shed that is rented by a local lad who has returned to the Highlands to start his metalworking business. "It's vital that we attract young people back to the Highlands and support them in setting up businesses. It's the only way the area will have a future," says Philippa.

Being in the heart of the Cairngorms National Park, there are of course thousands of visitors that use the estate every year for walking, cycling, adventure sports, fishing and shooting. The estate also has a beautiful campsite next to a river and among the trees. It's a very special place. As we drive around, Philippa greets every walker or picnicker like an old friend and asks if they are enjoying themselves. They have no idea who she is, but they enjoy the welcome anyway. It makes this astonishingly beautiful place feel like it belongs to everyone.

Philippa and Johnnie have ensured that Rothiemurchus fortunately remains a positive tale in the history of Highland estates, an otherwise diminishing asset in Scotland's colourful Highland history.

Rothiemurchus Estate

Coylumbridge, near Aviemore, Highland PH22 1QH
www.rothiemurchus.net

The Druie Cafe

opening times 09.45-16.45

Breakfast 09.30-11.00
Serving hot filled bacon
& egg rolls.

Lunch 12-16.00

Using locally sourced &
produce from the estate

Homemade Baking

All day, delicious freshly
baked scones & cakes

Pitch Up

Rothiemurchus Campsite

Rothiemurchus Estate, Coylumbridge, near Aviemore,
Highland PH22 1QU • 01479 812800

www.rothiemurchus.net

Rothiemurchus Campsite is a real treat, whether
you are under canvas, in a campervan or caravan.
You'll be nestled among the Scots pines and juniper
bushes and sleep to the sounds of the river running
past your pitch. The site has achieved a subtle but
successful blend of wild camping with modern
amenities and even a laundrette. There are 17 level
pitches with electric hook-ups, or plentiful spots in
the forest for tents.

Glenmore Camping in the Forest Site

Aviemore, Highland PH22 1QU • 01479 861271

www.campingintheforest.co.uk

A wonderful Camping in the Forest site only 15
minutes drive from the busy town and tourist
resort of Aviemore.

Eat Local

Rothiemurchus Estate Farm Shop

Aviemore, Highland PH22 1QH

The farm shop is just a short bike ride down the
road from the site. The meat counter is fabulous, the
Highland beef is top quality and I can thoroughly
recommend the venison steaks, cut perfectly for
flash frying in the pan. Freshly smoked rainbow
trout from the estate lochs as well as salmon offer a
fish alternative. The rest of the shop is thoughtfully
stocked with a whole bunch of enticing Scottish
produce to sort out your campsite cook-up.

Eating Out

Druie Café

Aviemore, Highland PH22 1QH • 01479 810005

Taking its name from the sparkling burn of mountain
water that flows behind the restaurant, this great food
spot connects its menu very firmly with its setting.
Dishes using the estate's Highland beef, wild venison
and rainbow trout are cooked to perfection. Open
daily for breakfast, coffee and lunches and in the
evenings from Thursday to Saturday.

> **We wend our way past clumps of juniper
> bushes and Scottish heather to meet a fold
> of Highland cattle.**

VELVET
ROTHIEMURCHUS
VENISON STEAKS

This quick and easy yet delicious venison dish is the ultimate posh nosh at your pitch. Serve it with lots of buttery, fluffy mashed potato.

Serves 2

- Season the steaks with salt and pepper and rub with olive oil. Fry the steaks in a large frying pan. The time taken depends on the thickness of the steak, and personal preference, but roughly 3-4 minutes on each side for a 150g steak. Take the steaks out of the pan and put somewhere warm to rest while you make the sauce.

- Melt the butter in the pan and soften the shallots for a few minutes. Add the port/wine, orange juice and mustard, stir and let it bubble until the volume reduces and the sauce thickens slightly. Add the redcurrant jelly and stir while it melts. Simmer for about 4-5 minutes then take off the heat.

- Spoon the sauce over the venison steaks and serve with some mashed potato.

2 venison strip loin steaks

salt and pepper

olive oil

For the sauce

a knob of butter

2 shallots, finely chopped

75ml port (or red wine if you don't have port)

3 tbsp orange juice

1 tsp English mustard

4 tbsp redcurrant jelly
(buy a jar in the estate farm shop)

Keeping Highland cattle is considered one of the best ways to preserve the Highland landscape. On unproductive land, the cows eat the rough fodder and let the less competitive grasses and flowers flourish. This is known as conservation grazing.

50 GLEN COW

I'm standing on a set from the *Braveheart* movie. While there are no actors here now, the vast mountains on either side of me continue to provide the drama. This is the splendour of Glen Nevis, the valley that curls itself around the base of Britain's highest peak, Ben Nevis. To complete the scene, a herd of Highland cattle go about their business, standing in the river, chewing the cud and generally making the place look authentically 'Highland'.

"This is where they filmed a lot of the scenes from the movie," explains Ewen Cameron of the legendary Highland clan Cameron, owner of the 1,000-acre Glen Nevis Estate who, with his son John, has taken me to meet his cows. "And in that next field is where they filmed the Harry Potter Quidditch games."

With a background in movies, the 10-strong 'fold' (as a group of Highland cows are known) are obviously used to a bit of attention. We park in the middle of the field, and within moments Scott the bull is making a beeline for us at quite a pace. Ewen whips a comb out of his pocket and begins to comb Scott's fringe. The bull stands patiently as he is groomed, moving his head to allow Ewen to reach the difficult spots – rather as if he was having a wet shave. The matriarch of the herd heads directly for me, so I am passed a comb of my own – and get to work. It's one of my more unusual mornings, but a great way to get to know a bit more about this iconic breed.

One of the oldest breeds in Britain, this animal is very much 'of' this Highland landscape. They thrive in areas where no other breed could exist, high on mountain land with rough grazing, bitter winds and copious rain. They are designed for it. Their flowing red coats have two layers. The inner one is thick and woolly like a blanket to keep the heat in, while the outer longer layer sheds the rain off.

Highland cattle are becoming an increasingly popular breed to farm. Highland beef is prized as a top-quality meat because it is slow-maturing, which means it has plenty of flavour. Far-ranging grazing on hillsides keeps them fit and their meat lean. Grass-fed beef is high in omega 3 and Highland beef is also low in cholesterol.

The beauty of Glen Nevis is legendary, so tourism not farming seems to make sense. But the cows play their part. Not many breeds draw the crowds, but spotting a Highland cow is high on visitors' wish lists. Getting to comb its fringe blows the list out of the water.

Pitch Up

Glen Nevis Holiday Park

Glen Nevis, Fort William, Highland PH33 6SX
01397 702191 • www.glen-nevis.co.uk
It is only a couple of miles from Fort William but
you can camp in the mountain shadows and hear the
river gently babble. The site is huge, yet never feels
like it due to the way it is laid out. There is a variety
of pitches, some out in the open, others sheltered
by trees. The facilities are all to a great standard and
there's a good shop on site. A short wander up the
glen brings you to a cafe and a restaurant run by
the owners.

Red Squirrel Campsite

Glencoe, Highland PH49 4HX • 01855 811256
www.redsquirrelcampsite.co.uk
Utterly unbeatable for a memorable camping
experience, Red Squirrel Campsite has cult status
among regular campers. For tents and campervans
only, and located way up in the Glen Coe wilderness,
it's an oasis of trees with a river for swimming in and

a path to the equally legendary **Clachaig Inn**. It is
obviously a labour of love for the owner, who has been
running it since the 1960s. His sense of humour is
displayed in the wacky signs and pictures around the
place. Come here to build campfires, play the guitar
and feel small against the enormity of the landscape.

Glencoe Camping and Caravanning Club Site

Glencoe, Ballachulish, Argyll, Highland PH49 4LA
01855 811397 • www.campingandcaravanningclub.
co.uk
A glorious site with stunning mountain vistas
well suited to caravans and motorhomes, although
tents are also welcome. Glencoe Visitor Centre is
a short walk from the site.

Eat Local

The inhospitable and dramatic landscapes are what
draw us to this place. It's also what makes this area
unsuitable for growing fresh produce. Instead this
landscape offers up beef and wild venison, salmon
from the rivers and shellfish from the sea and lochs –
you just have to know where to find it and be prepared
to travel for it.

Lochaber Farm Shop

Torlundy, Fort William, Highland PH33 6SQ
01397 708686 • www.lochaberfarmshop.com
You feel like you are beginning to drive up the
mountainside (follow signs for Ben Nevis Mountain
Range Resort off the A82) to get to this one. It's worth
it, too. Make the most of the views by stopping for a
coffee and a home-made lunch in the great little cafe
and sit on the terrace to gaze at Ben Nevis. The shop
has everything you'll need for your camping cook-up.

John MacMillan Butchers

Unit 4a, Blar Mhor Industrial Estate, Lochyside,
Fort William, Highland PH33 7PT • 01397 703070
The last high street butcher recently closed in Fort
William, as the supermarket effect has taken its
toll once again. But, if you want great quality meat
and service you can head out to John MacMillan's
butchers' unit, open from 8am–3pm weekdays. For
the last 40 years John has operated a mobile butchers'
service, driving to remote outposts to supply his meat.
Now you can get it from his premises on this little
industrial estate, too. He makes all his own sausages,
burgers and black puddings.

Loch Leven Seafood

North Ballachulish, Onich, Fort William,
Highland PH33 6SA • 01855 821048
www.lochlevenseafoodcafe.co.uk
In a fabulous lochside location, this small shop sells
shellfish, smoked fish and home-made sauces to go
with them. They'll make up a picnic box of freshly
caught and cooked langoustines for you.

Eating Out

Loch Leven Seafood

North Ballachulish, Onich, Fort William,
Highland PH33 6SA • 01855 821048
www.lochlevenseafoodcafe.co.uk
Joined on to the shellfish business and little shop, this
cafe/bistro has a small terrace looking out over the
loch where the langoustines are caught every morning.
On the menu are hand-dived scallops with harissa-
roasted garlic and lime, or a hot and cold seafood
platter with surf clams, razor clams, lobster and crab.

The Clachaig Inn

Glencoe, Highland PH49 4HX • 01855 811252
This inn is an institution in these parts. It would
appear that the required dress code is walking boots
and rosy cheeks. Set up in the wilds of Glencoe, and
walkable from Red Squirrel Campsite, they serve
hearty fare to provide sustenance or revival after a
day of trekking in the mountains. Great selection of
local beers.

HIGHLAND BEEF KEBABS
WITH HERBY TOMATO SALAD

Kebabs are a perennial campers' favourite. This version has a great twist with some garlicky toasted breadcrumbs to add a bit of crunch.

Serves 2 generously

350g lean Highland beef rump steak, cut into 2.5cm cubes

2 tbsp mayonnaise

1 tbsp wholegrain mustard

salt and pepper

1 tbsp olive oil

2 large slices white bread, crumbed (I roll it up and grate it roughly)

1 garlic clove, very finely chopped

2 tbsp fresh chopped herbs, parsley or thyme (1 tbsp dried if you need to)

For the tomato salad

6 cherry tomatoes

2 large tomatoes

8 sun-dried tomatoes

a few sprigs of fresh parsley and coriander

olive oil and some good vinegar

- Preheat a barbecue grill or cast-iron hotplate grill. If using wooden skewers, soak them in water for 30 minutes beforehand.

- Meanwhile make the tomato salad. Cut the cherry tomatoes in half and put in a serving bowl. Quarter the large tomatoes, scoop out the seeds, chop the flesh and add to the bowl. Cut the sun-dried tomatoes into small pieces and add to the bowl. Season well with salt and pepper. Using scissors, snip a handful of fresh parsley and coriander into the bowl. Glug in a little olive oil and a splash of vinegar and mix together well.

- In a bowl, mix together the mayonnaise, mustard, and some salt and pepper. Mix the beef cubes into this, and stir, coating them thoroughly.

- Thread the beef on to skewers.

- Cook the kebabs slowly on the preheated grill, turning to cook all sides. Depending on how rare you like your steak, this should take up to 8 minutes.

- While the kebabs are cooking, heat the oil in a small frying pan and add the breadcrumbs, garlic and herbs. Fry gently, tossing frequently until golden brown, a few minutes only.

- Once the kebabs are cooked, put on to plates and sprinkle the breadcrumb mixture over the top to coat. Serve with the tomato salad.

INDEX OF PLACES

INDEX OF FOOD

WITH THANKS TO...

Gavin, my husband and perfect camping buddy, for his patience, humour, support and hours and hours of proofreading.
A big thank you to my children Maisy and Mack for their irrepressible enthusiasm, my mother Chris for recipe testing and
my dad Tim for entertaining the children while I write. I dedicate this book to you all.

A huge thank you to Simon McGrath at the Camping and Caravanning Club without whose stoic support, belief and drive
this would never have happened. Also Sue Taylor for mentoring and encouraging me for so many years – this is for you.
Thanks to Paul Jones and Robert Louden for saying yes to the project.

My editor Tom Bromley – thank you so much for keeping the faith, being so encouraging and making this such a great book to
work on; likewise to the wonderful Donna Wood, who has guided me through my first book and made it such a brilliant experience,
and James Tims for keeping me laughing. Thank you also to Susan Fleming for checking my recipes and David Riding my agent at
MBALit, Helen Jenkins for testing many recipes and Owain Jenkins for answering my constant livestock and farming questions.

Thanks to Fiona Morrison and Amy White for assisting with research. Also, to my parents-in-law Frank and Trish Unsworth for
additional fact-finding and photos.

Thank you to Clive Garrett and Outwell for generously supporting Eat Local by keeping me stocked with such great kit.

Thank you also to red wine.

And finally and most importantly to all bakers, makers, growers, farmers, fish smokers, deer stalkers, cheesemakers, grape growers,
campsite owners, market traders and fisherfolk who appear in this book, for inspiring me in the first place and making this such a tasty
country to live and travel in.

The Automobile Association wishes to thank the following photographers, illustrator and organisations for their assistance in the preparation of this book.

Abbreviations for the image credits are as follows – (t) top; (m) middle; (b) bottom; (l) left; (r) right; (c) centre; (AA) AA World Travel Library.

Af8Images/Alamy: 227; Alan Majchrowicz/Alamy: 326-7; B Lawrence/Alamy: 224; Bon Appetit/Alamy: 153br; David Kilpatrick/Alamy: 359; David Noton
Photography/Alamy: 22-3; Ed Rhodes/Alamy: 172-3; Joan Gravell/Alamy: 269; John Morgan/Alamy: 329b; Keith Morris/Alamy: 262-3; Liquid Light/Alamy: 249; Loop
Images Ltd/Alamy: 72-3, 126-7; Neil Holmes Freelance Digital/Alamy: 191; Pick and Mix Images/Alamy: 30tl; Realimage/Alamy: 232-3; Sebastian Wasek/Alamy: 280-1

Ali Ray: front cover br, 7tl, 8cl, 8cr, 8cr, 8bl, 8br, 18, 24tl, 24tr, 24bl, 24cr, 24br, 40, 50, 52tl, 52tr, 52cl, 52c, 52cr, 52bl, 52br, 54l, 54r, 58tl, 58tr, 58cl, 58cr, 58bl, 58br, 61b, 64,
67tl, 67tr, 67bl, 67cr, 67br, 69tl, 69tr, 69cl, 69c, 69cr, 69bl, 69br, 71, 75tl, 75tr, 75cl, 75c, 75cr, 75bl, 75br, 79, 98tl, 98tr, 98cl, 98c, 98cr, 98bl, 98br, 101, 103, 104, 107tl, 107c,
107tr, 107bl, 107br, 109, 113, 114bl, 115, 117, 118tl, 118tr, 121, 122, 124, 133, 135tl, 135tl ii, 135tr, 135bl, 135c, 135cr, 135bc, 135cr, 137, 140tl, 140tr, 140cl, 140cr, 140cr ii,
140bl, 140br, 143, 144, 149, 150, 153tl, 153tc, 153tr, 153bl, 155tl, 155tr, 155cl, 155bl, 155br, 156, 158, 160tl, 160tc, 160tr, 160cl, 160cr, 160bl, 160br, 163t, 166tl, 166tr, 166cl,
166cr, 166bl, 166bc, 166br, 169, 189, 206tr, 214, 219, 223, 234, 240tl, 240tr, 240cl, 240c, 240cr, 240bl, 240br, 243, 244, 247tl, 247tr, 247b, 257tl, 257tr, 257b, 275, 276tl, 276tc,
276tr, 276b, 283tl, 283c, 283r, 283bl, 285, 289, 291, 295tl, 295tr, 295cl, 295cr, 295bl, 295br, 297, 299, 304, 311, 323, 329tl, 329tr, 331, 341tl, 341tr, 346tl, 346tr, 346b, 349, 352tl,
352tr, 352cl, 352c, 352cr, 352bl, 352br, 354, 357, 365, 366tl, 366tr, 366cl, 366c, 366cr, 366bl, 366br i, 366br ii, 370, 372

Alisdair Cusick: 7tr, 7b, 21, 29, 42tl, 42tr, 42b, 49, 62, 96, 164, 180, 184, 186, 231, 239, 287t, 287b, 324

Courtesy of British Asparagus Association: 198, 202, 204; Courtesy of Chatsworth House Trust: 183tl; Courtesy of Chatsworth House Trust/Claire Wood Photography:
183tr, 183b; Courtesy of Day's Orchard: 206tl, 206b, 209; Courtesy of Malcolm Mcbeath Collection: 334tl, 334tr; Courtesy of Packington Free Range: 174t, 174bl, 174br;
Courtesy of Pembrokeshire Beach Food Company: 272; Courtesy of Ray Edmondson: 300tl, 300c, 300bl, 300br; Courtesy of Riverford Farm Shops: 57; Courtesy of
Rodda's Clotted Cream: 30tr, 30b, 34; Courtesy of The Sandringham Estate: 128t, 128bl, 128br; Courtesy of Tash Daly: 200; Courtesy of The Camping and Caravanning
Club: 13, 33, 45, 46, 84, 130, 211, 250, 320; Courtesy of The Camping and Caravanning Club/Monty Rakusen: 229; Courtesy of The Camping and Caravanning Club/
Steve Wright: 308, 342, 360; Courtesy of The Cheddar Gorge Cheese Company: 37; Courtesy of The Glenlivet Distillery: 341tc, 341bl, 341br; Courtesy of Uncle Henry's
Farm Shop: 194, 195; Courtesy of Wookey Farm/J Wickham: 39

Ella Grabsky: 118b

Frank Unsworth: 307, 334b, 337

AA/James Tims: front cover tl, front cover tr, front cover bl, back cover, 8tl, 8tr, 8c, 11, 14, 17, 28, 35, 41, 48, 51, 56, 63, 65, 70, 78, 80, 81, 82, 86, 87, 89bl, 89r, 89ct, 89cb,
89cl, 90, 93, 94, 95tl, 95tc, 95tr, 95cl, 95bl, 95br, 97, 105, 110, 111, 116, 125, 132, 138, 139tl, 139tc, 139tr, 139cl, 139bl, 139br, 146tl, 146tc, 146tr, 146b, 147, 152, 159, 165, 170,
171, 178, 179tl, 179tc, 179tr, 179b, 181, 187, 188, 196, 197tl, 197tc, 197tr, 197b, 205, 212, 213tl, 213tr, 213b, 220, 221, 222, 230, 238, 245, 246, 252, 253, 254, 255, 260, 261, 266,
267, 273, 278, 279, 286, 292tl, 292tc, 292tr, 292b, 293, 298, 300tr, 300cl, 300cr, 302, 305, 310, 312tl, 312tr, 312bl, 312cr, 312br, 315b, 316tl, 316tc, 316tr, 316b, 317, 319tl, 319tr,
319cl, 319b, 322, 325, 332, 333, 338, 339tl, 339tr, 339b, 344, 345, 350, 351, 356, 362, 363, 368, 369, 374, 375

Matthew Midgley: 4, 23, 27, 55, 61tr, 68, 73, 77, 92, 100, 114br, 123, 127, 131, 145, 163b, 168, 173, 177, 193, 203, 208, 216, 226, 233, 237, 242, 251, 258, 271, 281, 290, 296,
303, 309, 315t, 327, 330, 336, 343, 355, 361, 373